Riding Above Air

Genevieve Mckay

Chapter One

"Fine, Caprice, I'll throw the ball one last time but that's it. I mean it. You're supposed to take it easy, remember?"

The little poodle crouched on her haunches, muscles flexed, toenails digging into the ground, ready to spring away. She gazed intently at the ball in my hand, her eyes glittering in the pale morning light.

"Go." I hurled the ball down the barn aisle and watched it bounce wildly out the front door.

Caprice sprang away, barely touching the concrete as she skimmed over the ground like a shadow, disappearing across the driveway into the woods.

Great, now maybe I can get some work done...

The thought was cut off as she returned almost immediately, prancing toward me in that exaggerated way poodles do with her front feet flicking high in the air in an extended trot, the orange ball clutched triumphantly between her teeth.

"All right, that's it; on your bed. The vet said not to overdo it, remember?"

She dropped the ball obediently at my feet and flopped down

happily on the travel-sized dog bed I'd set up for her beside the tack room, her sides still heaving from her run.

Back when she'd lived with my parents, before we'd run away together to live with the Ahlbergs, she'd torn a ligament in her hind leg and had narrowly avoided having surgery to repair it. Technically, she wasn't really supposed to be playing ball so much, but it was hard to say no to those big, brown eyes, especially when I'd been almost too busy to play with her over the last few weeks.

Huh, huh, huh, Red said from behind me. He'd swished through his knee-deep bed of shavings and now stood with his head hanging over his stall door into the aisle, peering hopefully at the orange ball at my feet. He tilted his nose to one side and pricked his ears, bobbing his nose encouragingly.

"Sorry, buddy, that's not an apple," I said, stifling a laugh. I moved over to rub his wide blaze and gently tug on his floppy ears, first one and then the other.

"You're bored, aren't you, handsome? I bet you want to go for a ride." I leaned forward, resting my cheek against his soft, warm neck. "Rob will be here soon with your friends. When I get my chores finished, I promise we'll do something fun. I know you've been a little neglected lately."

Between taking care of a stable full of horses, teaching at archery camp, recovering from my traumatic breakup with my parents, and dealing with all Hilary's drama, the last few weeks had flown by in a blur. I'd barely had time to *think* let alone ride Red and Ellie as much as they deserved.

Red gave me a friendly nudge on the arm and extracted himself from my hug, turning to saunter out to his paddock.

"Enjoy your nap," I called since this was exactly what he did every morning after breakfast. Red had become much more forward and animated since we'd moved to Hilary's stable, but he still really liked to sleep. He could curl up and power nap just about anywhere. It was just one of the thousand things I loved about him.

I went into the tack room to wash the stack of sticky feed tubs, mentally running through the list of chores that still had to be done.

The horses are almost finished with breakfast, I thought, plunging my hands into the sudsy hot water and giving each bucket a hard scrub and a rinse. *As soon as they're done I'll turn them out, and then I can get the stalls and paddocks done. I should have time to get all the waters in the barn scrubbed and refilled before Rob gets here with his horses.*

I'd worry about checking the pasture waters and tidying the tack room once we were done riding for the morning. Our new, potential, coach was supposed to come later in the afternoon to see the place and I wanted everything to look perfect. We needed a lesson program here badly and my old coach Liza had thought her friend Oona would fit the bill perfectly.

"She's been teaching overseas for years and she knows her stuff. You'll love her once you really get to know her," she'd told us over the phone. "She can seem a little strange at first, but her heart's in the right place." It wasn't a statement that exactly inspired confidence.

I drained the sink and set the buckets upside-down on the counter to dry, absently wiping my wet hands on my breeches.

Still thinking about Oona, I paused in the tack room

doorway, running my gaze down the aisle.

They're so happy, I thought, watching the contented horses with a mixture of love and pride. Sometimes I'd get so caught up in working that I'd forget how lucky I was to even *be* here. I had my own horses to ride (even though Ellie was only a temporary sales project), an indoor arena to school in and miles of trails to explore. Sometimes I had to pinch myself to make sure it wasn't all going to disappear like a dream.

The stable was my friend Hilary's barn, but she didn't have very much to do with it lately. Ever since she'd hurt her ankle practicing for a musical this summer she'd been moody and unpredictable and had left the running of the barn, and most of the chores, to me.

She'd buried herself in the business side of running the stable and taken less and less of an interest in the actual horses. I'd thought it would help that her new boyfriend Darius liked to ride and everything, and was a genius at horse-archery, but it had only seemed to make things worse.

Darius was a professional squash player who travelled a lot, so when he was away she didn't seem able to focus on *anything* except when he'd return. She hardly ate, she kept her phone glued to her hand just in case he texted, and every conversation would somehow turn to what Darius must be doing, thinking, wearing at that moment.

I actually liked the guy, especially since he'd spent so much time helping me train the horses to love mounted archery, but it had come to the point where her obsessive talking about him was driving me nuts and I could hardly hear his name without wanting to vomit.

Jerry can stay inside until after his ride, I thought, watching the big, grey warmblood lip up the last few strands of his breakfast hay. Jerry was such a friendly horse and he loved attention. Hilary used to spend all sorts of time riding and just hanging out with him, but now she barely looked at him at all.

Riverdance and Rabbit won't get ridden until this afternoon, so they can go out. Annie and Callie won't ride today, so Norman and Sox can go out now, too.

"All right, everyone," I said, "turnout for everyone except Red, Ellie, and Jerry. Let's get your halters on."

Caprice leapt up off her bed, spun a few circles and danced beside me as I grabbed Norman's halter and lead.

Now that the new pasture fencing was finished, and the horses could spend long blissful hours just grazing and loafing in the sunshine, the entire atmosphere of the barn had changed from tense to peaceful.

Without being cooped up in their tiny paddocks all day and hardly being ridden, the whole herd was now relaxed and easy to handle. One by one they sauntered beside me out to their fields like they'd never been the rearing, prancing nut-bars they'd been just a few months before.

Even Rabbit, who sometimes could act like the high-strung racehorse he'd once been, didn't even bother to run and buck when I shut the gate behind him; he just strolled out to the middle of the field and buried his face in the grass, half-closing his eyes in satisfaction.

"Right, Caprice, that's everyone," I said as she looked up at me expectantly, one paw poised on the toe of my paddock boot, "time for stalls and paddocks."

She danced on her hind legs, yapped at me once, and then took off on her own toward the barn.

The early morning air was still blissfully cool; a fresh little breeze skipped off the ocean and played across my skin, ruffling my hair. I hummed to myself as I trekked out to the manure pile for the fifth time, pushed my final wheelbarrow-load up the ramp we'd made and dumped it off the edge of the heap with satisfaction.

"Ouch," I said, flexing my hand a little and frowning down at the new row of tender, red spots that had sprung up along the fleshy part at the base of my fingers. It meant that more blisters were starting. I hated wearing gloves, so my hands had gone through a steady progression of blister to callous to new blister all summer long.

I walked back to the barn and propped the wheelbarrow back in its spot outside and hung the manure fork neatly beside it.

I didn't mind doing chores at all. I loved taking care of the horses; it was probably one of the most satisfying things I'd ever done. It was especially nice in the early mornings when it was just me and the horses and Caprice, and everything was still and quiet. I had time to think about all sorts of things and dream crazy dreams about a far-off future when I had my own barn.

On the other hand, taking care of seven horses a day, seven days a week, all by myself, was getting kind of exhausting. Especially when I also had to somehow fit in working at archery camp, helping the Ahlbergs turn their new farm into a bed and breakfast, and try to fit in my own riding time. Even though I tried not to think about it, the fact was that school was starting up again in a week and I had no idea how I was supposed to keep everything running smoothly once that happened. I barely had enough time to eat and shower as it was.

Hilary had been promising for *weeks* that she was almost ready to start helping with chores again, but so far it hadn't happened even though she was off her crutches and seemed to get around fine otherwise. Once in a while, she would feed and water the horses, but she sort of acted like she was doing me this great favour when she did it, which was incredibly annoying even though I pretended that it wasn't.

Stop it, I told myself, *it's too nice of a day to be worrying about all this. It will work out somehow. Hilary is just having a hard time; she'll be back to normal soon.*

I finished the rest of my chores quickly and stood back to survey my immaculately clean aisle with satisfaction. The roomy stalls were bedded deep with shavings and the water buckets cleaned and filled. I'd soaked the beet pulp for the evening feed and prepped the hay. Now I was finally ready to ride.

Right on cue, Rob's big dually truck came chugging up the driveway, his trailer full of horses in tow.

A throb of excitement went through my chest, both at the thought of the full morning of riding ahead and of seeing Rob.

"Hey, Mr. Harris," I called as he pulled up right in front of the barn, parking the trailer sideways so there was plenty of room to unload, "good morning."

"Right back at you, kiddo," he said, jumping to the ground. He was wearing jeans, Blundstone boots and a cowboy hat, but he wasn't a rider. He supported Rob's sport a hundred percent and he liked the horses, but he was quite happy to stay on the ground. "How are you holding up?"

"Great," I said, quickly ducking into the trailer to avoid his sympathetic look and put off any more questions. I knew Rob's dad still worried about me after that horrible night I'd taken Caprice and ran away from my crazy parents to come live with the Ahlbergs. And I appreciated that he cared about me, but that didn't mean I wanted to go around sharing my *feelings* every time I saw him.

Everyone at the barn had been so nice and supportive. Sadie had even given me the number of a counsellor just in case I wanted to talk to someone. But honestly, I didn't want to talk about it at all; it was easier to pretend that the whole thing had never happened.

All I wanted to do was to play with horses, practice archery, and enjoy what was left of my summer in peace. There was no need to ruin all that by constantly dredging up the past.

"Hey, you," Rob said from inside the trailer. He had a cup of coffee in one hand and Ferdi's lead in the other, but he somehow still managed to lean over and wrap me in a tight hug.

I let myself rest against him for a second, inhaling deeply and feeling like I always did when he was around, sort of safe and normal. I didn't know how I'd gotten so lucky as to have him in my life.

I pushed back reluctantly, already feeling the earlier tiredness of the morning dissolve like magic and be replaced by a new shot of energy.

"You ready to have fun, Artimax?" I said, turning to Rob's little Appaloosa-Warmblood cross, who was bobbing his head impatiently. I tickled his speckled nose and then reached up to scratch him under his neatly-pulled mane. He was my favourite horse to exercise, after Red, and I always chose him for these conditioning rides. I unclipped him and led him down the ramp, following Ferdi into the barn.

On the days when the barn was full, we'd often put Rob's horses in the unused back paddocks while we rode, but it was much quicker, and more fun, if he just used the main barn and we could get tacked up together. With half the horses already turned out in the pasture there was room enough for everyone today.

I went back for the little buckskin mare, Possum, and took a moment to admire how nicely muscled she'd become since coming to stay with Rob this spring. She'd been sent down with two other young, green horses from my Aunt Lillian's ranch to see if they'd sell more quickly here on the Island. Now Possum looked less like a working ranch horse and more like a little show pony, with her silky, black mane freshly trimmed and her buttermilk coat shiny with dapples. Rob would probably have no trouble finding a good home for her.

"Sorry, you'll have to get Maverick yourself," I said quickly as I passed, sending him a teasing look.

Maverick was another one of Aunt Lillian's projects, but he was my least favourite horse. He was a good-looking animal with a slick, black coat that glistened in the sun and delicately carved features that spoke to his good breeding. But the sullen, untrustworthy look rarely left his face, and he usually kept his pointed little ears flattened tight against his head unless there were treats around.

The vet, the chiropractor, and the massage therapist hadn't found anything physically wrong with him; it looked like this was just his permanent, charming personality. I didn't think it made him a good sales candidate, but Rob still had faith in him for some reason.

"You kids have fun," Rob's dad said once we were all unloaded and he'd unhooked the trailer from his work truck. "Your coffee and pastries are in the tack room, Astrid. We didn't forget."

"Ooh, thanks," I said, disappearing into the tack room to find the greasy, brown paper bag that contained my favourites. I came back out with Red's brush box in one hand and a sticky piece of raspberry glazed fry-bread in the other. I'd become addicted to the stuff since Rob's dad had brought me some from his friend's gourmet food truck this summer and now I could never get enough.

"Right, ring or trails?" Rob said, taking a sip of his coffee.

"Trails," I said quickly, not even hesitating. It was too nice of a morning to waste inside.

"Aye, aye, Captain," Rob teased. "Who's up first?"

"Red, of course," I said since he was my obvious favourite. "What about you?"

"I'll tack-up Jerry, then; Red's a good influence on him. When is Hilary planning on riding again, anyway? It's getting a little silly that she's still paying me to exercise her horse when she's perfectly able to ride."

"Soon, I hope," I said, taking my last bite of pastry and ducking into Red's stall. Even though Hilary was being incredibly irritating lately, I still felt a bit guilty talking about her behind her back, even to Rob. She'd been a really good friend to me all these years and her family had taken me in when I had nowhere to go. I just hoped she'd get over herself soon.

I knew Rob cared about her, too, but he was getting frustrated with how she was acting. And I hadn't even told him yet how much extra work I still had to do. I was avoiding that conversation as long as I could. Surely things would get better on their own eventually.

Red was already fairly clean, and it only took me a few minutes to run a soft body brush over his sides to whisk off some stray bits of dust, pick his feet, and put his boots on. I frowned at the frayed edges at the bottom of both front boots where some of the stitching had come apart. I used them nearly every day on either Red or Ellie and they were looking a little worse for wear.

Probably the salt water from the ocean eating them away, I thought with a sigh, *but they'll have to do.* I just didn't have the money in my non-existent budget to buy any new stuff now.

I slipped a clean, sky-blue pad on his back and then settled his saddle in place, shifting it back a little until it fit perfectly. Then I did his girth up loosely and put his bridle on, fussing with the straps until they were tucked neatly into their keepers and the bit sat evenly in his mouth.

Finally, he was ready to go, and he clopped out of his stall after me, his eyes bright with anticipation.

"Ready?" Rob said with a grin. He was already up on Jerry, his legs hanging loosely against the horse's sides, stirrups crossed over the front of his saddle.

Jerry stood with his head high, staring off in the distance with his gaze fixed on something only he could see. I tightened Red's girth and swung up from the mounting block, leaning down to give him an appreciative pat, thankful that I was riding him and not a younger, more reactive horse like Jerry.

Rob rode the big horse easily, the reins held lightly between his fingers. He was not at all concerned with any quirks or shenanigans some of the horses pulled on him like I would have been. I'd never actually seen him afraid of anything.

"Come on, big guy," he said, brushing his calves softly against Jerry's sides.

Jerry snorted loudly through both nostrils and took a couple of big prancing trot steps as if he were about to get airborne. Rob adjusted his reins slightly but acted like he didn't even notice the big horse's energy.

"So, where should we go this morning?" he asked casually, not losing his position as Jerry skipped sideways away from a scary tuft of grass.

"The whole route," I said without hesitation since this was my first time out in days and I felt like I owed Red a decent ride. And myself for that matter.

Whatever Rob's strategy was with Jerry it seemed to work: within a minute the young horse's excitement drained away. He let out a big sigh and dropped his head, strolling along like a relaxed trail horse, his moment of drama completely forgotten.

I breathed in the fresh, country air happily and leaned back in the saddle, looking up at the clear, blue sky with utter contentment. These were the perfect moments I lived for; being out in nature with the people and animals that I liked best.

"Hey, are we still going to do that schooling show?" Rob asked casually, bringing me back to the present with a jolt. "It's coming up in a few weeks."

"Oh, shoot," I said, clapping a hand to my forehead. "I'm so sorry. I printed off the entry forms and everything and then totally forgot about them. There's just been so much going on..." I stopped, my eyes losing focus as I gazed off into the distance, all at once remembering that final night I'd run away. My skin prickled. I could almost hear Marion's scream, the horrible sound of Caprice's panicked yelps when my dad had hurt her, the terrible utter helplessness I'd felt.

I shook my head to clear it, shivering despite the relentless August sun beating down overhead.

Pull yourself together, I told myself sternly. Most of the time I thought I was totally over what had happened but sometimes, out of the blue, it would all come rushing back.

"It's no problem," Rob said easily, turning to look over his shoulder at me, never guessing the things running through my head. "You can still send them in if you hurry. The entries haven't closed yet."

I looked down at Red's neck bobbing away happily beneath me and sighed. The truth was that I had barely schooled him or Ellie at all in the last month. I'd been so busy that I usually just spent all my precious riding time going out on the trails or practicing mounted archery on our home-built course in the woods. I hadn't seemed to have the heart for schooling lately, I got distracted too easily and it just felt a bit pointless.

"I can go over your tests with you if you like," Rob said encouragingly, not understanding my silence. "I mean if you want me to."

"Rob, I'm really sorry," I said miserably. "I just don't have time right now. We have the last of archery camp all this week and then school's starting. I haven't even picked up my uniform yet…" I was astonished to hear the quiver in my voice. Why on earth was I making such a big deal about this? My emotions always seemed to run so closely to the surface lately, any little thing could set me off.

"Hey, it's okay," Rob said, drawing Jerry level with Red and laying a hand softly on my arm. "I know you've had a lot going on. I just thought it was something you were looking forward to. Something we could do together."

"It was," I said guiltily. "I can't believe I forgot about it. I even told Aunt Lillian I'd take Ellie to get her some show miles; I hope she's not too disappointed."

"Of course she won't be. Everyone understands that this summer has been hard on you, Astrid. Besides, there's a whole winter full of schooling shows you can sign up for. I bet it will be easier once your new instructor arrives and you can take lessons again. Or, I can ride Ellie in it for you if you want, if you're worried about getting her more mileage."

"That's a good idea, actually," I said gratefully, glad to be off the hook, "thanks. Oh, I forgot to tell you, new coach, Liza's friend Oona, is supposed to be coming today, after lunch."

"Really? That's great, I didn't think she'd be here so soon. Let me know once her lesson schedule is set up. I'd like to try her out."

"Sure, I don't know what she'll be like, though. Liza hinted that she might be a little weird."

"It's okay," Rob shrugged and sent me a sideways look. "I'm used to hanging out with weird girls by now."

"Hey!" I punched him playfully on the shoulder. "What's that supposed to mean?"

"Nothing, nothing," he said innocently, sending me a wink and a smile. "Seriously, though, she's probably going to be good. Liza wouldn't have sent her otherwise. And weird doesn't have to mean bad. Nori thinks *we're* pretty weird after all with our crazy horse-training ideas."

"Yeah, she totally thinks we're nuts sometimes."

Nori was the twelve-year-old daughter of Norman's owner Annie, and she'd been pretty angry at the world when she and her family had first arrived. She'd mostly been mourning the death of her young event horse, Lumi, but she also hadn't thought much of the way we handled the horses; her opinion was that we were too soft on them and spent too much time on slow conditioning work, building the horse's bodies and minds so that they were prepared to tackle harder jobs in the future. It wasn't Nori's style to do *anything* slowly.

She'd changed her mind about most of it over the summer, especially since Rob had started letting her ride Maverick.

"Hey, are we still on for the movie tomorrow night?"

"Yep, I think so. As long as Hilary's parents still let her go. They've been arguing about Darius again and she's been sulking in her room since yesterday."

"She's still being moody, hey?"

"That's putting it mildly. I honestly don't know what's gotten into her. She has everything that she wants out of life and she doesn't seem happy at all. She has a fantastic horse she doesn't ride, a beautiful barn that she hardly sets foot inside anymore. And yeah, her parents are being a little strict about Darius but at least they're letting her *see* him. My dad wouldn't have let me date anyone. Ever. Not even you and you're perfect.

She has no idea how lucky she is."

"Perfect, hey?" Rob said, grinning. He eased Jerry to a halt so I could catch up.

"Come on, you know what I mean," I said. "You're like the most honest, trustworthy person on the planet. Anyone would be safe with you."

"I don't know, Astrid, that sounds pretty boring. You just haven't seen my wild side yet," he said, wiggling his eyebrows at me suggestively.

"Oh, please, you're about as wild as Red here. You're dependable and smart and you're brilliant with horses and that's why I lo—" I bit the word off before it could come out, "…like you so much." I corrected, my heart contracting painfully in my chest. What was I doing? I'd almost accidentally said that I loved him. Who said things like that? He'd think I was the stupidest person ever.

He looked at me steadily, his smile slipping away, and then he leaned over from Jerry's back and kissed me so softly that it was like the gentlest of silk brushing across my lips. But there was nothing soft about the jolt of electricity that sizzled and crackled between us, so intense that it took me by surprise. We broke apart, just staring at each other wide-eyed until impatient Jerry bobbed his head up and down and started up the trail of his own accord.

I let Red find his own way while I sat there on autopilot, my thoughts and emotions churning so fast that I could hardly think.

"Come on," Rob called casually over his shoulder, "let's trot this stretch."

I was glad to follow his lead and by the time we'd trotted and cantered a couple of times I was back to my old self again.

We stopped on the beach to let the horses wade knee-deep in the water. Even though they'd been there a million times before, Jerry still made a show of lifting each front hoof high in the air and slamming them down in the water one at a time, snorting dramatically and getting us all wet. Red was too dignified for that, but he dipped his nose carefully in the sea-foam and licked the salty brine off his lips like it was the most delicious thing he'd ever tasted. When he lifted his head, he had a funny little mustache of foam stuck to his upper lip that suited him perfectly.

We trotted up the hill to the woods and then let the horses canter up to the make-shift archery range where we'd set up a handful of targets in a line between the trees.

"Sorry, Red, I didn't bring my bow," I said, scratching his neck as he automatically stopped parallel to the first target and stood motionless, expecting me to shoot. We'd worked hard to get Red, Ellie, and Rob's horses comfortable with us shooting off their backs. Darius had taught me how to school them slowly, building up their tolerance to the arrows whizzing overhead until they were rock solid. We'd started first on the ground, then when mounted, and then at faster and faster gaits.

Red never forgot anything he'd been taught, especially when there were treats involved, and now he arched his neck and swivelled an ear back at me, convinced he was being a perfect pony.

"Fine, yes, you're a good boy." I laughed and fished a treat from my pocket which is exactly what he'd been waiting for. He turned his nose so I could lean forward and slip it between his searching lips. "Don't tell anyone that I'm teaching you bad habits, though."

Past the archery range was a nice wide path that was perfect for cantering; we let them move out for one last stretch and then, reluctantly, brought them back down to a walk to let them cool out.

"I'm glad you're here today," I said, staring dreamily up at the blue sky overhead. "I wish this is how life was always."

"Do you?" Rob asked, and I looked up at the strange, almost sad, note in his voice.

"Of course I do, who wouldn't want to do this forever?"

Rob didn't say anything for a few minutes and we walked on a loose rein, letting the horses stretch.

I glanced over at him a few times, but he looked so deep in thought that I didn't want to bother him.

"The thing is," he said finally, drawing Jerry to a halt, "I think I want to work with horses full time once I graduate."

"Well, that's not shocking, Rob. I think we all knew that."

"Yes, but my dad doesn't. I know he wants me to go to university."

"Come on, he's the best parent on the planet; he's not going to expect you to do something you don't want for the rest of your life. You ride horses all day long, every day; surely he knows that you don't want to give it up to work in some office somewhere."

"Not an office, no, but I'm sure he was hoping I'd take over his business one day. I think the plan was that I get an Economics degree or go into Architecture or something so that at least I could be in the same industry. My sister's definitely not interested in taking over so that leaves me."

"So, what do you want to do instead then? Train horses for

other people or buy and sell your own?"

"I don't know, really, maybe a bit of both. I just know that they're the best part of my day and I can't see losing that to just ride for an hour after work every night or on the weekends. That's not a life."

"Well, you're good enough, Rob. You're as good a rider as Liza—"

"Hardly," he laughed, "but maybe I'll get there one day. If I train hard enough."

"What about showing professionally? Maybe I could go to the Olympics for archery and you could go for eventing."

He laughed again, his eyes crinkling in the corners as he looked at me.

"That's a nice dream; if anything, it would be dressage. That's what I want to focus on once I've graduated high school."

"Why not now?" I asked, already guessing the answer.

"My dad loves watching me go cross-country, and he likes that crowd, he thinks dressage shows are too snooty. He supports me so much that it's the least I can do since he's driving me everywhere and pays for most of my riding. I don't hate eventing, I just like dressage better, that's all. It speaks to me somehow."

"Yeah." I sighed, reaching down to scratch Red's shoulder. I *wished* I felt that inspired by ring work right lately. I remembered how it used to feel. Every moment on Quarry had been like a journey unfolding, a secret language unravelling, brand new territory to explore. Everything had always felt so new and magical.

But now it was different. I loved spending time with Red more than anything, but I just couldn't seem to find the passion for dressage that I'd had before. I felt much happier being out in the woods with him or practicing on our archery course than I was trotting in circles in the ring.

Back at the barn, we took turns hosing the horses down, making sure all the salty ocean water was cleaned off their legs before carefully drying them and putting them back into their paddocks.

As soon as I unclipped his halter, Red arched his neck and pricked his ears at me, bobbing his nose expectantly, knowing our routine.

"Okay, okay," I laughed and handed him the carrot chunk I'd stashed in my grooming tote. "I didn't forget."

He crunched it happily, dripping white and orange foam onto the fresh shavings, his eyes half-closed in bliss.

"You hang out here while I finish my ride," I whispered to him, running a finger down his blaze, "and then you can go out in the pasture for the rest of the day. Okay?"

"You want Artimax next?" Rob called from the aisle, already knowing my answer.

"Definitely. You're taking Ferdi out?"

"Yeah, I wouldn't mind taking him over a few of the lower jumps to stretch his legs. You up for that?"

"Sure," I said, slipping out of Red's stall into the aisle. I wasn't much of a jumper. It was fun enough popping over the low, natural logs that we'd set up in the woods around the property, but I didn't get excited over it the way Rob and Nori did. After my first few nervous attempts when we'd first set up the course, I'd realized that Artimax knew what he was doing and I pretty much just had to sit there, stay balanced, and not get in his way.

"Are you going to take care of me out there, buddy?" I said, moving into his borrowed stall. He was already waiting for me, eyes bright and ears pricked. Artimax was my favourite of Rob's horses. He wasn't very tall, but he had a huge powerful chest and hindquarters and an arched, well-muscled neck. He was a strange cross, part Warmblood and part Appaloosa, but, after a couple of years of conditioning, he'd ended up looking like a compact baroque horse, like an Andalusian or a Lusitano, but with striking white spots on his mottled grey coat. He had a lot of personality and had been a bit of a handful when Rob first bought him, but now he was a fun, dependable horse and I loved him.

As usual, he couldn't just stand still when I brushed him, he had to turn around and inspect each brush with his speckled pink nose, and softly bite the hoof pick, and check my pockets for treats whenever I moved within range of his searching lips.

He bobbed his nose up and down appreciatively whenever I found an itchy spot and lifted each of his big feet helpfully for me to pick out before I even asked.

"You're such a funny guy," I told him, giving him a hug around his neck and leading him from his stall, fully tacked up. I took him outside to the mounting block and climbed easily onto his back, crossing the stirrups over the front of his saddle and letting my legs drape lightly over his sides.

Rob came out a few minutes later with his young chestnut gelding, Ferdi, who looked half-asleep. A year's worth of gentle, steady schooling had built muscle in all the right places. Even at six, he still looked like a baby, but his chest had finally filled out so his mile-long legs looked more in proportion to his body and his well-muscled topline meant that he didn't look so thin and reedy.

The sun was climbing and all the cool morning air had pretty much evaporated. Bees hummed around us and a trio of small sap-suckers flew from tree to tree alongside the driveway, knocking at the bark in search of bugs.

Over the summer I'd ridden our winding network of trails so often that it probably should have been boring by now. But I never got tired of it; each ride was an adventure.

We turned to the right and rode down a sandy trail edged with young, green pine saplings, then headed steeply downhill until we reached my favourite spot, the place where the smaller trees gave way to the last remnants of an ancient rainforest. The temperature dropped a few degrees as soon as we entered the grove, enough to make me shiver and goosebumps prickle up my arms. The light barely filtered in through the dense canopy of trees and the birdsong was replaced by a deep silence. We almost never spoke in here; there was something about it that was like the inside of a cathedral, you felt like you were entering some sacred place.

The horses picked their way carefully along the damp trail, hooves sinking a little into the spongy earth, and then, too soon, we were heading upward again, the path turning back to sand under the horse's feet. The horses pricked their ears and picked up their pace, already knowing that soon it would be time to canter again. They needed no encouragement to move into a quick, excited trot.

"Hang on there, friend," Rob said, as Ferdi let out a small excited buck. He waited until Ferdi was moving in a nice, steady rhythm again and then signaled him to canter. Ferdi sprang forward enthusiastically and surged up the hill, sand flying up behind him. It was much more of a gallop than a canter, but Rob didn't seem to mind.

I held Artimax back a little so we wouldn't get a face full of dirt and then shifted one seat-bone back slightly, asking him to pick up a canter. Artimax was in a relaxed mood and not worried about catching up with his friend at all so I let him move along on a loose rein. I noticed with satisfaction how much easier his upward transitions had become for me. He was so much more balanced, and it was easier for him to rock back on his hocks and pick up the canter rather than fall into it on his forehand and root at the reins for balance.

He was the type of horse that was easy for anyone to ride, but not so easy to ride *well*. It had taken me a while to figure out how to help him balance like Rob did.

I think that's one of the things I like best about riding so many different horses, I thought, *they're all such unique puzzles, and you have to think your way through putting the pieces together so they work. And every puzzle is different than the one before. I can understand why Rob would want to do this forever.*

I came out of my daydream just as Rob moved smoothly off the path and popped Ferdi effortlessly over one of the logs we'd set up alongside the trail.

Oh, right, I guess I should pay attention.

Arti's ears pricked as he spotted the jump, but he barely even had to adjust his stride, it was just like taking one huge canter step. For a second, we were suspended in the air and then back down to earth again with hardly a jolt.

"Good boy," I said, scratching his neck appreciatively. "Thanks for taking care of me." I didn't think I'd ever be a graceful jumper but at least I'd learned to sit quietly and let him do his job.

There were only a handful of low jumps scattered through the woods, nothing too challenging, just enough to give the young horses a taste and let the experienced horses stretch their legs.

"You should come with me to the cross-country schooling tomorrow," Rob said, "it's a nice track, you'd probably like it."

"No thanks," I said quickly, "I'm teaching at archery camp tomorrow, but I'd love to watch another time."

"Oh yeah, I forgot about that. I couldn't remember why you weren't going with me."

I turned at the strange note in his voice. He sounded almost sad again, but when I looked over, his face was smooth and unworried.

"Which horses are you taking?" I asked.

"All of mine and I can take Ellie, too, if you like. I have time."

I thought of delicate little Ellie hurtling across a cross-country course and shivered.

Rob glanced over at me and laughed, guessing my thoughts. "There's a modified course for schooling baby horses, you know," he said, "and scaredy-cat riders."

He laughed as I rolled my eyes and stuck my tongue out at him.

"They're basically the height of cross-rails to help the greenies gain confidence. There won't be anything there that she couldn't handle, and it would give her some new experiences."

"I guess." I sighed. "You're probably right. I know Aunt Lillian wants her out doing all sorts of stuff. But how are you supposed to take all five horses on your own? You'd need like six extra hands to get them all ready and cool them out."

"No big deal," he said, grinning at me. "My dad will be there to help. The baby horses will go in the morning and Artimax and Ferdi in the afternoon. I'll drop the young horses back off at home before taking the other guys out. Don't worry, I'm used to it."

We walked in silence for a few minutes while I thought it over. Of course, Ellie should go. I trusted Rob completely not to put her in a situation she couldn't handle. And yet, I couldn't help but worry about her. Would she have a good time? Would she be scared? She'd be with Possum and Maverick...

I sat up straight in the saddle as a sudden thought hit me.

"Rob, did you tell Nori that you planned to take Maverick tomorrow?"

"Oh, shoot." Rob's face creased. "I totally forgot about that. I didn't even think to run it by her. Is she going to flip out?"

"Um, probably. She is Nori, after all, that's kind of what she does."

Nori's horse Lumi had died the year before in a horrible freak accident on course. Even though it hadn't even happened at a fence, Nori had blamed herself and sworn off eventing forever. She wouldn't be happy if she found out Rob was taking her favourite horse cross-country, even if it was just an easy schooling day.

"Argh, all right, I guess I should call her and talk to her tonight."

"Good luck," I said sympathetically. "You know, you should really just let her buy him. She's the only person Maverick likes."

"I know. I guess it makes sense, but I'm just afraid she's going to change her mind and want to compete again in a few months and then she'll have to sell him. Maverick is a good all-around horse but he's never going to be a top athlete. The Nori I knew, before the accident, was as competitive as they come, and she was talented, too. I can't see her giving all that up forever."

"Well, she's pretty stubborn once she sets her mind on something. I believe her when she says she's quit for good."

"I'll think about it. I just don't want him to be passed around from home to home. He's the type of horse who could end up in a bad situation in the wrong hands. He's not exactly a joy to work with."

"I know. That's exactly why I think he and Nori were made for each other."

We let the horses walk the last ten minutes on a loose rein, dangling our feet out of the stirrups and chatting about all sorts of things. Being with Rob was so easy. The dark shadows that often crowded around me when I was alone just seemed to melt away when he was around.

After we'd cooled Ferdi and Artimax out and put them away, we took a break to refuel on coffee and the last of the pastries.

"All right, Ellie and Possum next and then I'll work Maverick in the ring," Rob said. "I forgot that we're short a horse now that Sadie's back from vacation and can ride Riverdance herself."

"Yeah, I'm okay not having one more horse to ride." I laughed, heading into Ellie's stall. I'd loved riding Riverdance, Sadie's flashy Lusitano who'd once been a legitimate bullfighting horse, but working four horses a day after doing all the stalls and paddocks and other barn work, on top of all my other chores, were more than enough.

I'd always admired that Rob could happily ride eight horses a day without breaking a sweat but that was definitely not me.

Ellie met me at the front of her stall with a happy little nicker. She nuzzled her soft golden nose against my arm and I smoothed her long forelock down the center of her face. She was a sweet, uncomplicated mare who'd originally been Hilary's project horse until the whole ankle accident thing. Then I'd inherited her somehow.

I hadn't wanted to ride a green horse at first, but now I loved working with her. I had to remind myself daily that she was not *really* my horse, she was Aunt Lillian's, and she was there only to be sold. Still, it was hard not to get attached.

I ran a brush over her glossy coat, picked her feet and hesitated before putting the still-damp boots on her legs. I hadn't gotten her a set of her own because I didn't know when she'd be leaving, but it was times like these when I wished I had.

I led her over to the mounting block and she stood motionless, tilting her head sideways a little so that she could watch me get on her back. She turned her nose and bumped my foot gently, lipping softly at the toe of my boot.

"You're a silly girl," I said, scratching her under her golden forelock. She was pretty much any kid's dream horse and I hoped that she'd be sold to someone who loved and appreciated her. I could hardly stand the thought that a new owner might treat her badly.

Stop thinking like that, I ordered myself. *Nobody is going to treat*

27

her badly. She'll be sold to the perfect home. Besides, that's probably months away, you can worry about that when the time comes.

Possum and Ellie were evenly matched in size, temperament and good looks. Neither of them was the flashiest of movers in the world, but they were steady and honest and got the job done. They seemed to enjoy being in each other's company, too, preferring to trot along side by side whenever possible instead of single file.

The sun had climbed steadily higher in the sky and the temperature had now reached the near-roasting point. Sweat dotted my face and trickled down my back and I was glad now that this was my last ride of the day.

We didn't push the horses too hard in the heat, just trotted and cantered them a little in the shady spots and let them walk the rest of the time. In her last email, Liza had reminded me to include some lateral work on our conditioning rides so now I gently added some leg yields on the wider trails, smoothly moving Ellie from side to side, focusing on her hind end to make sure her hind legs were crossing properly. And then added some slight shoulder-ins as well.

When we got back, I said I'd give them both baths and get them put away myself while Rob went and tacked up Maverick.

By the time I had both girls clean, dry and back in their paddocks snacking on hay, Rob was already cantering the grumpy little black horse around the cooler indoor arena.

I grabbed a root beer for me and a bottle of water for Rob from the fridge in the tack room and went inside the arena to watch the end of his ride.

They were cantering around in a wide figure eight, Maverick

snorting rhythmically at every stride. Rob brought him back to a trot in the middle of the ring and then asked him to canter again, this time on the opposite lead.

I frowned, watching the angry swish of Maverick's tail as he passed me. The horse was doing everything he was asked to, but it was obvious that his heart wasn't in it. He kept his ears back and there was a certain tightness around his mouth and nostrils that showed that he wasn't thrilled about his job.

"How does he look?" Rob asked, bringing him down to a walk.

"Cranky," I said honestly.

He looked down at Maverick's silky neck and frowned. "Yeah, that's what I thought. He's perfectly obedient, but it feels like there's something missing. He doesn't enjoy any of this."

"He doesn't always look that way with Nori, though," I said slowly. "I think he maybe tries harder for her. And he loves, or at least doesn't hate, the archery."

"You're probably right," Rob said unenthusiastically. "But Nori is just a kid. She could drop horses completely tomorrow and take up knitting."

I coughed hard, nearly choking on my root beer. "Knitting? I think she'd rather use the needles to stab someone."

"Yeah, okay, bad example. Maybe she'd take up kickboxing or Olympic rowing or whatever. I just mean she could get bored of him and sell him at any time. I just worry about him. He's so moody. Can you imagine him with someone who didn't understand that? Who hit him or punished him?"

"I know," I said. "I get it, but they're here to be sold, Rob. They have to go *somewhere*."

"And that, there, is the reason I hesitate to go into horses full time. It's fine when they're your own and you have the final say what happens to them. But when they're not yours…. Well, maybe I don't have the stomach for the business side of training."

"I think you do," I said thoughtfully. "I think that you'll be good at it because you *do* care. You'll always go that extra mile to do what's right for the horses."

"Like you do," Rob said, smiling down at me. "I see how hard you work hard to make sure they're happy."

"Yes, we make a good team."

Before Rob could answer we heard the sound of his dad's truck chugging up the driveway and we had to hurry to cool Maverick out and get everyone ready to load back on the trailer.

"See you tomorrow night for the movies," I said once the final horse had been loaded. I let Rob pull me into a hug, resting my cheek against his shirt one final time and inhaling deeply.

I waved them down the driveway and went to turn Ellie, Red, and Jerry out on pasture and make sure all the paddocks and stalls we'd used for Rob's horses were still clean.

It wasn't until I climbed wearily onto my bike and pedalled the long, slow incline up to the house that I realized how truly exhausted I was.

"What's the matter, sheep?" I asked, pausing to take a break under a shade tree right beside their pasture at the top of the hill. Normally they would be out grazing in their field, but today they were all lined up against the fence, staring at me expectantly.

I dropped my bike on the grass and went over to the fence to visit them, reaching out to scratch my favourite one, Portia, under her chin. They were hair sheep, not the type with wool, so they really looked more like goats than traditional fuzzy sheep. Their coats were silky soft in the summer heat and their black and white fur glistened in the sun.

"*Baa*," Portia said the second I stopped petting her. She used her nose to nudge me sharply on the arm, demanding more scratches.

"You're so bossy, Portia," I told her. "Why are you standing out here in the heat? Go in your nice, shady barn."

The flock continued to stare at me blankly. I had no idea what they wanted, but I checked to make sure their big water tub was full just in case and then continued on up to the house.

Chapter Two

When I opened the front door, the temperature inside the house was blissfully cold against my sundrenched skin. I stopped in the doorway, closing my eyes and just letting every last drop of heat evaporate from my body.

The house was silent except for the hollow *tock, tock, tock* of the big stand-up clock in the entryway. I pulled my paddock boots off, wiggling my hot, cramped toes luxuriously against the cool wooden floor and then padded directly into the family room, the place where it was okay for Hilary and me to lounge in our dirty horse clothes and for Caprice to get up on the furniture.

Caprice was already there, stretched out asleep with her head on a pillow at the end of one of the big leather couches.

"Is there room for me?" I asked, sinking gratefully down into the cool, soft cushions. Caprice immediately sprang up and came to snuggle with me, curling her soft body against mine and nudging her head under my hand so I'd pet her.

"Good girl," I said, yawning and closing my eyes. The house was so quiet and peaceful; I could just drift away and sleep for hours.

"Don't you want lunch, Astrid?" Mrs. Ahlberg said, appearing beside me out of nowhere and jolting me awake.

"What?" I sat up, looking around in confusion. "Oh, no thank you. I don't have any energy for food right now, maybe later."

"Food gives you energy. Honey, you look worn out. Have you been drinking enough water? It's so hot out there today, you need to stay hydrated."

"Is coffee considered water?" I asked sleepily.

"No, it certainly is not. Where's Hilary anyway? I thought she went down to the barn when we got back from grocery shopping. Wasn't she outside helping you get everything ready for the new coach?"

"I haven't seen her yet today," I confessed reluctantly, not quite meeting Mrs. Ahlberg's anxious gaze. I was frustrated with Hilary, but I didn't want to get her in trouble.

"That girl. I don't know what's gotten into her lately, Astrid. But I really don't want you being left shouldering all the extra workload. You look exhausted."

"No, I'm good," I murmured, closing my eyes and pretending to fall back into a doze so I could avoid this conversation. In a moment, her footsteps trailed from the room and I snuggled deeper into the couch, trying to regain the peaceful sleep I'd come out of.

"Here you go." It felt like only a second had passed but Mrs. Ahlberg was back with a plate of food in one hand and a bottle of water in the other. "Sit up, dear. Hilary's in her room getting changed. Your new coach is going to be here in an hour and I know you'll want to go down to the barn and make sure everything is tidy for her. Have your lunch and make sure you drink all the water."

Thanking her I pulled myself into a sitting position and set the plate, filled with a thick deli meat sandwich, my favourite salad with pecans, cranberries and goat cheese, and a small pile of chips, onto my lap.

I did feel better after I'd eaten and drained all the water. The heavy feeling in my head passed and my muscles didn't ache quite so much.

Hilary trotted down the stairs, looking fresh and radiant in a clean pair of grey checked breeches and a plum-coloured polo shirt, her long blonde hair pulled up in a pony-tail and just the faintest trace of make-up on her face.

I eyed her carefully, but she didn't look sulky and moody like she had that morning. She looked like her easy-going, happy self again.

"She's almost here," she said, plopping down breathlessly on the chair across from me, "aren't you excited? Come on, let's head down to the barn and make sure everything's perfect."

"Okay, I just have to run upstairs and have a quick shower. I'll be right down."

"Well, hurry," she said, rolling her eyes a little. She brushed an invisible bit of dirt off her breeches and frowned. "I'd have thought you would have been ready ages ago."

I went to the kitchen to put my plate in the dishwasher and then ran upstairs to jump into the shower. There was no point in washing my hair since it would take hours to dry my curls properly, so I just pulled it back in a pony-tail to keep it out of the cool jets of water.

I could have stayed in there all afternoon, but the clock was ticking, and I knew Hilary would be getting impatient. I towelled off quickly and padded barefoot back to my room to find something decent to wear.

"No, definitely not," I said out loud, holding up the breeches I'd just changed out of. They had dirt smears all over them and would not make a good impression. I only owned one more pair for schooling and they were in pretty much the same state since I hadn't had time to do laundry at all this week.

White show breeches? I thought, considering they were the only clean pair I had left. No, it would look pretty pretentious to show up in those since I hadn't touched the ring in weeks. *Jeans it is, then.* I found a clean pair that I thought I looked decent in and a red t-shirt that only had one small hole in the armpit that nobody could see unless I lifted my arms too high.

I guess I'll have to go shopping before school starts, I thought ruefully. *I've almost worn everything out. Maybe I'll pick up a few things when I go to get my uniform.*

Technically, my dad and step-mom had left me a credit card to spend on school supplies, my uniform and other clothes, but the thought of using any money that came from *them* made me sick. I'd decided when I'd first run away that I would never touch another penny of their money again; I didn't want anything to do with them at all. But realistically, I would probably have to give in and use it unless I figured out a way to get a job. They were already paying for my school fees after all; there wasn't much I could do about that.

Aunt Lillian had been so upset about what had happened that she'd insisted on covering all Red and Ellie's farrier and vet bills, and the Ahlbergs were feeding me and Caprice and letting us stay on the farm as their guests. It was all very generous of everyone but a little mortifying, too; I hated to be a charity case. I wanted to pay for my *own* things and take care of Red and Caprice with my *own* money. I just didn't know how to make that happen yet.

"Astrid, what are you *doing* up there? We're going to be late," Hilary called up the stairs impatiently.

"Yeah, yeah," I muttered under my breath, staring at my reflection in the mirror over the dresser. *Good enough, you'll do,* I told myself. *The new coach won't care about what you look like, only what you ride like.*

Chapter Three

We'd hardly been at the barn for five minutes when a battered blue truck drove slowly up the driveway, squeaking and rattling as it moved toward us. From a distance, it reminded me of Aunt Lillian's ancient ranch truck that was always losing pieces and never quite worked properly.

That's a good sign, I thought, scuffing the worn toe of my boot into the gravel. *Anyone who drives a truck like Aunt Lillian's has to be nice.*

"That must be her," Mr. Ahlberg said helpfully from his spot on the golf cart. Hilary and I sat baking side by side in the sun at the picnic table, but her dad had parked the cart under a shade tree where he'd been casually thumbing through one of his farming books. Since they'd bought the farm last year, Hilary's parents had had to take a crash course in agriculture to learn how to take care of all the animals they'd collected. They'd been city people before the move and hadn't quite realized how much work a flock of sheep, chickens, quail, bees, and turkeys would be.

Normally, they left the running of the stable entirely in

Hilary's hands since it had been her project from start to finish. But today they'd thought it best if at least one of them met the new instructor since she was going to be living above the barn and everything. Just to make sure she wasn't some sort of psychopath.

Caprice squirmed on my lap when she heard the strange truck chugging up the driveway and let out a sharp warning bark.

"Wait, Caprice," I said but she twisted in my grasp, leaping off me just as the truck shuddered to a halt. She barrelled over at top speed then stood at the driver's side door, wagging hard and barking at the same time. She stood on her hind legs in an effort to be the first to greet the new arrival.

"Ow," I said, rubbing the spot where her claws had dug into my leg. I looked ruefully at the dirty paw prints on my jeans and sighed. I really wasn't meant to stay clean apparently.

Even though she hadn't ridden since her accident Hilary had zipped on her tall, custom leather boots over her checked breeches and added a pair of little gold horseshoe earrings and a matching gold chain. She looked like a professional rider while I looked… well, best not to think about that.

I held my breath as the truck door opened and a pair of legs in immaculate white breeches and tall burgundy boots swung out. The strawberry-blonde girl didn't match the truck at all. She should have been driving a little designer sports car rather than a rusty old beater. Her long red-blonde hair was scraped back into a tight pony-tail that had been braided down the length of her back. She had on a pair of oversized sunglasses and even at a distance, I could see the tiny rhinestones sparkling around the edges.

She didn't even glance at the little poodle spinning in circles at her feet. Instead, she stood with her hands on her hips, swivelling around slowly so she could take in the barn, the big sand ring and the woods nearby. Finally, she caught sight of us. She pressed her lips together in a thin line and straightened her shoulders like she was bracing against an unseen wind.

She doesn't like it, I thought in surprise and disappointment. To me, the Ahlberg's farm was pretty much perfect, but Liza had said that Oona had been training in Europe for the past few years. She was probably used to some crazy fancy dressage barns.

"Hello," she called stiffly, raising her oversized sunglasses and studying us solemnly from a pair of pale green eyes. She moved slowly, reluctantly, toward us looking like she'd rather get back in her clunky, old truck and drive away as fast as possible in the other direction.

"Hello," Mr. Ahlberg called out warmly before Hilary or I could respond. He jumped nimbly off the golf cart and went forward to shake her hand. "You must be Oona; we've heard good things about you from Liza."

"Oh," she said, struggling for a response. "It's a pleasure to meet you, I suppose." She cleared her throat a few times before adding, "thank you for inviting me."

She turned to look at Hilary and me, surveying each of us from top to bottom with a wide-eyed gaze as if she'd never seen anything quite like us before. Her gaze lingered for a moment on the smear of dirt on my jeans and she wrinkled her nose a little.

"This is my daughter Hilary and her best friend Astrid," Mr. Ahlberg said reassuringly, acting like there wasn't anything weird at all about this whole interaction. "They run the show here.

Hilary even designed the barn herself."

"It was my project for school," Hilary said hesitantly, for once not sounding like her usual overconfident self. "Well, for my homeschool program. We had to set up and design our own business." She faltered, pinned down by Oona's wide-eyed stare.

"Fascinating," Oona said in an obviously disinterested voice. There was an uncomfortable silence and then she added, "How many horses do you have here?"

"Just seven right now," Hilary said, uncertainly. "And our friend Rob trailers his horses in to ride here. We have one more space in the barn available and room for more boarders in the paddocks, but they're not filled yet."

"And your staff? How many people work here?"

There was another short uncomfortable silence and then Hilary said, "Well, nobody, officially. We all pitch in and the work gets done. Doesn't it, Astrid?"

"Um, yes," I said, squirming a little as Oona's appraising look swung back to me. It was like her sea-green eyes had x-ray vision and she could look right through me. Even though I'd showered, I imagined that she knew exactly who it was that had cleaned all the stalls and paddocks this morning and ridden three horses in the late August heat. I shifted from foot to foot uncomfortably, my cheeks stinging with embarrassment.

"I see. So, you don't have any proper grooms at all," Oona said quietly. "Who gets the rider's horses ready, then?"

"Um…" Hilary and I exchanged a glance. "Everyone brushes and tacks up their own horses."

"Huh." Oona snorted sharply through her nose and shook her head. "Well, I'm not going to lie. This is not what I expected."

"Oh," Hilary said, her voice quivering a little. "You don't like it?"

"I didn't say that. It's a very beautiful setting, very…picturesque. It's just that I'm used to a more…formal atmosphere."

She stared at us and when nobody spoke, she pressed her lips together and sighed heavily. "Well, I suppose I'm here now. Show me the apartment and then you can take me on a tour of the facilities."

"Oh, okay," Hilary said, gulping a little. I shifted toward her so our shoulders bumped lightly together, lending her some support.

"Well, I'll let you girls get to it," Mr. Ahlberg said jovially, clapping his hands together, clearly done with his role as a supervisor. "I have a chicken pen to finish building."

"You don't want to come with us?" Hilary asked a little desperately, turning to look at him.

"No, no, I'm sure you have it all under control," he said, smiling broadly and sending her a wink as he made a beeline for his golf cart. "Text me or your mother if you need anything."

Hilary sighed, and her shoulders sagged as she led Oona upstairs to the small apartment over the barn. Hilary's mom had overseen the renovations herself and the flat was compact but beautiful, with one small bedroom, a kitchen and a little nook off to one side with bookshelves built into the wall that served as both a living room and dining room. Best of all, there were a set of sliding doors that led to a wooden balcony just big enough for two chairs and a small table. It had a view of the back paddocks and I'd already decided that if I ever got to live above my own barn that I'd have a balcony just like that where I'd eat breakfast every single morning.

Oona stood in the middle of the room and turned slowly in a circle, saying nothing, her mouth pulled into its signature frown.

I glanced at her sideways, trying to gauge her expression. Her face was a mask that gave away nothing about what she was feeling. I'd bet she'd make a terrific poker player.

"Well, this is the suite," Hilary said finally, swallowing hard.

"Yes," Oona said solemnly, still not smiling. "I see that. It's as nice as Liza told me. Small but satisfactory."

"Um, okay, good," Hilary said in a small voice. "I guess we can show you the rest of the farm then."

We went down the stairs in another uncomfortable silence.

"I like your truck," I said, finally thinking of something to say. "It reminds me of my Aunt Lillian's truck back at the ranch where I lived last year. That's where Liza lives now, of course."

"Oh right, the *cattle* ranch." Oona wrinkled her nose a little, not sounding interested in the least. "It's my father's truck. He loaned it to me since I haven't found anything suitable yet. I can't wait to give it back."

"Oh," I said and there was nothing more to say.

The silence stretched out painfully as we took Oona on a tour of the empty stables and paddocks. All the horses were turned out and, even to my eyes, the barn didn't seem as nice somehow without them.

She clearly hates it, I thought glumly, *and that means she won't stay, and we'll be without a coach again and we'll lose all the boarders. Hilary must be freaking out.*

"You're well organized," Oona said unexpectedly when we showed her the neatly arranged tack room that smelled of freshly oiled leather, "that's good. I don't enjoy disorder."

Hilary and I exchanged a furtive glance and led our guest down to the driveway to the lower pastures.

I wished that Mr. Ahlberg hadn't sped away on the golf cart quite so quickly, leaving us to walk. The afternoon sun was high in the sky and it beat down on us mercilessly on the trek to the pastures. Sweat beaded my face and slid down my back, partly from heat and partly from nerves.

"Here's our crew," Hilary said, leading Oona to Jerry's pasture first. "They're all friendly and easy to handle. That's my horse there, Jerry, he's a Swedish Warmblood."

"Hmm," Oona said, standing a few feet back from the fence. She crossed her arms over her chest, and tilted her head slightly to one side, going over them one by one with her laser-like stare. "They're nice horses, but they all look a bit soft, they need more muscle. What sort of conditioning programs are they on?"

"Programs?" Hilary said blankly. "Um, I'm still recovering from a very bad injury, so Astrid knows more about that..." She gulped and turned to look at me for help.

"We take them on the trails mostly," I said, finding my voice, "and sometimes we work in the ring. We haven't had a coach in a while, so we sort of just... well, have fun."

Oona's eyes flickered open wide as if this was a completely foreign concept. "Fun. I see."

I swallowed hard, wondering how this so-called interview could possibly get any worse. Liza herself had said that our trail rides were great for the horses to build up their strength and stamina. That had been our only plan for Red this summer. Get him moving forward and building up muscle. Maybe Oona thought we just sauntered along on the trail. I probably should have explained better.

We turned to the other pasture where Red and Ellie were turned out with Mister Sox and Norman.

"Oh," Oona said, sounding almost human for the first time, "you have a pony." She moved to the fence with an actual ghost of a smile on her face and leaned on the top board as cheeky Sox marched up looking for treats, a greedy glint in his eyes.

"You're pushy," she said, scratching his forehead as stuck his little nose over the fence and snorted his hot breath right next to her face. His long forelock hung over one eye making him look especially roguish. "I had a pony like you once. He was very bad, just so you know. But smart and handsome, too."

Hilary and I exchanged another glance; this was the first time Oona sounded remotely nice. Maybe there was hope for her yet.

"He's a Section C Welsh Cob," I said tentatively, "and he's nice even though he's pushy. Liza gave his little girl, Callie, some lessons and he's been much better since then. He just has a sense of humour."

Oona raised an eyebrow and turned around to look at me. "You think horses are capable of having a sense of humour? That's very anthropomorphic of you."

"Um," I said, staring at her blankly, my mind scrambling to remember what anthropomorphic meant. Was it treating animals like they were people? That sounded right.

I thought of all the bright, clever animals I'd known and yes some of them definitely had had a sense of humour. I didn't really want to argue with her, though; she didn't look like the type to welcome a fun debate.

Sox had no problems proving anyone wrong; before she could stop him, he reached out with his little yellow teeth and snapped up the end of Oona's long braid, gripping it triumphantly.

"Oh no, Sox, let go," Hilary ordered but the little pony just looked off into the far distance, not moving a muscle, Oona's hair firmly clamped between his teeth.

"Very funny," Oona said dryly. She turned around as much as she could and stuck her fingers into the corner of the pony's mouth in the foolproof method horse people had of prying open a horse's jaws. Only this time it didn't work. If anything, Sox bit down even harder.

"Sox, drop it," Hilary commanded like he was a dog.

Oona frowned and shifted her fingers to the left, poking again at that sensitive spot between his teeth that would automatically cause him to open his mouth.

I could see the determined resistance on his face as he fought to keep his mouth closed and then finally, with a sigh of disappointment, he reluctantly spit out her hair along with a wad of half-chewed grass and pony slobber.

"Monster," Oona said mildly as she examined the end of her braid, which was now stained a minty green colour.

"I'm so sorry," Hilary said, looking at Sox miserably. He stood at the fence watching us with his ears pricked and his lips working the air, hoping for another try.

"It's my fault," Oona said, looking almost pleased. "I know better than to turn my back on a pony. Let's see your schooling areas now."

She didn't say anything at all when we looked at the huge outdoor ring, but she nodded in approval when we took her to the indoor and even crouched down to pick up a handful of the footing, which was light sand mixed with strips of felt.

"Nice," she said, "this was a good choice."

"It's very bouncy, the horses like it," I said, then blushed once again when she gave me another slow, wide-eyed stare as if I'd said something bizarre.

"Well, um, I think you've seen everything," Hilary said, twisting her hands together nervously. "I don't know what you were expecting exactly. But we need a coach, badly. I thought Liza told you all about us and, er, the farm."

"She did," Oona said slowly. "I'm just not used to…well, doing things on such a small scale." She hesitated. "I was at my last position for over ten years. The Ecole was housed in a restored castle in rural Belgium. We had over seventy horses in our care at all times and an army of staff to take care of them."

Hilary and I exchanged a sideways look but said nothing.

"Anyway, you can see why this is such a change for me. It was quite a shock to have to leave so suddenly, and I haven't quite recovered yet. But, if you're willing, we will give this arrangement a six-month trial and see how it works for all of us."

"O…okay," Hilary said, sounding surprised that Oona actually wanted to stay.

"Liza said something about you possibly needing a barn manager. Is that something you wanted to make a part of the position?"

"Did she say that?" Hilary said, looking surprised and a little hurt. "I don't need a manager, I can handle things perfectly well on my own. We just need a coach."

"Suit yourself. I will take the next two days to get settled.

Schedule my lessons starting at seven o'clock on Monday morning at forty-five-minute intervals and a half-hour break at lunch. Lateness will not be tolerated. Make sure the horses are immaculate; any horse not up to inspection will be dismissed. That goes for the riders, too." Her gaze flicked toward the dirt smudge on my jeans, lingering meaningfully for a moment before moving away. "They must be clean and presentable; otherwise, no lesson."

"Okay," Hilary said again, her voice coming out a squeak, "that won't be a problem. I'll let everyone know. I'm...I'm glad you want to stay, though. We've been missing having lessons so much. After my accident..."

"I'm very tired," Oona interrupted stiffly. "I need to rest. I have a signed copy of the contract you sent me in the truck. Do you have a key for me?"

"Here," Hilary said, fishing a glittery, pink unicorn keychain out of the back pocket of her breeches and holding it out awkwardly between them.

Oona's eyes widened, and she took the key chain with just the tips of her fingers, wrinkling her nose in distaste at the charm attached to it.

"Lovely," she said in a flat voice, "goodbye."

Hilary and I looked at each other again and then hurried out of the ring, not looking back or saying a word until we were out of the barn and walking so fast up the driveway that we were practically running.

"Oh my gosh, she's nuts," Hilary whispered, stopping and clutching my arm as soon as we were out of sight of the barn.

"That was awful," I said and then for some reason I started to laugh and after a moment so did Hilary. We leaned against the fence lining the driveway and laughed until we were both nearly in tears.

"Liza did warn us that it might take a while to get used to Oona," I said, wiping my eyes. "She wouldn't have recommended her if she wasn't a good coach."

"I hope so. She'd better be freaking fantastic if we have to put up with her personality. I can't imagine things being very fun around here with her lurking around the barn. We'll lose boarders for sure if that's how she acts around everyone."

"Well, I guess we should give her a chance. That was interesting about the stable being in a castle, though. I'd like to see something like that."

"And that's another thing. Why did she mysteriously have to leave her last place if she loved it so much?"

"I don't know; Liza never said anything about that. But it did sound mysterious. I wonder if she left on her own or if they fired her?"

"Hopefully she didn't do anything too awful. I guess I don't have much choice but to hire her for now. We need a coach and she's already here. I just hope this doesn't end badly. I don't need any more stress in my life."

Chapter Four

"Hello, girls," Mr. Alhberg called out happily as he crossed the driveway in front of us, a hammer in one hand and a large paper bag in the other. "Hope everything went well with the new coach; she seems nice. You're just in time to help me put up the extension on the chicken run. I could use an extra pair of hands."

"Maybe Astrid can help, she's your favourite anyway." Hilary said it like a joke, but there was a strange undertone in her voice that made me look over at her quickly. "I have some paperwork to catch up on. And Darius said he'd call today…"

"Nice try, missy," her dad interrupted mildly, "if there's one thing I've learned in life it's to find a balance between work, play, and spending time with your family. We haven't had much family time lately. Come on out and help your old man with his silly project."

He wiggled his eyebrows at her in a funny way to make her laugh.

"Oh, fine," Hilary said, rolling her eyes, "but I have to go change first. I'll be down in a few minutes."

I was sure she'd disappear into the house and never come

back, but she reappeared at the chicken coop ten minutes later wearing scruffy jeans and a t-shirt that looked like it had seen better days. Her make-up was gone, and she looked just like my everyday best friend again.

"Here," she said, setting down a cloth bag filled with drinks and snacks. "This is for when we need a break."

It wasn't hard work, and thankfully the new chicken run was in the shade of a handful of towering pines clustered together around the coop. Mr. Ahlberg had already used a machine to sink neat rows of fence posts into the ground and all we had to do was stretch out the giant roll of wire and tack it to the posts, making sure to keep it even.

An hour later and we were standing in the middle of a huge, fully finished deluxe chicken run.

"Nice job, girls," Hilary's dad said, draping an arm over each of our shoulders. "Teamwork makes every job go that much quicker. The chickens will be very happy with their new playground. They were getting a little cramped in the old one. Stay here and I'll let them out to explore."

He went to the attached coop and flung the door open. There were some startled clucking noises from inside and then one by one the chickens flowed out the door and began excitedly exploring their new yard.

"Do you love it?" I asked a little speckled grey hen who stopped right at my feet and looked up at me, tilting her beak to one side, probably expecting the treats Mr. Ahlberg was always bringing them from the kitchen. "Did we do a good job?"

She made a soft trilling noise and began industriously scratching at the ground at our feet, looking for bugs.

"Do you always talk the animals like they're people?" Hilary said, laughing.

I looked at her thoughtfully, thinking back to the things Oona had said to me earlier, about whether I really believed that horses were capable of a sense of humour. "Yes, I guess I do," I said slowly, "I think they all understand, in their own way. I think animals are way smarter than we give them credit for."

"You're probably right. But you should be careful, people will think you're weird if you keep talking to the *livestock* out loud." She was still laughing, but somehow her voice had hardened a little and didn't sound so nice. "Darius probably thinks it's a bit...immature."

I looked up uncertainly to find her staring at me with her eyebrows raised, a superior look on her face.

"What do you mean?" I asked in confusion. "Darius *likes* animals. Talking to chickens is the same thing as talking to Jerry or Caprice, isn't it?"

"Well, I suppose. But that's all kid stuff, Astrid. We have to grow up sometime, right? We can't hang out in a barnyard all our lives, not if we want to be taken seriously."

"Huh? Why not? I don't mind hanging out with animals at all. And you used to talk to Jerry all the time."

"Yes, well," she frowned and looked down at her fingernails, picking at a spot where the purple polish had fallen off, "I guess I've just grown up. I still *like* animals, I just don't need to talk to them or spend all my time playing in the dirt with them getting filthy. There are better things I can do with my life."

"Oh, really?" I said, rolling my eyes. "And you've just decided to act all grown up overnight because Darius said so, did you?"

"Well, what if I did?" she asked furiously, her temper flaring up. "He's older, Astrid, and has certain standards. Besides, I'm trying to run my own business here. You might be doing all the heavy labour, but I'm doing the hard *mental* work of making sure everything stays running. I pay the bills and do all the ordering and keep things from falling apart. That sounds pretty grown-up to me."

"Wow, poor you," I countered, all that irritation I'd suppressed over the last month simmering to the surface. "I think you actually spend more time writing love notes to Darius than you do running the barn. And you're too self-absorbed to even visit your own horse. I don't even know you anymore, Hilary. I don't understand why you've changed into this new person and abandoned Jerry and the farm and everything you used to love."

"I didn't *abandon* Jerry, I've just been busy. I make sure he's taken care of. I pay Rob good money to ride him. He has everything he needs."

"Yes, but he doesn't have *you*," I insisted. "When is the last time you brushed him and hung out with him, let alone ride him? Why bother having a horse if you never even spend any time with him? It's not fair to him."

"That's it, I don't have time for this," Hilary said, turning on her heel and stomping toward the coop. "This conversation is over."

"Girls? Hilary, what's going on?" her dad asked in bewilderment, coming out of the coop. But she just marched toward the house without looking back at either of us.

Chapter Five

I didn't see Hilary again for the rest of the day. I kept myself busy until late afternoon by helping Mrs. Ahlberg with the vegetable garden and then went back down to the barn to bring the horses in and give them an early supper.

There was no sign of Oona's battered truck when I got there, and when I glanced up the stairs to her suite, the door was firmly closed.

Pender and Sadie were already in the aisle; they'd brought Riverdance and Rabbit in from the field themselves and were leisurely tacking up and reminiscing about the riding holiday to Portugal they'd taken earlier that spring.

"You have to go one day, Astrid," Pender said, brushing back a stray lock of frizzy hair impatiently with the back of her hand. "The place is something out of a fairy tale. The horses were incredible and being able to really feel those upper-level movements on a highly trained horse was an experience I'll never forget. It gave me some great goals to work toward with Rabbit, too."

The big thoroughbred swivelled one oversized ear toward her when he heard his name.

"Yes, that's right, you heard me," Pender said, laughing and poking him playfully on the shoulder, "no more slacking off for either of us, we're going to get both of us to Grand Prix one day, just you wait."

"Astrid, we met the new coach," Sadie said, peering at me over Riverdance's glossy neck, "she seems nice."

"Does she?" I asked incredulously, wondering if we were talking about the same person.

"Oh, well, being the new girl is always hard," Sadie said with a smile. "I'm sure she'll warm up once she's settled in. I actually remember meeting her a few times back in the day when she trained with Claudia. She used to trailer in for lessons when she was younger.

"I do remember that she had trouble getting along with some of the other students, but she and Liza were great friends. I heard she did very well on her European tour, then took a break to go to school, and then she was taken on by a trainer somewhere over there and just never came home. Until now. We're both going to take lessons with her on Monday. Did you book a spot yet?"

"Um, Hilary thought that she and I should wait and see how many other people wanted lessons first. She wanted the boarders and some of Liza's old students to have the first pick. She really wants Ally to bring Severus."

"Well, it would be great to see Ally again; I miss her being a part of barn life. But you're a boarder, too," Sadie said, frowning, "you have two horses here, actually."

"Well, sort of but I work off my board so it's different."

"It shouldn't be," Pender insisted, strapping on the last of Rabbit's boots, "you work so hard, Astrid, we all think…"

"We'd better get going, Pender" Sadie interrupted, "we don't want to be riding home in the dark. We'll see you later, Astrid."

"Bye," I said to their retreating backs, wondering what Pender had been about to say.

That night at dinner, Hilary was almost back to her old self, acting as if we'd never had an argument at all. She joked back and forth with her parents and the conversation kept rolling so naturally that you almost couldn't tell that she avoided talking to me directly. Almost.

"Hilary, why don't you and Astrid watch a movie before bed," her mom suggested, smiling fondly at us both. "You girls have had so much on your plates this summer. I don't think you spend enough time just hanging out being kids anymore."

"No thanks," Hilary said, not quite looking at me. "I have some prep work to do to get ready for school. Good night."

"Good night," I murmured, keeping my eyes cast downward at my plate until she was gone.

I was too tired to stay up watching movies anyway; I could barely keep my eyes open. Although I usually fed the horses their night snack as late as possible so that they wouldn't go hungry overnight, I knew I would fall asleep and never wake up if I let myself wait so I headed down to the barn as soon as I could.

Oona's truck was back again. This time the bed of the pickup was piled high with items hidden under a wide blue tarp that had been tied neatly over the entire stack.

I resisted the urge to snoop underneath the plastic and walked into the open front door of the barn.

The horses were all still awake, listening with interest to the hurried footsteps moving back and forth upstairs. This was the first time they'd ever had anyone living overhead and they looked pretty entertained with the whole thing.

"Eat your dinners and then get a good sleep everyone," I told them, tossing in their flakes of hay. "You all need to be rested for your lessons on Monday. You have to make a good impression."

There was another loud thump from the ceiling above and then muffled voices. Did she have someone up there with her or was she just on the phone?

It's none of your business, I told myself firmly, stifling my curiosity.

"Good night, Red," I said, moving to the front of his stall for a last look at him. "Sleep well. Hopefully, she doesn't keep you up all night."

He whuffled happily under his breath and looked at me with his large, dark eyes as if to tell me not to worry so much.

"All right," I said, still reluctant to leave him. "I guess I'll see you tomorrow."

The stars were bright overhead as I rolled the door softly closed and crunched my way up the driveway to the house, stifling a yawn. Thank goodness Hilary had already agreed to do morning feed tomorrow because I could really use the extra hour of sleep. I hoped she still planned to keep her promise even though we'd fought.

Chapter Six

"Now, this filling is a mascarpone mixture of glazed pears, walnuts, brie, and brown sugar, and a dash of lemon curd. How does that compare with the chocolate-strawberry one you tried?"

"Delicious," I said, sighing with complete satisfaction as I took another bite of the newest breakfast crepe Mr. Ahlberg had set in front of me. I'd agreed to help him taste-test and now I was stationed at the big kitchen island with a fork and a platter of crepes.

"Not too sweet? Not too much brie?"

As if there could ever be a thing such as too much brie.

"No, it's perfect. They're all perfect. This is amazing."

"Well, good. I hope our clients feel the same way. Our first guests arrive next week."

The food was beyond amazing. If the bed and breakfast guests didn't appreciate meals like this then there was something seriously wrong with them.

"Right, the blackberry one is up next. This is a special—"

The front door burst open and then slammed so hard that the whole room shook, making us both jump.

"Dad!" Hilary bellowed from the hallway at the top of her lungs, causing him to jerk backward and drop his whisk into the bowl of yellow batter. It sounded like she was being killed.

"Dad! Your stupid sheep are in my *barn*." Hilary appeared in the doorway like an avenging angel, long hair billowing out in all directions, her cheeks red and her eyes glistening with murderous rage.

"Hilary, don't shout like that. I thought you'd been hurt. What's wrong?"

"Sheep!" she said, pointing at him accusingly from the doorway.

He coughed and put a hand over his mouth, stifling a laugh. Hilary was nothing if not dramatic. Her years in amateur theatre had clearly not been wasted.

"It's not funny." She clomped across the floor in her dusty paddock boots and flung herself into the chair beside me, impatiently pushing her hair off her face.

"You're right. I'm sorry. I was overwhelmed by the theatrical execution. Tell me the story, slowly."

"Your. Dumb. Sheep. Are in my barn destroying everything," she finished in a rush. "Why aren't they in their own pasture?"

"Oh, right," Mr. Ahlberg winced and drummed his fingers on the table, "I forgot about that. Sorry, I let them out this morning. The "How to Care for Sheep" manual said they do best if they're allowed to range over vast terrain. They've grazed down their own field and seemed hungry, so I thought they could do some foraging around the property."

"Well, they're *foraging* in my barn. How am I supposed to run a fancy dressage barn if there are disgusting sheep everywhere? The new instructor is going to think we're nuts."

"That's a little melodramatic, Hilary. Can't you just shoo them outside?"

"I'm telling you they won't leave." Hilary's voice climbed to a higher octave, "and the big one tried to knock me over on purpose."

"Oh dear." Mr. Ahlberg shifted his gaze reluctantly over to the open cookbook. Clearly, all he wanted was to be able to finish testing his breakfast recipes in peace. "That sounds like Portia," he murmured, "she can be bossy."

"Well, whatever. Just get them out. My ankle is too sore to be chasing them around." She reached down and rubbed her leg reflexively, her forehead knitted into unhappy lines.

"Fine, fine." Mr. Ahlberg sighed and looked longingly down at the mixing bowl. "I guess I can wrap up here. It's almost time to get ready for church anyway. We still have to help your mother pack up the food for the soup kitchen."

"Ugh, I forgot it was Sunday." Hilary made a face. "Do I have to go? I have so much to do here. Darius said he'd call as soon as he got in town and I haven't ordered shavings yet or booked the farrier. I'm too busy. And there's this weird lady that keeps calling me to ask about board..."

She broke off and frowned at her father who was staring at her incredulously as if she were a stranger who'd just walked in and sat down at his table.

There was a strained silence as Mr. Ahlberg slowly crossed his arms over his chest and looked at his daughter with a serious expression.

"What?" she asked, a faint blush tinging her cheeks. "I just don't feel like going to church, okay. I don't see what's wrong with missing a day here and there."

"Well, maybe that's exactly why you should go," her dad said quietly. "Do you think the homeless people we feed *feel* like sleeping on the street every night?"

"Okay, whatever, Dad, I don't need a speech. If you want me to go then I guess I'll go. Even though I have a million other things to do."

But Mr. Ahlberg had already started his lecture and there was no stopping him now.

"Do you think our mission crew who spent the last six months helping sick and starving children at the refugee camp in Kenya *felt* like doing it every day? Don't you think they'd rather have been safe and comfortable at home?"

"Dad, come on, I said I get it. I'm sorry if I'm not thrilled about spending a whole day at church."

"No, Hilary, I think you need to put your life in perspective here. We are extremely fortunate to be able to live this lifestyle. I made a pact with myself when I first began to succeed in my career never to forget where I came from. There were many nights growing up where my mother had to decide whether to put food on the table or pay the hydro bill…"

"I know, I know." Hilary interrupted. "I've heard this story a million—"

"Maybe you forgot the part where the church helped my mother enough so that my brothers and sisters and I were able to stay together rather than go into foster care. They made sure I had food to eat and clean clothes and supplies for school. I made a promise that I'd always look out for others the way I was looked out for, even when it's not convenient for me or when I don't *feel* like it. Without those people stepping in at that time, none of this might even exist."

"Okay, I said I don't need a lecture," Hilary snapped, setting her jaw in a determined line the way she did when she was about to launch into a debate. "If I hadn't spent the last hour chasing *your* stupid sheep around then maybe I'd have more enthusiasm—"

"All right," I stood up, pushing my chair back, "I'll go down to the barn and take care of the sheep."

"You don't have to do that," they both said at the same time, turning to look at me with the identical stubborn expressions.

"Um, no, that's fine," I said, "you guys need to talk, and I have chores to do anyway."

Hilary might have fed, but I still had turnout and cleaning to do before Annie and Nori picked me up for archery camp. Anything would be better than sitting here and listening to these two fight. Again.

Hilary had always gotten along with her parents; that was one of the reasons why I loved spending so much time with their family growing up. They always seemed to be part of the same team. Lately, though, it felt like all they did was argue with each other.

"Astrid, the barn is supposed to be Hilary's responsibility. You do too much around here as it is."

"Hey, what's that supposed to mean?" Hilary said angrily. "I've been injured, I'm trying to run a stable, and I'm taking extra courses on so I can finish high school early. Most parents would be thrilled to have a daughter like me."

"I'm always thrilled that you're my daughter, Hilary, that won't change. But I'm not happy with your attitude lately."

"Yes, I know, that's what you keep saying. Well, I'm sorry if I can't be perfect like Astrid all the time."

"Hilary, that's enough—"

"Well, that's what it feels like. I'm doing the best I can, Dad. I don't know why you and mom are being so hard on me."

"Because you haven't been yourself, Hilary. Ever since you met this boy—"

"Okay, bye," I said quickly before they could start in on the Darius argument. In my opinion, Hilary's parents had actually been pretty good about letting her see him. She just wasn't allowed to go over to his place on her own or anything. He was quite a bit older than her and had a lifetime of experience behind him that made her parents nervous, but you could tell they were trying their best to protect her while letting her live her own life. Something she was completely ungrateful for.

I dumped my uneaten food in the compost, put my plate in the dishwasher and headed outside as fast as I could before I could hear any more arguing.

I bypassed the golf cart and grabbed my bicycle from where it leaned against the porch railing, thankful my dad and Marion had dropped it off with the rest of my stuff before they'd headed off on their relationship-saving road trip to Alaska.

I coasted effortlessly down the gentle slope to the barn, the early morning sun on my face and a light breeze ruffling my hair.

The first thing I noticed was that Oona's truck was gone again, which hopefully meant that she'd left early enough to avoid running into a flock of embarrassingly bad sheep.

The barn door had been pushed open a few feet and there was a lot of thumping going on inside. I leaned my bike up against the wall and peered inside.

Oh no. My heart sank. As Hilary had said, the barn aisle was packed full of sheep and the scene was pure chaos.

"Oh, my gosh, you guys," I said out loud, "what have you done?"

"Bah," the closest one said, looking up at me with glittering, unrepentant eyes. At its feet was Pender's empty plastic brush box that had been dumped on its side, brushes tossed in all directions. A bottle of hoof polish had been squashed under someone's hoof until the lid popped off and a pool of clear, sticky liquid had spread across the floor.

Lead ropes and halters had been pulled off of every stall door and dumped into the aisle. The broom lay in the middle of the floor, its bristles clearly chewed, and the hose had been yanked off the wall and completely unravelled. Luckily, they hadn't figured out how to turn on the water. They'd also managed to roll open the hay room door and half of them had their heads jammed in there, eating scraps off the floor.

Worst of all, they'd gone to the bathroom everywhere and little piles of sheep nuggets littered the entire aisle.

The horses all had their chests pressed against their stall doors, heads hanging into the aisle, watching the commotion unfold with fascination. Rabbit's eyes were wide with delight and he kept snorting dramatically, dipping his nose down to snort at any sheep brave enough to wander close to him.

No wonder Hilary had been so upset.

"Okay, monsters, that's it. Time to go," I said loudly,

clapping my hands together to get their attention. Most of them completely ignored me but the one closest to me, the big black and white-bearded ram Hamlet, raised his head slowly to stare at me with a calculating look in his gold-flecked eyes. From one corner of his mouth dangled the well-chewed end of Riverdance's fancy leather lead line.

Still staring at me, he spat out the lead and snatched up a fallen hoof pick, waving it back and forth menacingly in my direction.

"Um, nice boy, Hamlet," I said, gulping and taking a few steps backward. Maybe he was just playing but he resembled some thug holding me at knifepoint. The hay room door rolled back another foot and the pile of sheep tumbled inside.

Portia reared up and put her hooves against the stack; clearly about to climb the whole thing and probably knock it over.

"Portia, Beatrice, Cordelia, go home," I said loudly in what I hoped was a commanding voice. Edging my way around Hamlet I marched to the hay room threading through the jostling, shoving sheep until I reached Portia.

The reclusive old lady Mr. Ahlberg had bought his flock from had been obsessed with Shakespeare, so she'd named every single one of them from her favourite plays, and somehow the names had stuck when they'd moved here, too. Today I thought they were way too elegant names for such bad sheep.

"Get down," I said firmly, pushing at Portia's furry shoulder. But it was like trying to move a squishy tree trunk. She leaned her weight into me stubbornly and didn't even look up from the bale she was demolishing with her teeth.

"Come on you guys," I pleaded, "there's lots of grass out there for you. You're messing everything up."

Grain, I thought, suddenly inspired. Squeezing back through the mob, I slipped into the feed room, slamming the door firmly behind me just as Hamlet tried to push his big head inside. Grabbing a bucket, I filled it full of sweet-feed and alfalfa pellets, took a deep breath and pushed my way back into the aisle.

"All right, sheep," I said loudly, "breakfast time. Come get it." The second I shook the bucket, all eyes turned toward me, glinting greedily in the morning light. And then there was a stampede.

I didn't know if they would have actually knocked me over and mauled me to death, but I didn't stick around long enough to find out. I ran for the front door, leapt on my bike and took off toward the lower pasture as fast as I could, a flock of crazed sheep galloping behind me at top speed.

When I reached the field, I skidded to a stop, dropped my bike and pulled the gate open just as the first one arrived. I ran into the pasture, dumped the grain on the ground and then leapt out of harm's way. They dived onto the grain like vultures, pushing and shoving one another in order to fill their faces.

"Now, *stay* there," I said, clanging the gate firmly behind them and resting my arms on the top rail so I could catch my breath. Who would have guessed that farming could be so terrifying?

Once I was sure they weren't going anywhere, I walked my bike slowly up the hill and stared in dismay at the dismantled aisle way. It actually made me feel a little ill to see it so filthy; maybe all those years living with my neurotically clean stepmother, Marion, had finally rubbed off on me.

"This is so gross," I said out loud, gingerly picking up all the fallen halters and leads first. Anything that was extra-disgusting went directly to the tack room sink to be scrubbed. The scattered brushes and grooming totes soon followed close behind.

As soon as the aisle was clear of debris, I used the half-chewed broom to sweep up what I could, used nearly a whole roll of paper towels to sop up the hoof polish, and then lightly sprayed the aisle down with water from the freshly coiled hose. I swept the whole thing out again; hoping it would dry quickly in the heat of the day before Oona came back from wherever she was and decided that she *really* didn't want to coach in this madhouse after all.

I looked down at my watch and sighed. I had an hour to turn the horses out and get paddocks finished before Annie came to take Nori and me to archery camp. Hopefully, I had just enough time to get Ellie brushed and ready for Rob to pick up for her day of cross-country schooling.

"You have a nice, relaxing day today," I told Red, leading him out to the pasture. "Nothing wrong with hanging out with your friends all day. Just don't get too used to being lazy."

He made a little nickering noise under his breath that I chose to interpret as agreement.

The Ahlbergs were gone when I got back, and the house was silent. They must have left for church when I was in the tack room or something because I hadn't even heard their car leave.

There was no time for a shower. I got dressed in record time and brought my practice bow and quiver downstairs to set by the front door. I hadn't actually started formal practice yet this summer. I'd taken my horse bow with me a few times just to show the kids how it was different than a regular recurve bow, and Earl had watched me shoot that, but he hadn't said anything about me starting to practice for real yet.

The last few days I'd brought my old battered practice bow with me; just in case Earl happened to put me on the schedule again. I wanted to be ready.

I made a sandwich, grabbed some apples and granola bars and put them all in my backpack with a bottle of water.

"You be a good girl and stay here," I told Caprice, tossing her the rubber toy stuffed with treats that I always gave her before she was left alone for the day. She used to have a lot of anxiety whenever she had to stay behind, but now she seemed to accept that eventually, someone would come back for her.

I slipped outside and locked the front door behind me just as Annie's black SUV pulled up.

"Astrid, did you hear the news yet?" Nori yelled, throwing her door open before the car had even stopped moving. "Did Hilary tell you?"

"Nori, wait until I stop the car, that's dangerous," her mom said but, as usual, Nori ignored her.

"We're going to lease Maverick," she shouted, hopping out of the car and running to give me a tight hug, which must have meant she was beyond happy because it was a very un-Nori-like move. "My mom talked to Rob last night and he's dropping him off today when he comes to pick up Ellie."

"Oh, a lease. That's a great idea. That's exciting, Nori."

"Yeah, Rob thinks I'll change my mind about showing and blah, blah, blah. But I won't and when the year's up we'll buy him. Maverick, not Rob. We just called Hilary to tell her we're taking the empty stall, I can't believe she didn't tell you."

"I haven't seen her since early this morning, but I'm so happy you get to keep him, Nori. I think you two are great together."

I loaded my stuff into the open hatch at the back of Annie's SUV and then slid into the back seat since Nori had claimed the front passenger side.

"Hey, where's Callie?" I asked, seeing that her booster seat was empty.

"Oh, she's spending a week with her father," Annie said, rolling her eyes a little and laughing. "I'm not sure how it's going, though. I'm getting panicked phone calls from him every day."

"Yeah, Callie's a little high-maintenance," Nori said and I stifled a laugh. Both Annie's kids were pretty strong-willed but if there was a prize for being high-maintenance it would definitely go to Nori.

"You didn't want to go visit, too?" I asked.

"No, why would I?" Nori said, looking at me blankly. "Frank isn't my dad, he's Callie's. I see mine all the time."

"Oh," I said, not asking any more questions. It seemed like nobodies family life was ever straight forward.

"Today is seriously the best day of my life," Nori went on blissfully as we headed down the driveway toward the road. "I get the horse I want and then I get to spend the day shooting at things. It's perfect. Even if I'm the most terrible archer on the face of the planet."

"You're not that bad," I half-lied, "everyone has to start somewhere."

"It's okay." Nori shrugged. "I just like shooting things. I don't care if I'm good at it or not. You don't know how nice it is to be in a sport where the worst that can happen is that you miss your target."

"What do you mean?"

"Well, let's see, in my last sport I made one small mistake and my horse ended up dead. This is much, much better."

"Nori," Annie said in surprise, looking over at her daughter with concern. "That accident wasn't your fault at all. He just slipped, it could have happened anywhere."

"Yeah, maybe. But I heard what people said afterward. That we were pushing him too hard and he was too young and inexperienced to be ridden at those heights by someone who wasn't a pro. Or his growth plates weren't closed all the way at his age, so it made it easy for him to break a leg. We messed up, Mom. Admit it."

I stared at the back of her head in astonishment. Nori had never talked about what had happened when Lumi died; it had taken almost the whole summer for her to even say his name without getting upset. What little I'd heard about that day was from Rob.

"Nori, people say hurtful things without thinking sometimes," Annie said slowly. "It doesn't mean their words are true."

"Yeah, whatever. All I know is that my best friend died while I was responsible for him. I will never, ever forgive myself for that. And I will never let anything like that happen to Maverick."

She set her jaw stubbornly and stared at her mom as if daring her to argue.

Annie chewed on her lower lip and frowned at the car ahead of her, clearly at a loss of what to say to her daughter.

"It's okay, Mom, you don't need to *fix* anything or come up with something wise to say to make it better," Nori said impatiently. "All I'm saying is that I like archery. It's not a big deal."

We pulled into the parking lot and Nori's mood shifted again. A smile lit up her face, and she bounced up and down in her seat excitedly like a little girl.

Annie looked over at her daughter and laughed, the tension leaving her face.

"Have fun girls, I'll see you this afternoon."

"Come on, Astrid," Nori said impatiently, "we're going to be late."

"We're not late," I grumbled, "we're always way too early. We're the only car in the parking lot."

"Good, I like being first. This way we can help Earl set up. Maybe he'll give me some more tips. Maybe he'll let you start practicing for *real* today."

"Maybe." I sighed and pulled my gear out of the car. I'd hurt my arm last year, twice actually, in the world's stupidest freak accidents and Earl had felt that I'd have the best chance of healing if I stuck to my lighter horse-archery bow for the summer and gave my arm a rest from the indoor range.

I loved horse archery, but I was itching to get back to my old practice and competition schedule.

Nori turned on her heel and trotted toward the shooting range, the place where I'd spent some of the best years of my life in, and I had to laugh at her bossy impatience. She and Maverick really were incredibly alike.

"Thank you for the ride," I said to Annie.

"Any time, sweetie, take good care of my girl in there."

"Sure," I said, privately thinking that Nori could more than take care of herself in any situation.

She'd turned to wait for me, holding the big metal door open and swinging it back and forth impatiently. "Come on, I want to see Earl before everyone gets here."

"Okay, okay," I said, laughing. Earl was a fantastic coach, but he was also an amazing human and he'd been the best thing in my life before I'd discovered horses. He was always so positive and kind, and the range had been a sanctuary for me from my turbulent home life.

"I hope Miranda isn't here today," Nori said a little too loudly, "she's so full of herself."

"Shh, Nori, keep it down," I said, looking anxiously down the empty hallway. Growing up, Miranda had been my closest competitor and, once upon a time, I'd *thought* she'd been my best friend, too. But that friendship had ended abruptly, right before I'd gone to spend a year at the ranch when she'd basically set out to ruin me on purpose.

"What, it's true. I don't like the way she looks at you. She's creepy."

Great, I thought, *just what I need; Miranda being weird and jealous again. Why can't she just live her own life and leave me alone?*

Although we'd never really talked about what had happened, Earl had done his best to schedule Miranda and I for different camp days so we didn't have to run into each other too often. He'd given her the little kids, which she probably hated and assigned me the older kids. But once in a while, like this week, the groups overlapped and then I just had to do my best to ignore her.

71

Earl was *my* coach, too, and I wasn't going to give up something I loved just because she hated me for no logical reason.

"Earl," Nori called out happily, dancing toward him, "can I try a different bow today? I don't think the one I had before was working properly."

I stifled a laugh and shook my head. Nori had been through almost every piece of equipment on site trying to improve her aim. She was convinced that there was a magical piece of gear out there that was going to make her shoot perfectly overnight. I didn't tease her about it, though; as long as she kept practicing, she'd eventually get better one way or another.

Chapter Seven

The group of kids I'd been given was a really fun group of archers. I had three girls, including Nori, and two boys all between ten and thirteen years old and all eager to learn. This was a beginner camp so, like Nori, most of them had a lot of work to do, but I really loved helping them to improve their skills.

Earl had us drill inside for the morning working on technique and stance and going over practical things like how to clean and take care of the equipment.

In the afternoon, we moved outside to the 3D archery range to shoot targets there. It was more fun outside than shooting at a paper target inside.

These targets were made to look like living things; some wild animals and even a life-size zombie that always creeped me out but thrilled the kids.

Here we could practice shooting from different angles and across different terrain. Next week we were going on a field trip to one of the big wilderness ranges where we would have to hike through the woods to get to each target. I'd been there many times before. I still loved it and I was excited to show it to Nori and the other kids.

"Isn't this better than slaving around at the stable all day?" Nori asked happily, launching an arrow at an upright foam black bear. The point headed right toward the bullseye in the center of the bear's chest and then swerved at the last second and buried itself lower down, right in the bear's kneecap.

"Oh, I don't mind working for the horses; they're worth it," I said, smiling at her kindly. "I think you need you to fix your anchor point a little. Pull back a bit further on your string until your knuckle is resting on your cheekbone. Yes, there. Perfect."

This time the arrow shot true and plunged into the foam bear's core.

"That was good, Nori, you're really improving."

"Thanks," she said, beaming. "Anyway, I overheard Mom telling Pender that you're working too hard. They were going to talk to Hilary's mom."

"Oh, no." I groaned. Why did adults always have to *interfere* with things that didn't need fixing? "I'm perfectly fine. Really. The Ahlberg's took me in and I work off Red's board. Once Hilary's helping with stalls and paddocks again, it won't be so bad."

"Yeah, right," she said under her breath, "as if that's going to happen."

I opened my mouth to argue and then shut it abruptly. Honestly, were things ever going to change if I left it up to Hilary? Maybe Annie and Pender were right. My schedule was so full these days between organizing the barn, helping with archery camp and riding the horses that sometimes I felt pulled in a million directions. When school started it was obvious things were going to fall apart if something didn't change soon.

"All right, come on you guys, next target," I said, changing the subject, "you need to focus."

Halfway through the day, my phone pinged about a dozen times in a row and I pulled it out to see multiple pictures of Ellie looking like a happy and adorable little eventer in Rob's borrowed gear.

There were a few candid shots of her hanging out with Possum by the trailer and other, better, photos that must have been taken by someone else because they were of her and Rob on course.

Oh, wow, I thought, pausing at one of her sailing over a small jump, ears pricked and knees tucked, looking like she was having the time of her life. *Maybe I've been holding her back. She looks like she was made for this.*

She just blazed through the water, Rob sent. *Super brave. She has a lot of fans here. There's a food truck and she discovered mini-donuts. She's a good one.*

"Ooh, she looks fantastic," Nori said, peering over my shoulder and studying the pictures. "She has a decent jump on her, too."

"Thanks. Wait, I thought you hated eventing."

"Of course I don't, eventing is awesome. *I'm* never doing it again, but I don't mind if other people do."

She really was a strange kid.

Later that afternoon as we were cleaning up and getting ready to go home, I found a second to pull Earl away from the mob of kids.

"Hey, kiddo. How's it going?" he asked. "Great job today with your crew. Everyone's improving quite a bit."

"Thanks. I love being here. Thanks for talking me into it."

"No problem. Now, what's on your mind?"

"Earl, you've seen me shoot a bit with the horse bow lately. Do you think I'm ready to start practicing again for real? My shoulder doesn't hurt anymore. Or at least not much, anyway."

"Taking the summer off definitely did you good. I think you're ready to ease back in. Want me to put you back on the training schedule here?"

"Yes, please," I said, feeling a ripple of excitement at the thought of practicing on a regular schedule again. "I'm just not sure how it's going to work, though. I have to take care of the barn and ride and, I guess, go to school. The city bus doesn't go out to where I'm living now very often so I'll have to ask the Ahlberg's if they don't mind driving me."

"Well, you let me know," he said. "Maybe there's someone who lives out your way who can carpool. That little girl is improving, if she wants to keep on with lessons maybe you can ride with her."

"Who, Nori? Don't let her hear you calling her a little girl. She's like an angry old lady in a kid's body. She really likes archery, though, maybe she will take lessons this year. I'll have to ask."

"She rides horses, too, right?"

"Yes, she's a good rider, completely fearless, really. Once she improves her shooting, she'll be killer at horse archery."

"Huh, I should come out and watch this in action one day. Would you want to start a league of some sort?"

"Well, sure, maybe someday," I said, "but it's not that simple. The horses have to be trained really carefully. And so do the people. And then there's the insurance. I looked into it when I first got here, but it seemed so complicated."

"Complicated doesn't mean impossible."

"I guess not," I said slowly. "I bet a lot of people would be interested. But I'd have to ask Hilary since it's her farm and she's been pretty moody lately. And I'm no expert so we'd need a real instructor." I sighed thinking of how difficult it all sounded.

"Don't sell yourself short," Earl said seriously. "You'd be a good teacher; you're a natural. The kids like you and they listen to you."

"Oh, well, thanks. Maybe someday."

"It doesn't hurt to start thinking about it now," he said seriously.

"Ooh, do you get to start practicing again, Astrid?" Nori asked excitedly, popping up from wherever she'd been eavesdropping. "I was telling our group all about you and how amazing you are."

"Earl says it's okay if I start slowly. I can hardly wait."

"Well, why wait? Get your bow, there's still a few minutes left. I'm sure everyone wants to see you shoot."

"Yes," the kids who'd trailed behind Nori said, gathering back around us, "let's see."

"Oh, yes." Miranda slid up to the outskirts of the group and fixed me with a malicious stare. "That sounds just fantastic. Let's stand around and watch perfect Astrid sail back on her way to the Olympics."

"That's enough, Miranda," Earl said sternly.

"What?" Miranda opened her eyes wide, struggling to look

innocent. "I wasn't being sarcastic; I'm really interested in seeing what she'll be like after all that time off. Go ahead, Astrid, show us. Show us how good you are."

Nori looked up into my face uncertainly and bit her lip, probably sorry she'd started all this.

"It's late," Earl said, "we can do this on Tuesday."

Miranda's mouth twisted in a triumphant smirk, and right then I wanted nothing more than to wipe that stupid expression off her face.

"It's fine, Earl, I don't mind," I said quietly, retrieving my bow and quiver from the corner. I pulled the stringer from the pocket on my quiver and strung the bow quickly, trying to keep my hands from shaking. There was no reason to be nervous, I'd shot in front of thousands of people before, including Miranda, but suddenly this seemed terribly important.

We filed silently to the spot in front of the first target and I reached down into my quiver and selected an arrow carefully. It was one of my favourites, an older wooden arrow with orange feathered fletching.

You've done this a million times before, I told myself firmly, lining myself up with the target and taking a few deep breaths to calm my nerves.

Horse archery was different than this. When you were shooting from the back of a moving horse there was no time to carefully line up your shot. You shot on instinct, firing arrows in quick succession with hardly any time to think. I wasn't even sure how to do it any other way anymore.

Trying not to overthink things I drew the string back, remembering belatedly that this bow's pull was much heavier than that of my horse bow, and sent the arrow flying. I knew the shot was all wrong even as it left the shelf and bit my lip as it wobbled through the air and thunked into the thick foam of the target.

"Aww," one of the kids said sympathetically and I bit the inside of my cheek in frustration.

"Not bad," Earl said, staring at the board with his arms crossed. The arrow had at least hit the face of the target, but it was on the upper edge, no where close to the center.

"Not bad?" I said incredulously, ready to argue.

Earl raised an eyebrow at me meaningfully and nodded toward the kids surrounding us, staring with wide eyes, taking in every word we said. They were all still beginners and most of them would love to be able to even *hit* the target consistently let alone the bullseye. They didn't need to hear me whining when I missed one shot.

I realized all at once what a big responsibility it was to teach; they were always watching and listening, soaking up their surroundings like a sponge. It was up to me to set a good example.

"Right," I said, clearing my throat, "I'd forgotten how heavy the pull was on this bow and I released too soon. I should have taken time to line up my shot more carefully before I'd even pulled back my string."

I glanced over to where Miranda stood, arms crossed, at the back of the room, a small smile playing across her face.

"Half the battle in archery is being able to control your mind and your emotions under pressure," Earl said, "it's one thing to shoot at home or when you're with your friends at the range, but when you get into a competition setting it's easy for things to fall apart."

The kids nodded, their faces serious.

"Try a few more," Earl said patiently, "let's see what you're grouping looks like, then we can finesse it."

I pulled another arrow from my quiver, took a deep breath to release the tension in my body and nocked the arrow without pulling back the string. I raised the bow, lining up my arm and studying my target, feeling the familiar weight of it in my hand. When I was ready, I touched the string almost reverently and pulled it back, waiting until the knuckles of my right hand touched the corner of my lip before I paused for one intake of breath and let the arrow go.

"Better," Earl said, "keep going."

I did it four more times until my quiver was empty.

"Good, let's go down to the end, everyone, and see what we've got."

We filed down to the end of the range, and Earl stood back and pointed at the arrows bristling from the target so everyone could see. "Astrid has a pretty tight grouping here. So you can all see that if she lowered her aim that they would have all landed in the right spot. This is a pretty easy fix compared to if her arrows were scattered all over the place. Not bad for your first day back, Astrid, good job."

I looked at the buried arrows and took another deep breath, trying not to feel disappointed. Of course I wasn't going to be perfect on my first try; I'd been shooting the horse bow all summer which wasn't the same at all. But still...

Before this summer, I couldn't remember the last time I had

less than a perfect shot. Not ever. My aim had been almost magical. What if I'd somehow lost that forever?

"Yeah, nice job, Astrid," Miranda said, sidling up beside me. Anyone who didn't know her might have thought she was being sincere, but I could feel the animosity practically rolling off of her in waves. "I just can't *wait* to compete against you this winter. It's going to be epic."

Nori looked up sharply and sent Miranda a glare.

"All right, everyone, good work," Earl called. "See you all on Tuesday."

We piled out into the sunshine, but I could hardly feel it, that grey cloud of unhappiness had descended on me again.

Chapter Eight

"Mom, Astrid is going to the Olympics and we're going to sponsor her," Nori announced to Annie as soon as the car was moving.

"What?" I sputtered, tugged out of my dark thoughts by this shocking announcement. "You saw me in there, Nori. I was hardly Olympic material."

"Doesn't matter," she shrugged, "it was your first day back. You'll get better."

"Don't get your hopes up," I said gloomily. "I thought taking the summer off would be a good thing, but I think I've wrecked it. I've lost my touch."

"Oh, Astrid, did your first practice not go well?" Annie asked sympathetically. "I know you were looking forward to starting again."

"It was okay," I said with a sigh, turning to look out the window. "I don't know why I thought I'd be perfect the first time out."

"So *anyway*," Nori interrupted, huffing impatiently, "when we sponsor you, Mom and Callie and I will travel to wherever you're competing and hold up banners and things to cheer you on and heckle your competition. We'll have to sit down with Earl next week and figure out which shoots you need to do to qualify for the Olympics, though."

"Whoa, whoa," Annie said, laughing. "Nori, slow down. I think you're getting a little ahead of yourself."

"Yeah, I wouldn't bet on me yet," I warned, "I have no idea if I'll ever be good enough again."

"You will be," Nori said confidently.

"I would like to know what your plans are though, Astrid." Annie glanced at me in the rear-view mirror. "Are you going to focus on your archery again this year or are you sticking with the horses?"

"I'll never give up horses," I said positively. "And I don't know if I have an archery career to go back to. But I'm going to try; I do miss it."

I looked out the window, sighing heavily, wondering how life had become this complicated.

"I see, well, if there's a will there's a way, Astrid. You've always struck me as a person who finds a way to get things done."

"I do?" I asked in surprise. I'd never thought of myself that way at all.

"You're a hard worker, Astrid," she went on. "If you do decide to get very serious about your archery career again, I might be able to help you. My chain of fitness centers does take on some athletic sponsorships from time to time. I'd put in a good word to the board if you wanted to apply."

"Oh, really?" I said, sitting a little straighter. "Thanks, maybe I could look into that. Like they would pay for coaching?"

"Yes, some lessons and some entry fees for competitions, a gym membership for cross training, athletic wear, that sort of thing."

"Wow, that sounds amazing."

"We have a lot of applicants every year so you'd have to be actively competing already and maintaining a certain level of success. And your coach would have to be on board; there'd have to be a competition and training schedule in place before you apply."

"Oh," I said, feeling a little deflated. Two years ago I could have easily walked into a sponsorship like that. Now, that felt depressingly far away; next to impossible. "Okay, thanks. I guess I'll have to see how it goes. I'll have to sit down with Earl and figure out some sort of plan."

"Well, let me know if you need help. I'm a bit of an expert at making things happen."

"Yes, Mom loves organizing other people's lives," Nori said but, even though she was teasing, there was a note of pride in her voice.

Chapter Nine

When we got back to the farm, Nori leapt from the car before it had even rolled to a stop.

"I'm going to go see how Maverick's settling in," she called over her shoulder.

"Thanks again for the ride," I told Annie, opening the hatch and pulling out all my gear.

"Astrid, I can drive you up to the house with all that."

"Oh, don't worry, I have to bring the rest of the horses in and feed dinner. Are you going to ride Norman?"

"Not today. I'll just brush him while Nori's hanging out with that cranky horse of hers. Honestly, she could have had any horse she wanted and *that* was the one she picked."

"He's not that bad," I said, laughing, as I piled my things on the picnic table. "Have fun with Norman."

I trotted down the hill to bring in the horses, leading the calmest ones two at a time and bringing Rabbit last by himself.

Hey, where's my stuff? I thought, noticing that Annie's car was gone and the picnic table was empty.

"Astrid, my mom took your things up to the house for you,"

Nori called from the depths of Maverick's new stall. "She wanted to talk to Hilary's mom for some reason. Come look at this stunning horse, he's so happy here."

Maverick lifted his head and flattened his ears in Rabbit's direction as we came into the barn. He sent me a withering look as if it were somehow my fault he was there.

"Yeah, he looks thrilled," I said, raising my eyebrows.

"Oh, that's just his face," Nori assured me, "he really does like it here."

"Uh huh." I broke off, as there was a rumbling sound outside and Oona drove up in her rickety old truck. The bed of the truck had been stacked high with contents that had been covered by a shiny, blue tarp.

I guess I should offer to help, I thought, moving reluctantly outside.

Oona was leaning over the side of the truck-bed, struggling to lift something out. Her hair had half come out of its braid and her cheeks were red with exertion.

"Do you need a hand?" I asked hesitantly, wanting to be polite.

"No," Oona said abruptly. She straightened up, pushing the corner of the blue tarp back into place quickly, covering whatever she'd been trying to lift. She turned to look at me with her eyebrows raised as if just the act of me standing there was offensive. "Your assistance is unnecessary; you can go."

She continued to stare at me accusingly until I moved back into the safety of the barn.

Seriously, what is wrong with her? I thought as I tossed dinner hay to all the horses that hadn't been fed yet.

I moved into Red's stall and brushed him while he ate his dinner, half-listening to Nori's excited chatter from Maverick's stall down the aisle. Once Red had had a nice massage to work all the knots out of his muscles, I left his stall and went to fuss over Ellie.

"You were such a good girl on your adventure today," I told her. "Rob said you were a superstar."

I knew Rob would have made sure she was groomed properly after her ride but I gave her a good brushing anyway, happy to just spend time with her. If she'd made that good of an impression today then who knew how much longer she'd be around for me to enjoy?

Chapter Ten

By the time dinner came, all I wanted to do was fall into bed and sleep until morning, but Hilary, who was magically speaking to me again as if we'd never fought at all, and I still had to meet Rob and Darius for the movies.

Darius was still technically playing on his North American squash tournament tour and he wasn't able to fly into town that often so I knew Hilary would be furious if I even suggested bailing on her.

Everyone who met him thought Darius was charming but, because he was a few years older than Hilary, and was a war refugee and everything, Hilary's parents didn't quite trust him yet, which meant she wasn't allowed to go out with him alone.

If she wanted to see him then she had to drag someone with her, and that person was usually me. Something that drove Hilary crazy.

"It makes no sense," she complained to me nearly every day. "No offense Astrid but I don't need a babysitter; I'm practically a grown adult."

"Just go along with it for now, Hilary," I'd told her patiently, "as soon as they know him and trust him then your parents will let you hang out with him on your own. They're just trying to protect you."

That night, Hilary changed her outfit at least a dozen times before settling on a dark blue form-fitting dress with spaghetti straps and flats.

"I wish I could wear heels." She sighed dramatically and stared at herself in the mirror critically. "I think my ankle would just collapse in them, though."

"Isn't that a bit fancy for the movies?" I asked, looking down at my own jeans skeptically. I'd put on a nice shirt and a little make-up but otherwise, I looked the same as always. "I wonder if I should change."

"You look fine, Astrid. Besides, Rob likes you no matter what you're wearing. I just like to dress up, and Darius is older so he's probably used to a little more sophistication."

"I doubt it, Hilary. He spent the last five years at boarding school, refugee camps, and avoiding being killed by bombs. He likes you for you; not for what you wear."

"You're right, I know you are," she said, her hesitant gaze meeting mine in the mirror, "And I know it's stupid of me but he only comes home every so often so I feel like have to look good to keep his interest. He's surrounded by those gorgeous squash players all day and they're like real athletes; I can't help but feel that I have to keep up."

There was a long silence while I let that sink in.

"Hilary," I said slowly, "I really don't think Darius is like that. And since when do you care what anyone thinks? You've always done your own thing no matter what. You're smart, funny, kind, and generous." I thought about how many times she'd talked sense into me when I was feeling down on myself. It was strange to be the one giving advice for once.

"Thanks, Astrid," she said, coming over to throw an arm over my shoulder. "I don't know what's come over me lately. Sometimes I don't even know who I am anymore."

"You've been a little…distracted," I said diplomatically.

"Don't say it. I know I've been a nightmare. It's my parents being stupid about Darius, who I'm *obviously* meant to be with. And it's all the stress of running the farm and this stupid accident; I miss acting, I miss dancing, I miss everything."

"Like riding Jerry?" I said quietly.

"Yes, yes, of course, that too." She pulled away and turned to pick up her purse. "Come on, my mother's probably waiting to take us on this stupid date. I can't believe I have to be ferried around like a child."

I sighed at her retreating back. For someone who wanted to be treated like an adult, she sure did a lot of whining.

Mrs. Ahlberg widened her eyes when she saw what Hilary was wearing and took a deep breath.

"You look lovely, girls," she said, "it's getting a little chilly at night though, Hilary, are you sure you don't want a sweater?"

"No, I'm fine," Hilary said, smiling at her mother innocently as she flounced past. "Once I'm with Darius I don't think I'll feel the cold at all."

Hilary's mom shook her head and reached over to give me a quick hug as we headed out the door. "I'm so glad you're going along to keep an eye on that one for me, Astrid," she said half seriously.

"I heard that," Hilary called over her shoulder as she climbed into the front passenger seat of the car. I slid into the back seat, leaning my head back against the soft leather and hoping they weren't about to start arguing again.

"Did you girls invite Oona to go with you?"

"Oona?" Hilary said blankly. "No, why would we?"

"Because she's new here and might be feeling a little lonely. She might appreciate the invitation."

Mrs. Ahlberg slowed the car as we reached the barn and looked pointedly at Hilary. "You should at least ask her, that's the kind thing to do."

"No way," Hilary said, "you didn't meet her, Mom; there is not a chance that she wants to come to the movies with us."

The silence drew out as Mrs. Ahlberg just sat there staring at the barn, casually tapping her fingers on the steering wheel as if she had all the time in the world.

"Okay, *fine*," Hilary said, sounding irritated, "but I don't want to wreck these shoes on the gravel. Astrid, can you run up?"

Wreck your shoes? I thought in astonishment. *Who are you and what have you done with my friend?*

"Hilary, you really need to stop having Astrid do all your work," her mother warned, suddenly sounding serious.

"For the last time, she doesn't do *all* the work..."

"It's okay," I said quickly, "I'll go ask her. It's fine."

They were still arguing as I shut the door firmly behind me.

I slid quietly into the barn, my shoulders relaxing as I heard the gentle crunching sounds of horses contentedly eating their hay.

Oona is lucky to live above this, I thought, *it would be so peaceful to fall asleep listening to a barn full of happy horses.*

I flicked on the light at the bottom of the stairs and made my way upward, feeling nervous. Oona didn't seem like the type of person who would appreciate surprise visitors. Hopefully, the worst she'd do was snap at me again like she had earlier.

Taking a deep breath I knocked on the wooden door. At first there were no sounds from inside and I'd almost decided to give up when there was a muffled thump and the door swung open.

"Oh," I said, stepping back in surprise. Because the cold, perfectly made-up person I'd met earlier had been transformed. Her long hair was pulled up into a messy bun on top of her head and a thin paintbrush had been stabbed through it to pin everything in place. She had on a pair of dark-rimmed glasses and zero make-up and she was wearing a pair of ripped jeans and a tee-shirt with a horse print on it that was spattered with paint. Her feet were bare against the wood floor, her toenails painted a vivid shade of purple.

"Can I help you?" she asked, raising her eyebrows. Still, she didn't sound as intimidating as she had earlier. This time she looked more distracted than irritated.

"I'm so sorry to barge in," I said, twisting my fingers together nervously. "I know you don't want to be bothered, it's just that we're going to the movies and we thought maybe that you'd like to go."

"The movies?" Oona tilted her head to one side and crinkled her forehead as if she'd never heard of the concept before. "Oh, like the cinema. Thank you but no. I'm busy. Goodnight."

She started to close the door when something over her shoulder caught my eye. She hadn't unpacked yet, or at least not completely. Boxes were stacked around the edges of the room but in the middle, in front of the open balcony doors, were what looked like cavasses carefully lined up against the wall. Between them was an easel that had a half-finished painting balanced on it.

"Is that Sox?" I asked in astonishment, pointing at the canvas.

Oona made some muttering noises under her breath before reluctantly opening the door a little wider.

"Sort of," she said, "It's the essence of him I guess, and of all the ponies like him that I've known over the years."

"But you just met him *yesterday*. How did you do it so fast?" I asked in amazement. "You didn't even take a picture, either, how did you remember all the details?"

"It's just how my brain works," Oona said with a shrug. "I see something and my mind takes a picture of it and I can always remember exactly the way things looked in that moment."

Without thinking, I stepped around her and moved closer to the painting, leaning down to study the details.

It was just a pony in a pasture. But he was looking right out of the picture with such a bold, mischievous expression on his face that I felt he would step out of the canvas at any moment.

"This is so amazing," I said, hardly daring to breathe. I turned to look at the other canvasses nearby and shook my head in amazement. There were horses everywhere; dozens of them, some at liberty, some under saddle but all looked so vividly alive that I could hardly contain myself.

I paused to stare at a noble white horse with a curved roman nose and wide, intelligent eyes. He stood poised in the middle of a lavish indoor arena that had stone pillars and arched stained-glass windows in the background.

"Wow, is that a horse that you know in real life?" I asked, studying his imperious expression. He was commanding like a king, but also kindly and wise, too. He reminded me a little of my old friend Quarry in a way.

"Yes," Oona said sharply. "He is. He was." She stepped forward abruptly and threw a nearby cloth over the painting, covering it up fully. "His name was Furioso; I don't like to talk about him."

"Oh…I'm sorry," I said. *He must have died or something and she can't talk about it. I understand that. I wonder if that's why she left her old stable?*

"It's fine," she said, tapping her foot against the floor. "Don't you have a movie to get to?"

"Right, yes," I said, realizing all at once that I'd barged into her apartment without even asking. "They will be wondering what happened to me."

She raised her eyebrows and didn't say a word so I headed for the door as fast as I could.

I'd almost made it out when a small painting hanging just beside the doorway caught my eye. A rider and another white horse, not Furioso this time, alone in the middle of a darkened arena, suspended in the middle of a beautiful piaffe.

The rider had all four reins held lightly in one hand, the other hand resting gently on her thigh. The horse's neck was arched proudly and his ears were pricked, his gaze focused inward.

"Oh," I said excitedly. "I know that horse; that's Quarry. That's Claudia."

"Yes," Oona said in surprise. "It is. I forgot that you knew them both."

"Claudia taught me to ride. And Quarry was my first horse," I said, my gaze fixed on the painting. This was a younger Quarry in his prime and I drank in the sight of both him and Claudia; it brought back so many good memories. "I mean, I didn't own him but he was the first horse who…"

I stopped, not quite sure how to find the right words. Oona probably wouldn't understand what I meant anyway.

"Sorry," I said, letting myself quickly out into the stairwell, dying now to get away before I embarrassed myself any more.

"No, I get it," she said quietly from behind me. "I've loved many horses that I didn't own. You must miss him. And Claudia. I was so sorry to hear of her passing; she taught me so much."

"I do miss them both," I said, feeling my eyes prickle with tears. I quickly turned to the door. I had to get out of there before I found yet another way to mortify myself. "Goodbye."

I ran the rest of the way down the stairs and headed for the door. At the last minute, I turned quickly toward Red's stall. He was busy pulling at the hay in his manger but he came to the door happily enough when I hung my arms over the top of it. I leaned forward, resting my forehead on his neck and ran my fingers up under his jaw bone, scratching the hollow spot between his jowls.

"See you later, buddy," I whispered, kissing his soft, warm nose.

"What took you so long?" Hilary demanded as soon as I was back in the car. "Is she coming or not?"

I shook my head. "She's busy. But she said thanks for inviting her."

"Well, that took forever. What were you doing up there?"

"Nothing," I said, suddenly not wanting to explain about the paintings and about how Oona had seemed almost like a different person. It felt like it wasn't my secret to tell somehow.

Mrs. Ahlberg dropped us off at the door to the theatre where Rob and Darius were already waiting. They hadn't seen us yet; they were deep in conversation by the doors. Rob had on jeans and a tee shirt like me but Darius wore a sports coat and looked like he'd spent about eight hours perfecting his hair.

"I'll be back in a few hours girls, have a good time," Hilary's mom said, smiling nervously at her daughter.

"Yep, see you," Hilary said, slipping out of the car and slamming the door a little harder than necessary.

"Thanks for the ride," I added.

We waited until she drove away before we headed toward the door.

"Now, we're going to have some fun," Hilary whispered to me, reaching down and squeezing my hand briefly. "Thanks for coming."

"Of course," I said, "it's nice to be hanging out with you again…"

I broke off because Darius and Rob had just noticed we were there and Hilary dropped my hand and danced toward them.

"Darius!" Hilary called out as if she couldn't hold the words back, a tremor in her voice. And then it was like one of those scenes in a movie where the hero and the heroine have been kept apart by awful circumstances and are just being reunited.

Darius came striding toward her and would have swept her up in his arms except she beat him to it and threw herself at him, clinging to his neck tightly like he was saving her from drowning. If you saved a drowning person with your mouth that is.

A few people stopped to stare and some teenaged boys busy smoking behind a pillar started whooping and clapping enthusiastically.

"Okay, I guess we'll just wait for you inside," I said, pulling Rob into the building so I did not have to witness them practically undressing each other in the parking lot. It might have been a great scene in a romance movie but in real life, it was just incredibly awkward to watch people you knew making out in public.

"That was dramatic," Rob said, laughing, "you'd think they hadn't seen each other in months."

"Yeah, welcome to my world. I get to hear about Darius every minute of every day."

"Oh come on, you don't like him?"

"Of course I do, he's great. I just don't want to hear about him non-stop. Why can't they just be a normal, boring couple without all the drama?"

"Let's get you some popcorn," Rob said, laughing, "that will cheer you up."

"Only if there's extra butter. And if we can dump our candy on top."

"Okay, that is completely wrong on so many levels but whatever makes you happy."

Chapter Eleven

"You were right, this does make me happy," I said, gleefully dumping the rest of our box of chocolate Maltesers on top of the popcorn and giving the bag a shake so they'd get nicely coated in butter and salt.

We were alone in the half-empty theatre. The movie had been out for a while so it wasn't very crowded. "Do you think I should text Hilary? They won't know where to find us when they finally come up for air."

"I think maybe you should leave it, Astrid. She'll text if she's looking for us."

"You don't think she'll be wondering where we are?"

Rob shrugged. "I'm not sure that I care, honestly. I'm just glad that I'm here with you."

"Oh," I said, remembering all at once how lucky I was to *be* here with Rob at all. Not so long ago my dad would have forbidden me to even do something as innocent as go on a simple date to the movies. "You're right, me too. They'll find us if they need to."

The film was something Hilary had chosen for all of us, one of those soppy romantic comedies that I wouldn't have usually picked out. But it turned out to be really funny and it was good to just forget about my everyday life for once and lose myself in the story.

Hilary and Darius never showed up, but by the time the movie was half-over I was having too much fun to care. It wasn't until Rob and I came out of the theatre hand in hand that I felt a twinge of worry again. I didn't want her mom to blame me if anything had happened to her.

"Astrid, Rob!" Hilary jumped up and down, waving at us. Darius stood close beside her, one arm over her shoulder. "Over here."

"Where were you?" I asked as we came toward them, not sure if I really wanted to know.

"It's okay, we just went to a restaurant to have dinner. Darius is only in town for tonight so I didn't want to waste it on a silly movie."

"Oh," I said, frowning.

"Well, you missed out," Rob said, squeezing my hand, "it was good."

"I'm sure it was," Hilary said quickly. "Astrid, I'm sorry we bailed on you, I didn't want you to know ahead of time just in case my parents started grilling you or something. Don't mention it to them, though, okay?"

"She shouldn't have to lie for you—" Rob started but Darius cut him off.

"Of course we'd never expect Astrid to lie," he said smoothly. "Hilary just had a headache so we left the theatre early and got some food, that is all. Hilary will tell her parents this herself. Right?"

"Sure," Hilary said, smiling sweetly. "If they ask. We didn't get dessert, though, we wanted to wait for you guys so we could go get ice cream together. You up for it?"

She beamed at both us, looking a million times happier than she usually did lately, and I found it was nearly impossible to stay irritated, even though I didn't like how they were both way too comfortable about lying.

"There's that gelato place you like just around the corner," Hilary wheedled.

Hmm, that was an amazing place. They had over a hundred delicious flavours of Italian ice cream. Who could say no to that?

The shop was crowded and noisy but Darius found us a table and kept us entertained with stories of his travels across the States and Canada playing with the squash tournament. Then he politely asked after all the horses by name, wanting to know how the horse archery was coming along. He was clearly turning on his charm full-strength tonight in order to make up for bailing on us.

Oh well, at least he genuinely cares about her, I thought, watching them together, *and he makes her happy. I guess the rest isn't any of my business.*

We hung out for another hour before Mrs. Ahlberg came to pick us up, and it wasn't until Hilary and I were back in the car heading home that the weariness I'd pushed away earlier came rushing back. I leaned my head against the leather seat and shut my eyes gratefully.

"Mom, can you stop the car here so that Astrid can throw the horses their hay?" Hilary asked, jolting me awake.

"Sure, honey, but I think it's your turn this time. Astrid ran up to ask Oona about the movies, remember?"

"But I'm wearing a dress and these are my favourite flats," Hilary argued, her voice rising up a few notches.

"Well then, I'll just run you up to the house so you can get changed and you can come back down on your own then," her mother said firmly.

"No, just forget it," Hilary muttered, "they probably don't even need a night feed anyway, it doesn't matter if we skip it just this once."

I sat up, now fully awake and very angry. "Oh, yes it does," I said from my place in the backseat. "Stop the car, please. I'll get out and do it."

"Astrid, you don't have to do that," Mrs. Ahlberg protested, slowing down in front of the barn, but I was already out of the car and marching toward the waiting horses.

"Don't bother waiting," I said over my shoulder as Hilary rolled down her window to apologize. "I'll walk back to the house. I need the fresh air anyway."

There weren't any sounds from Oona's loft and I threw everyone their hay quickly and checked their water buckets, silently cursing Hilary under my breath the whole time.

I couldn't believe she'd be so thoughtless as to skip feeding them an entire meal just because she was lazy or she was wearing the wrong shoes, for heaven's sake. She'd changed so much in such a short time that I hardly knew her. Had I ever really known her?

"Good night, everyone," I whispered but the only answer was contented chewing.

The night was still very warm but clouds had rolled in

overhead, covering the stars and making things seem darker than usual. Caprice met me halfway up the driveway, prancing and wiggling in her excitement to greet me.

"Hey there, what are you doing out here by yourself?" I whispered, leaning down to pet her. She sat still as long as she could and then wriggled free, galloping back the way she'd come.

The house was quiet when I got back. I ushered Caprice inside and locked the front door behind us, tiptoeing up the creaky wooden stairs to my room.

I showered and dumped my clothes into the overflowing laundry basket, vowing that tomorrow was the day that I'd actually get caught up on all that washing.

I'd just crawled into bed and shut the light off when there was a quiet knock on my door.

"Astrid?" Hilary said, standing uncertainly in my bedroom doorway. "Are you asleep?"

"Barely," I said, pulling myself upright and flicking the bedside light back on, "'what's wrong?"

"Oh, nothing really," she said, coming a few steps inside and shutting the door carefully behind her. "I just wanted to apologize is all. I'm sorry about skipping the movie tonight and for fighting with you yesterday. I'm sorry I've not been pulling my weight around here. I do know that I'm not being fair making you do all the work. I'll work on that, I promise. I just get so overwhelmed that sometimes it's an effort to do anything at all."

"But why?" I asked. "I mean, I know you're busy but so am I. I'd think it would be relaxing for you to spend time with the horses. It's the best part of my day."

"I know it is. And it used to be that way for me, too, but it isn't now. Whenever I'm down there, I just see all these mouths to feed, depending on me to make all the right decisions and not make any mistakes. I see them using all those expensive shavings and eating all that imported hay and supplements that they probably don't even need. Then there's deworming and the vet and farrier list, and then this business of trying to find a good coach.

"As soon as I'm around them I just start to think about everything I have to do, and my throat closes up and I feel all panicky, and I just want to curl up on a ball and sleep or throw up or something."

"Oh, Hilary," I said, "why didn't you tell me about it? Have you talked to your parents?"

"No," she said quickly, "and I'm not going to. It's my problem to deal with. I took on this project, I made my parents build me a barn, for heaven's sake. They basically bought this property because I talked them into it. I owe it to them to make it work. But it's taken all the fun out of having horses. The only thing that's good in my life right now is Darius. I feel so happy when I'm around him like he's tossing me a life ring. Whenever I'm away from him I just feel lost. It will be better when he's done the tour and is back in town for good. Then I'll feel like I can breathe again."

"But wouldn't spending time with Jerry help?"

"It doesn't, he knows the second I start to tense up and then he gets spooky or tries something stupid. He knows how I feel inside. He doesn't want to be around me..."

"That's not true..."

"I think it is. But what I'm worried about now are tomorrow's lessons. What if she's a terrible coach or mean to the boarders or the horses? How am I supposed to get rid of her if it doesn't work out? And that weird woman who keeps calling me about horse board is coming to look at the barn tomorrow, and I already know it's not going to be what she wants."

"I think you need to stop worrying so much," I said gently, stifling a yawn. "You're doing a great job with the farm; all the horses and the boarders are really happy here. I'm sure Oona will be fine or Liza wouldn't have sent her in the first place. And if that boarder doesn't work out then someone else will."

"You're probably right," she said, looking down at her bare toes. "I guess I should go. Thanks for accepting my apology." She paused, looking as if she'd like to say something more. "Good night."

"Hilary…" I said, not wanting her to go when there was clearly something else on her mind but she'd already disappeared into the hallway, shutting the door gently behind her.

Chapter Twelve

The next morning my alarm went off before the sun was up, and I leapt out of bed, reaching automatically for the clothes I'd set aside the night before.

This is it, I thought, *lesson day*.

Caprice was still sleeping so I went downstairs to grab a coffee and to make myself some toast with peanut butter and bananas.

It was probably going to be a long day so I wanted to make sure I had a chance to eat now because who knew the next time I'd get a chance. I wanted to get the barn tidy before all the activity started and any outside riders came in for their lessons.

"Eat up, everyone," I told the horses, tossing their hay hurriedly into the stalls and heading in to mix up their grain. "I'll turn you out after your workouts."

I swept the aisle while they ate and made sure the gravel out front was raked neatly and that the tack room looked perfect.

"Come on, you two," I said to Red and Ellie who'd barely finished their breakfast hay. "We'll get you out on pasture early. You too, Sox."

It wouldn't hurt them to get some extra outside time today.

That way I could get a head start on stall cleaning, too.

Rob had been the only one willing to take the early morning spots so it wasn't long before his truck and trailer chugged up the driveway.

"Hey, you're driving," I said in surprise as he grinned down at me from the driver's side window.

"Yep, I have my Learner's permit now so I'm halfway to being an actual driver."

"Soon, he won't need me at all," his dad joked, leaning across his son to hand me a coffee through the window.

"Well, *I'll* need you then," I told him, "I meant to get my Learner's this summer but everything was so crazy that I forgot."

"Anytime," Rob's dad laughed, "just say the word."

They'd only brought Ferdi, since the second horse Rob was riding was Jerry, and I led them to Red's vacant stall so they could leave him relaxing with a hay net since we had some extra time before he had to be tacked up.

Rob's dad plunked a large bag of pastries down on the picnic table and we all sat down to have coffee and second breakfast in the early morning sunshine.

I heaved a deep sigh of contentment as I licked the last of the sugar off my fingers and leaned back to look up at the perfect blue sky overhead. It was shaping up to be a fantastic day.

"Right, time to tack up," Rob said, glancing at his watch after twenty minutes and we both got up to get Ferdi ready.

Rob's horses were always immaculate anyway. He kept their coats glossy, their tack supple and well-oiled, and their boots squeaky clean. But after I'd pulled Ferdi's cotton sheet off, I still went over his shiny copper coat a final time just in case. Then, while Rob put his tack and boots on, I brushed every hair in Ferdi's tail out until it cascaded down to his hocks. He looked perfect.

"Good morning," Oona said stiffly, marching down the stairs. She didn't look like the softer, artistic version of herself anymore; this morning she was all business. She narrowed her eyes critically at Rob and Ferdi and then slowly her expression softened and she actually managed a smile. "This horse is well turned out. He has a kind eye and looks eager to begin his work. Liza says you've done a good job training him so far."

"Claudia started him," Rob said, smiling back at her easily, "and I just picked up where she left off. It's hard to ruin a horse when he had such a good foundation."

Oona's smile dropped away. "It's easier than you'd think," she said sharply. "Fine, let's see what we have to work with here."

I started to follow them to the ring, eager to see Rob ride. I always learned so much from watching other people's lessons and I was excited to have a coach again. But I was stopped dead in my tracks when Oona turned on me, blocking the way.

"No spectators this week," she said sternly, "we don't need any distractions. But, of course, family can come in..." she added reluctantly, turning to Rob's dad, "if they must."

"But..." I said feebly, looking to Rob for help but he just raised his eyebrows and shrugged.

"Astrid's practically family," he tried, but Oona held up a hand to stop him.

"No exceptions," she said. "Astrid, make sure the others are clear that there are to be no interruptions."

Well, fine, I thought as the arena door shut firmly in my face,

I guess I'll just go back to cleaning the barn, like the unpaid hired help I am.

I wasn't even getting my own lesson that day. When Hilary had made up a list of all the riders who wanted a lesson it had been too full to fit everyone in. Liza had had quite a few students in the area before she'd left to live at the ranch and she'd called them all to let them know that there was a new coach in town. That meant we were full to capacity and some people had to be bumped off the list. And that included me.

"Sorry, Astrid," Hilary had said, "but there are too many people already. Ally wants to trailer Severus over to try Oona out so I had to fit her in. I'm really hoping Ally will like her enough to start boarding Severus here. Then it can be just like it was back at Claudia's. You understand, right?"

Even Rob had only gotten in because Hilary wanted Jerry ridden so Oona could admire him, and Rob had only agreed to do it if he could bring Ferdi for a lesson, too.

I was even more annoyed forty-five minutes later when Rob led Ferdi from the ring, both of them damp with exertion but Ferdi bright-eyed and Rob smiling enthusiastically. I didn't even have to ask him how it went.

"She's really good," he said, "different but good. You'll definitely like her."

"Yeah, if I ever get to ride."

"Oh, come on, it's not like you to feel sorry for yourself. You *live* here, and you have the whole winter to ride with her. I'm sure you'll get your chance soon."

"I know," I said, laughing a little at my own crankiness. "I've got my nose out of joint. Here, I'll take care of Ferdi. I've got

Jerry all ready for you; you just need to put on his bridle. I'm not sure where Hilary is but I know she wanted to watch his lesson."

"Well, she's going to miss out then, Oona wants me back in there right away."

I did a final check to make sure Jerry looked perfect and then watched them head off to the ring without me, wishing again that I could just watch their lesson. Back at Claudia's, there'd been the upstairs viewing room you could watch from, even when the lessons were supposed to be private. Here there was nowhere to spy from.

"Are they already in there?" Hilary asked breathlessly, rolling up on the golf cart just as I was finishing Ferdi's bath. "I was stuck on the phone with yet another phone call with that crazy lady who wants to board here. She interrogated me with like a million more questions. She's coming out tomorrow now instead of today to check us out and see if it's good enough for her precious baby. She asked if she could bring a ruler to measure the height of the bedding."

I laughed and shook my head. "She sounds high-maintenance. Do you even want someone like that here?"

"Well, I want her board money anyway," Hilary said, hopping out of the golf cart. She pulled a heavy-looking backpack after her and sat down at the picnic table. "I had no idea how expensive it is to run a place like this, Astrid. The next payment on the indoor is due at the end of the month, too. I think I'm getting an ulcer from all this stress. I can deal with high-maintenance people if I have to."

"Jerry's already in there having his lesson," I reminded her, "you should go in and watch. I don't think Oona could argue since he's your horse."

"Oh, I don't need to watch," Hilary said with a shrug, "not this time. Rob can just tell me all about it afterward."

I stared at her then turned off the hose and started stripping the water from Ferdi's coat, the droplets splashing rhythmically on the driveway under our feet.

Don't judge her, I told myself, *she's struggling.*

"Okay," I said slowly, "well, I'm almost done here if you want to hang out. I told Pender I'd get started on Rabbit for her; she had to drop her youngest kid off at camp last minute and he's filthy. She's supposed to be up next. You can help me if you like."

"No, that's okay. I have to catch up on some homework anyway. I started my courses early and I already feel behind. I doubled my course load this year so that I can graduate faster, but now I'm realizing how much work it's going to be. Hopefully I didn't make a mistake by taking all this on. I'll just do my work out at the picnic table if you don't mind."

"Fine," I said, holding back my disappointment. I guessed that hanging out with me had moved to the very bottom of her priority list, too.

At least Rabbit was well-behaved when I slipped on his halter and tied him to the front ring inside his stall. I didn't dare take him out and put him in the cross-ties since he'd snapped a set of them last week when Pender was just trying to put his boots on. Then he'd bolted outside and it had taken three of us nearly an hour to catch him again. It hadn't bothered Pender at all but it wasn't something I wanted to deal with this morning.

Today, he seemed mellow and was quite content to let me brush him and massage the kinks out of his body while we waited for his rider to arrive.

"Oh, thank you so much," Pender said, rushing in with her vest unbuttoned and her hair coming out of its bun. "I seriously don't know what we'd do without you, Astrid. Lunch is on me today. Let me just get changed and then I'll take over."

I carefully put on Rabbit's boots and smoothed his mane one last time before heading to the tack room to grab his gear. Pender had bought a new white saddle pad for the occasion and had draped it over his saddle so I gathered those up along with his girth, hung his bridle over my shoulder and ferried the whole lot of it back to his stall.

"Good boy, Rabbit," I said, glad to see that he was still standing quietly, snacking on what hay was left in his manger. I brought everything inside and hung the bridle over his door while I got the rest of his gear in place.

"Oh, Astrid, he looks wonderful," Pender said, appearing in front of his stall with her unruly hair slicked back into a tight bun and her clothes clean and somewhat unwrinkled. Pender had always been one of my favourite boarders, even back at Claudia's. It was probably partly because we had the same sense of fashion…so pretty much non-existent. But we both cleaned up nicely when we bothered to make an effort.

"Rob's already had his first lesson and he said Oona's really good," I assured Pender, because she looked white with nerves. "He's still in there with Jerry."

"Oh, good, I really don't like being yelled at. I was up all night worrying about this. Oh dear, there they are. Do I look okay?"

"Yes, you both look great, have fun."

"Thanks, I don't know about fun but wish me luck." She

gulped and trudged slowly off to the open arena door clutching Rabbit's reins tightly like she was headed to her own funeral. She nodded stiffly at Rob as she passed, her face pinched with worry.

It must be awful to be that scared, I thought, *I wonder why she even bothers with lessons if they make her so anxious.*

But the answer to that was obvious when Pender came out of the ring forty-five minutes later; beaming, her face flushed and her eyes bright. Rabbit was steaming with sweat too, but he looked content, his overly-long ears sagging to the side in the way they did when he was at his most relaxed.

"I'm so glad we have a coach again, Astrid. That was wonderful," Pender said as she clipped Rabbit confidently into the cross-ties and pulled his tack off. "When do you have your lessons with Red and Ellie?"

"Um, I'm not sure," I said, eyeing up Rabbit warily. Thankfully he looked much too tired to break any cross-ties at that moment. "Oona hasn't made up her schedule yet. She did today as sort of a trial and then she's going to let us know how she wants to organize things."

"Oh, well, you'll love her. Here's Sadie, she must be running late, too."

Running late seemed to be the theme of the morning for some reason. Rob had had to leave right after his lessons but we shared a quick kiss goodbye and he promised to text me later to fill me in on all the details of his lesson.

I helped Sadie get Riverdance ready and then Annie with Norman. And then it was time for the outside people to trailer in and have their turn.

"Astrid," Ally said happily, leading her huge, elegant

warmblood, Severus, down from his trailer, "it's so good to see you. You look fantastic."

"Thanks, Ally," I said, smiling at her. "You do, too."

She'd been another boarder back at Claudia's barn and she'd always been nice to me. She had Severus in full training with Claudia's son, my old coach Cole who was a bit of a psychopath. I thought she was crazy to stay there, but she refused to move Severus away from him unless we could offer something better as far as facilities and coaching went.

"Astrid, this is my groom, Riley. Can you show her where everything is? I need to get changed."

"Sure," I said, smiling at the rail-thin, nervous-looking blonde girl who now had Severus's lead rope clutched in both hands.

Severus already looked immaculate but Riley brushed him and checked his feet before carefully going over his coat with a damp cloth and rubbing polish onto his hooves. He looked like he'd stepped off the pages of Dressage Today.

Riley just shook her head when I offered to help but she didn't object when I said I could bring Ally's tack in while she busied herself spritzing some lavender scented detangler on his mane and tail.

"Thank you," she said in a quiet voice when I handed her the saddle pad.

Ally came back just as Riley unclipped him from the cross-ties. "Thank you, girls, wish me luck." She strode away confidently, not looking like she needed luck at all.

Riley disappeared back to the horse trailer and I kept myself busy cleaning the rest of the stalls and paddocks. It wasn't until

I heard hooves clopping down the aisle that I realized how much time had passed.

"How did it go?" I asked from Riverdance's stall as Ally led Severus past.

"Interesting," she said, frowning, "it gave me a lot to think about anyway. I guess I have some decisions to make. Well, I'd better be off. It was good to see you, Astrid."

She led him past me to the trailer and I saw Riley scramble out to quickly strip off his gear, throw a cooler over his back, and lead him up the ramp. Then they were gone without saying another word.

Huh, I thought, *they left pretty quickly.* Either the lesson had gone very good or very bad. It was hard to tell.

Another handful of horses and riders came and went while I kept the aisle swept in between grooming sessions and made sure everyone knew where they were going. Finally, it was over and the barn was quiet again.

Chapter Thirteen

Tuesday morning my alarm went off extra early for the second day in a row. I groaned and rolled over, stuffing my head under my pillow.

Oh, get up, I told myself. *Time to get moving. If you were a real athlete you would be leaping out of bed.*

I pulled myself upright with a groan and glanced over at Caprice who was still mostly burrowed under the covers, her little brown muzzle just poking out.

"Do you want to go outside?" I said in an encouraging voice, but she clamped her eyes tightly shut and snuggled deeper until she was completely buried.

"Fine." I sighed. "Glad *someone* gets to sleep in."

I threw on the first pair of half-clean jeans I found and climbed blearily down the stairs, still rubbing my eyes.

I went straight to the front door and pushed my bare feet into my paddock boots, slipping outside into the pre-dawn light and beginning my long walk. I was much too tired to operate a bicycle at this point in my day.

The further on I went and the more early-morning air I

breathed in, the better I felt. By the time I reached the barn door and heard the welcoming whicker of my herd of horses, I was fully awake.

"Hello, everyone," I said softly, rolling the door back and stepping inside. I flicked on the light and inhaled happily; that smell of horse was always like coming home.

I padded past their outstretched heads, avoiding Rabbit's flapping lips but pausing for a second to tickle the end of Red's soft, velvety nose. I rolled back the hay room door and quickly doled out the flakes to everyone, making sure they were each standing back politely before I tossed their hay inside.

All around me was the sound of happy crunching and I went to the tack room, flicked on the light, and moved to the big counter and sink area where all their buckets were lined up, each one half-full of expanded wet beet pulp. I didn't need to look at the feed chart before I mixed up their breakfast; I knew by heart what everyone ate, what supplements they got and how each horse liked their breakfast served. The needs of this herd were more familiar to me than my own.

One by one I opened their doors and dumped breakfasts into their rubber feed tubs, smiling at the eager little sounds Rabbit made under his breath. He was not a patient horse, but he'd learned to be polite and not barge for the tub the second I dumped his food.

"Good boy," I said, pausing to scratch his neck before moving on to Jerry's stall. Under Rob's careful conditioning program, Jerry was looking better than ever; in some spots, his dark grey was fading more to a milky-white, and I knew that in a few years he'd be almost silver.

"Hilary's missing out not riding a nice boy like you," I said to him softly. "I bet you miss her hanging out with you, don't you, buddy? You used to be her main guy."

Jerry raised his head and watched me thoughtfully, his soupy, green breakfast dripping from his mouth. As if he understood what I was saying he heaved a huge sigh and gave a shake, his ears flopping from side to side.

I didn't have much time to eat my own breakfast before it was time for Annie to pick me up for camp. I was lucky she was driving me and I didn't want to be late, especially when I was getting to practice for real again today.

Back inside the house, I ran upstairs to change and grabbed my practice bow and my quiver and filled it with a half-dozen arrows.

In the kitchen, I wolfed down a couple of pieces of toast and an apple juice and forced a sleepy-looking Caprice to at least go outside for a few seconds before I had to leave.

"Why are you up so early?" Hilary said, yawning as she came down the stairs wearing a long old-fashioned nightgown and a pair of fluffy cat socks that went up almost to her knees. When Darius wasn't around, Hilary had a mind of her own when it came to bizarre fashion choices. Most of the time her crazy combinations seemed to work for her but this look; not so much.

"Archery camp, remember?"

"Oh, right, you're still doing that." Hilary opened a few cupboards and started to assemble herself a bowl of granola.

"Just two more days. I do Tuesday and Friday this week and then we have our field trip on the weekend. Nori and Annie will be here any minute. I fed everyone already, but you'll remember to turn them out in an hour or so, right? I can do the paddocks when I get back."

"Um, sure. I guess," Hilary said, wrinkling her nose a little. "That's a lot of walking for me to do, though. They couldn't stay in until you get home?"

"*No*," I said firmly. "It will be late afternoon when I get back. You promised. Remember?"

"Yeah, yeah, okay. It's fine, I'll put them out."

"Great. Watch the sheep, they'll barge the gate and try to escape if you're not paying attention. Pender and Sadie are riding first thing this morning so their horses can stay in until they're done. Everyone else goes out. Unless you're riding Jerry?"

"Nope," Hilary said around a mouthful of cereal. "Not today."

"Fine, well, suit yourself. Thanks for putting them out at least."

I had meant it genuinely but even I heard the exasperated tone my voice.

Hilary looked at me, raising her eyebrows a little. "All right, enjoy your camp thing."

Annie's horn beeped outside and I pushed my chair back, grabbed my bow and quiver, and headed to the door. "Bye, thanks again. I'll see you this afternoon."

I shrugged off the niggle of worry that lodged itself in my heart. Of course, Hilary would do what she'd promised and take care of the horses. She was a good horse person at heart, even if she wasn't acting like it lately. I had to tell myself that, anyway.

Chapter Fourteen

Archery camp was just as fun and challenging as it always was and this time when I did my own short practice at the end of the day, I didn't have my expectations set quite so high.

That was a good thing, because even though my arrows sometimes veered where I wanted, they were still unpredictable and I found my frustration levels rising.

"Don't worry about it," Earl said good-naturedly, "this is only your second day back, give your muscles a chance to remember their job."

"Okay," I said, trying not to feel discouraged.

"There's a new competition series happening this winter for up and coming athletes. I think you should join. There's a shoot every month."

"Are you kidding? I wouldn't have a chance of winning."

"No, but winning isn't the point right now. Being there might give you some inspiration; get you back in the groove and give you some much-needed competition time."

But I'll embarrass myself in front of all those people, I thought, *they will be expecting me to be like I was before. What if people laugh?*

Earl looked at me patiently, giving me time to sort out my thoughts and I finally nodded.

"Okay, yeah, I guess I could do that."

"Good girl," he said, clapping me on the shoulder, "this will be great for you."

There was a loud scuffling sound and raised voices behind us.

"You don't know anything," I heard Nori say angrily.

I turned to see her glaring down at a girl half her size who was in Miranda's group. The girl gulped and looked up at Nori with wide eyes.

"Well, that's what Miranda told us," she said in a tiny, determined voice, "she said that Astrid wasn't any good at all and that it was all luck that she'd won so many times before."

"That's ridiculous, Miranda doesn't know what she's talking about. Astrid can shoot a target off a galloping horse from a hundred yards…"

"Whoa, whoa, whoa," I said, going over to intervene before she added any more to her story. "Nori, what's going on?"

"Miranda says you can't shoot anymore," Nori said angrily.

"Oh, did she now?" I raised my eyebrows at the little girl who was looking like she very much regretted starting this conversation.

"Umm, maybe I got it wrong," she said quickly. "I've got to go." She spun around and hurried back to the other side of the range.

"Just ignore Miranda, Nori," I said, patiently. "that's the only way to handle someone like her."

"But you can't let her talk about you like that. I know, you have to host a horse archery day, let them see what you're made of."

"Nori, I really don't care what Miranda, or some random kid, thinks of me. I've barely practiced in a year; Earl's not worried and neither am I."

Even though I was just trying to reassure Nori, at that moment my words actually felt true. Sometimes I really did believe in myself.

"But I want them to see you like I see you," Nori said, her face falling. "I wish they could just come to the farm and watch you in action."

I felt a stab of sympathy for her. Nori felt everything so intensely; her anger, her happiness, her sadness and sense of fairness was much stronger than most people's. It couldn't be easy to live like that.

"I wonder if Earl would go for that?" I asked thoughtfully.

"Go for what?" Earl said, coming up behind us.

"Maybe a field trip to the farm someday. Maybe over Christmas break. We could let everyone see the horse bows, and Nori and I could do a little demo. We could show them how we train the horses, too."

"Yes," Nori said, her eyes shining. "That would be so epic. Can we really do it, Astrid?"

"How about I ask Hilary's parents? As long as they say it's okay then I can't see why not. I bet Rob wouldn't mind helping organize it, either."

"It's actually a good idea, Astrid," Earl said, "I'd love to show the kids something different. I bet a lot of them would be interested if you decide to start your own program in the future."

During the ride home, I sat mostly in silence, letting Nori do most of the talking. I only came back to reality when we pulled up the driveway.

At least the horses got turned out, I thought, glad to see that

Hilary had kept her word and the pastures were full of horses grazing happily in the late afternoon sun.

"I'll help you with paddocks while mom rides Norman," Nori announced, bouncing out of the car, "then maybe we can go on a trail ride."

"Nori," her mother warned, "don't pester Astrid, she looks tired."

"Come on, Mom, I'm not two years old. I'm just helping to clean. Don't worry about me, just go ride your horse."

Annie shook her head but didn't say anything. Nori had become much more pleasant over the summer but she still had an attitude when she felt like it. Still, I wasn't about to argue with someone who wanted to help me clean paddocks and go for a trail ride.

We pulled the wheelbarrow out and grabbed two plastic manure forks and got to work.

"I'd come and train with you once you start your horse archery school here," Nori said out of nowhere as soon as we'd reached the first paddock.

"School? What are you talking about?"

"You know, in the future, when you and Rob are married and you have your farm and everything."

"What?" I sputtered, nearly dropping the fork. "Where on earth is this coming from?"

"Come on, it's completely obvious that's what's going to happen. After you win at the Olympics, you're going to get married and live on a farm, and Rob's going to train horses and you're going to have a horse archery school. Unless you decide to have lots of babies instead, and then you'll just want to sit around the house all day eating chocolate and watching soap operas."

"Whoa, whoa, whoa." I held up my hand to stop her right there. "I'm not even old enough to have my full driver's license yet so I certainly don't want to think about *babies* now. Gross."

"You're right, sorry; the 'babies' part was a bit much. But back to the horse archery—"

"I didn't know you had such a good imagination, Nori."

"I don't. I'm just following the current evidence to its logical conclusion."

"Great, well, let's start with the part about me going to the Olympics when I can barely hit a target."

"At the range, you mean. You hit targets all the time here."

"Hmm," I said, "that's true."

"So, eventually that's going to happen at the range, too. You'll start competing again and then you'll be unstoppable."

"Well, thanks, Nori," I said, smiling at her fondly. Even if she was way off base with all this, it was still sweet that she believed in me.

With Nori's help and non-stop excited chatter about her plans for *my* future, cleaning the stalls and paddocks went much faster than normal. We sauntered down to the pasture and brought the horses in two at a time.

"What do *they* want?" Nori asked, pointing at the sheep who were standing a few feet back from the gate, staring at us pointedly.

"They probably want back in the barn so they can destroy things. Or they want grain. I've never met such greedy animals."

"They're fat, too," Nori said, "it's not like they need any more groceries."

"They certainly are round," I said, flinching instinctively at the word *fat*. It had been used on me enough in the past that I had a pathological hatred of the word even when it wasn't directed my way. It was amazing how words could hurt almost as much as physical things.

I looked over at the expectantly waiting sheep and frowned. Something was different.

"Hey, guys," I said. "Where's Portia?"

"Bah," Hamlet said and stamped a front foot hard on the ground.

"Hmm, that's not very helpful, Hamlet."

"Are you talking to a sheep?" Nori said, raising an incredulous eyebrow in my direction.

"Yep. Come on, let's finish putting the horses away and get them their dinner. I'll have to go look for her; it's not like Portia to be away from her friends."

"You're so weird," Nori said affectionately but followed me obediently to the barn.

We settled the horses in their stalls and left them all happily eating their hay and trekked back down the hill to the field. The flock was grazing a little ways off now, noses down in the grass but there was still no sign of Portia.

"I guess we'll just have to walk the fence line," I said, resigning myself to a hike. The pasture was huge and the terrain dipped and rolled so it wasn't like you could stand in one corner and see the whole thing. There were wooded areas in some places, too; plenty of spots where a sheep could get stuck.

We headed off to the left first, combing the little copses of trees to make sure we didn't miss her.

When we reached the halfway point, Nori's phone chimed.

"Um, Astrid," she said, looking up from her phone with a smile. "I think we can stop looking now." She showed me her phone where half a dozen texts from her mom had popped up. All were photos taken from Norman's back inside the big sand ring and clearly showed Portia, also inside the ring, grazing on the thick grass growing around the bottom of the fence posts.

"How did she even get up there by herself?" I asked and Nori shrugged.

"I don't know. How are you planning to get her back? She looks pretty happy."

"Probably food," I said, laughing.

We trekked back up to the barn and sure enough, Portia was in the corner of the sand ring, not grazing anymore but lying down with her front legs tucked neatly underneath her while she chewed her cud, a satisfied expression on her face.

"Sorry about this," I called out to Annie but she just laughed and shook her head.

"Norman and I don't mind an audience. She's been perfectly well-behaved."

"Yeah, except for breaking out of the pasture and running away," I said and then stopped, remembering that I myself had been a runaway not too long ago.

"I'll go get some grain; I think she'll follow me back to them."

Leaving Nori and Annie guarding Portia, I went to the barn to grab a bucket of sweet feed and was surprised to find Hilary there in the aisle, her phone pressed against her cheek and a worried expression on her face.

"Yes, yes, I understand," she said in a small voice, quickly turning away when she caught sight of me. "Next week works fine. We'll be ready."

She hung up and turned around slowly, rubbing one hand across her forehead wearily. "Well, that woman finally said yes. She came this morning to check the place out and she just called back; she's going to board her precious horse here."

"That's good news, though, isn't it? You don't look that happy."

"Sort of," Hilary said slowly, not quite meeting my eye. "But she doesn't want a back paddock. She wants to be in this barn."

"What did she say when you told her there's not any room in here?"

"Um," Hilary said, and a stain of blush rose steadily up her neck and coloured her cheeks a mottled pink. She cleared her throat a few times before saying, "You know, I was thinking that maybe Ellie could move to an outside paddock; that would make space."

"Ellie," I said in surprise. "You want to move her? But she'd be all by herself back there. She'd hate that."

"That's true." Hilary moved to the open doorway and looked outside toward the back paddocks. "I guess we could move another horse over to keep her company. That would free up another spot for a boarder; I've had a few other calls this week."

"You want to move Jerry over?"

"I could…" Hilary said slowly, "I hadn't thought of that. He really likes being in the barn, though, and it's sort of *his* place so I hate to move him. But it would be super nice if I could fill the place with paying boarders…" She broke off, still not looking at me.

There was a sudden, uncomfortable silence and I realized abruptly what she was getting at. She wanted me to move *Red*. Because I wasn't paying board at all except through all the work I did. But I did *all the work*. Didn't that mean anything?

Inexplicable tears welled in my eyes. It wasn't that I even minded moving to the outside paddocks. Red would actually probably like it better. The stalls were huge and so were the paddocks. But the idea that Hilary just considered me so disposable, so easy to push aside nearly made me sick.

The door overhead banged loudly and Oona strode down the stairs, her boots thudding purposefully on each step. She glanced at us, raising her eyebrows first at Hilary and then at me, her mouth pulling down into its signature frown. She shook her head slightly as she passed us on her way to the tack room and I felt my mood slide even lower.

"Astrid," Hilary said urgently as soon as Oona had passed, "I didn't mean that you *had* to move. Of course I don't want you to. It's just that it would be easier…I mean, it makes the most sense."

"Lesson in fifteen minutes, Astrid," Oona said loudly from the open tack room door, making both me and Hilary jump. "Ride your chestnut."

"What?" I said, caught off guard. "But I'm not dressed, and I have to catch a sheep."

Oona pressed her lips together and I couldn't tell if she was angry or struggling not to laugh. "Of course you do. All right, half an hour then. Make sure your horse is immaculate. I'd hurry if I were you. You're already late."

"Okay," I said, but she'd already turned on her heel and

marched back upstairs to the loft, making me wonder why she'd come down in the first place. Had she somehow overheard our conversation?

"Astrid," Hilary said again as soon as she was gone, "I don't mean to sound like a complete cow but I'm trying to run a business…."

"Can we do this later?" I interrupted, suddenly wanting to be as far away from her as possible. I pushed past her to the tack room to get my bucket of grain. "I have to catch Portia, she got out somehow."

I bet it was Hilary who let her escape, I thought angrily, *she doesn't care about who she hurts anymore.*

As expected, Portia leapt up right away when she saw the grain bucket and waddled after me down to the pasture to be with her friends, her large belly swaying from side to side.

"I hate to even *mention* dieting, Portia," I told her seriously, "but there's such a thing as portion control, you know. You're not going to be able to walk properly if you get any bigger."

As soon as she was safely back with her friends, I dumped the bucket of grain on the ground for them all to share. I gave her one last scratch behind the ear and then hurried away to break it to Nori that I was having a lesson and wouldn't be able to go on a trail ride.

"It's fine," she said, surprisingly unruffled, "Mom and I will go. It's our first time we get to ride out together since…well, since this spring. And it will be the last chance we'll have for a peaceful ride once Callie is back from her dad's tomorrow."

Thankful that I'd escaped without her pitching one of her famous fits, I ran up to the house to get changed as fast as I could.

By the time I was back, Annie and Nori were just leaving on their trail ride and I had ten minutes to have Red tacked up and in the ring.

Chapter Fifteen

It was only when I'd hurried into Red's stall and begun whisking his coat clean that my conversation with Hilary came back to me.

"I'm being silly, Red," I whispered. "It doesn't really matter where I keep you, does it? You don't care as long as you have food and a nice paddock and lots of attention. So why does it hurt so much?"

I ran the soft body brush over his coat one final time and smoothed his mane so every hair lay flat and perfect.

Oona appeared from the tack room with a set of four immaculately clean white leather dressage boots under one arm.

"Here," she said, "he can wear these today."

"Oh, thanks, but I have some," I said, looking down at the battered, sun-bleached boots sticking out of my grooming tote.

"Just use the white ones," Oona said firmly. "I don't have a horse to put them on right now and I think they'll fit him just fine. He should always look his best. Make sure you clean them carefully after every ride and only use them in the ring. No *trails* and certainly no ocean."

"Okay, thank you," I said, wondering why she was being

extra nice to me all of a sudden.

I strapped the fancy white leather boots on all four of Red's legs and stood back to admire how handsome he looked. Even though we'd hardly schooled at all lately, he was looking more toned and powerful than he ever had. Our summer of riding the trails had been good for him.

I had a clean white show pad that I'd never had the chance to use so I put that on and then finished tacking him up.

"You look like a real dressage horse, Red," I told him, stopping quickly to use my phone to take half a dozen photos of him looking so handsome before leading him down the aisle to the ring. His hooves clopped steadily on the concrete floor, such a good solid sound, and I leaned over to kiss his soft neck, marvelling once again how lucky I was to have him in my life.

"Astrid, are you coming?"

I sped up, marching Red quickly to the ring; Oona stood in the middle, arms crossed over her chest, and one booted foot tapping the arena dirt, not looking so pleasant at all now.

I gulped nervously as I fumbled with the girth to make sure it was tight enough and ran down my stirrups. I wondered now if this was such a good idea. Oona seemed a little intense; maybe I didn't want to take lessons with her after all.

"All right, buddy," I said as I swung up into the saddle. "It's too late to turn back now. Let's do this."

"Pick him up and engage him right away," Oona said before I'd even taken ten steps. "He's absolutely allowed to stretch, but he should be moving and using those hindquarters; it doesn't benefit him at all to let him shuffle along."

"Oh, okay," I said and surprised Red by urging him forward

a little. He was used to us having a nice, relaxing stroll to loosen his muscles before he got to work.

"Better. He needs to know that this is his job when he enters the arena; it is not play-time."

Hmm, but his work should be fun, I thought, *like when we free lunge, that's playing but it's hard work, too.*

"Engage his mind right from the beginning, Astrid, he's just wandering along without purpose. This should be exciting and interesting for him."

"Um, we're just warming up," I said hesitantly, not sure what she meant.

"That doesn't mean it has to be boring. Do some circles, squares, serpentines, zig-zag lines. Anything except the dreaded plodding along on the rail that you're doing. Add in some figure-eights, leg-yields, shoulder-in; he can do all these things in an active walk. You are the captain of this ship, Astrid, do something to inspire him."

"Um, okay," I said, thrown off, and slightly annoyed, by this disruption in my routine. I guess I *had* let our rides in the arena become a little boring. Maybe that's why I'd spent almost all my time this summer out on the trail. Red swivelled one ear back at me, uncertain of what I was asking him to do so early in our ride but trying hard to figure it out.

"Do some triangles down the long side," Oona called out.

Triangles? I had no idea what she meant, *maybe like pointy serpentines?* I started to cross from one side of the ring to the other, glancing over at her to see if I was doing it right.

"No, like this," Oona said, moving to the rail and doing a series of small triangles from the wall to the quarter line, "like little shark's teeth. It helps them to engage their haunches. Can you feel that?"

"I actually do," I said, zig-zagging in precise little triangles, Red's weight shifted backward and I could feel his hind legs engaging at each turn, reminding me of the cow-horse he'd once been. He snorted softly when we reached the short wall and dropped his nose, mouthing gently at the bit.

"Give him at least five more minutes at the walk. I always use a stopwatch to time my warmup and I recommend that you do the same in the future. When you're ready and you think he's had a chance to stretch evenly on both sides you can do the same thing in a trot."

I nodded and, after a few more exercises in the walk, we moved into a loose, rising trot. I had to admit that he felt suppler and freer than he normally would at this stage in our ride.

"Right, good. Oops, and now he's dropped on the forehand, did you feel that? Circle there and rebalance him. Now, repeat that whole walk warm-up in the trot."

She watched us in silence for a while with her arms crossed. "You need to rebalance him there," she called out, striding over toward us, "that's going to be your challenge with him, I think. He has a powerful engine, but you'll need to encourage him to sit down and use it rather than dragging himself along on the forehand. He's naturally built a little downhill, too, so that makes your job harder. Can you feel the difference between when he's slogging along vs. when he's sitting and engaging his hocks?"

"Sometimes," I said honestly, bringing him down to a walk, grateful for the break. I hadn't done ring work like this in a while and I was out of breath. "And sometimes it feels just fine and I can't tell at all."

"Fair enough, that will come with time and experience. Besides, engagement of the hocks isn't easy for him to maintain, we can't expect him to use his body perfectly all the time at this stage, but you'll be able to help him more once you can consistently recognize when he's out of balance and needs your assistance. Okay, let's pick up the trot again."

I asked Red to move forward into a trot and he readily complied, his neck reaching down, his mouth soft on the bit.

"How does that feel?"

"It feels good to me; he's relaxed and stretching down."

"Does he feel energized, like he could leap out of the way at any moment, say, if he were charged by a runaway bull?"

"What?" I laughed. "No, well, it feels comfortable but I don't think he could do any leaping."

"Okay, so let's work on activating him a little more behind then, that way we can free up those shoulders."

More forward, I thought, encouraging Red to step out even more. We moved around the outside of the ring in a quick trot but it didn't feel as relaxed and balanced as what I was used to. It felt like he was just rushing.

"Remember that activating the hind-quarters doesn't automatically mean faster though, Astrid. What makes him have to sit and use his hind-end?"

"Um," I said, thinking desperately. I knew all this stuff, or at least I thought I had but that was back when I'd been riding Quarry. I hadn't really had to think about it lately with Red, we'd been having fun just playing. "Circles?" I guessed.

"Not necessarily but at least they'd be an improvement to you trundling along the outside of the ring on autopilot. Literally nothing can be accomplished by staying on the rail all the time, Astrid."

"Sorry, I know."

"That's fine, that's why we're here. One of the many acceptable answers I was looking for was transitions."

"Oh, right," I said as bits of Claudia's and Liza's lessons began to slowly come back to me.

We went through a series of upward and downward transitions, never staying in one gait too long. Oona didn't let me take more than six strides along the rail without reminding me to circle or cross the diagonal or, for heaven's sake, do something different. Despite my frustration, pretty soon Red was moving out like a little warhorse, his ears pricked as he leapt into another canter.

"Great, Astrid, so much better. Now he's really able to use himself properly. Can you feel that?"

"Yes." I nodded, bringing him down into a walk. "This is how he feels out on the trails when he's really fresh."

"Yes, that's exactly the energy you want to re-create in here. You've done a good job over the summer of getting him to be a nice, forward mover. Liza told me a little bit about how you struggled with him."

"It wasn't a struggle," I protested, not wanting to hear anything bad about Red. "He was fine bareback, he just didn't like moving forward under saddle. We fixed that, though."

"Yes, that's sort of what I just said. Anyway, if your plans are to show and move him up the levels then we'll need to sit down and discuss a training plan to help him develop a little more strategically. I really do think he has a lot of potential."

I sighed and looked down at his neck, running my fingers nervously through his neatly pulled mane.

"You don't look very happy. Isn't that what you want?" Oona asked in confusion. "Liza said there was a good winter series here. She thought you'd be ready to enter with both horses."

"There is," I said slowly. "I know I *should* go, at least to take Ellie who needs the experience. But—"

I swallowed hard. I hadn't confessed to anyone yet how little I was looking forward to this season. I *did* want to show, but just not now, not this year. Red was my sanctuary and I loved hanging out with him; I didn't want to risk wrecking the special bond we had.

"Astrid, you don't sound very inspired."

"No." I looked up tentatively. "I'm not. It all feels like so much work."

"Well, riding is hard work. I thought you'd know that by now."

"Yes, I do and it's not that I mind work. It's just…." I stopped, trying to piece out what I wanted to say. Despite the fact that she was abrupt, or maybe because of it, for some reason I felt that I could be honest with Oona. "I used to be excited every time I stepped in the ring, now I just can't feel that magic for some reason. I love riding and I love Red, and I don't want it to be just another chore I have to get through in the day. I don't want to drill with him in the ring, I just want to be out on the trails and hang out with him."

I stopped, knowing that this probably sounded crazy to her. She was a dressage coach; she probably found every second in the ring fascinating. I must sound like a spoilt child to her. "I know it must sound silly to you…"

I glanced up to find her staring at me with a strange, distant expression on her face as if she wasn't really seeing me at all.

"Why did you start riding?" she asked out of the blue, surprising me with the question.

"I didn't even like horses at first," I confessed, smiling as I remembered back to my very first day at the barn with Hilary. "I thought they were too big and that they stank. It was meeting Quarry who changed that, I fell in love with him right away."

"Do you remember why?"

"Well, he was so beautiful, and graceful; I thought he looked like a unicorn without the horn. He was wise and he took care of me. Claudia was so generous with him, too, she gave me so many lessons when she didn't have to. She—"

My eyes welled with tears. I brushed them away impatiently. Not this again. Did I have to cry every single time I felt an emotion now?

"She was a wonderful person," Oona said gently, "she did the same thing for me, actually. I don't think I would have had the same opportunities abroad if it hadn't been for her kindness."

"Do you miss her?" I asked, sniffling a little.

"I do. And I miss the girl that I was back then when I was just learning what this magical thing called dressage was all about."

"All I wanted to do when I started was piaffe and passage," I said, laughing. "I had no idea there was anything else."

"Well, upper level movements are pretty fantastic. I don't blame you."

I stared down at Red's neck and sighed. "I feel a little of that magic when I free lunge, actually."

"Oh? How so?"

"Because they're so beautiful," I said slowly. "Maybe because they're free to express themselves when they're loose. It's not like they're just trotting around like robots being told what to do. They get to keep their sparks, their personalities. And when they play with you it's because they *choose* to, not because you're forcing them to."

Oona was watching me with a smile on her face and I blushed, thinking that she must imagine me the most childish student in the world. I should never have told her all that stuff.

"Astrid, I really see why Liza likes you so much. You're one of her favourite students, you know."

"I am?" I said incredulously, but she waved a hand in my direction impatiently.

"I have an idea," she said, a genuine smile transforming her face; she looked more like she had when I'd caught her painting in the loft.

"What kind of idea?" I asked warily.

"The next step in your dressage journey. Look, I can see that you're bored in the ring right now. You've just hit a rut and that's natural; we all go through it at one point or another. I don't think you're going to get any benefit out of riding lessons right now, your head is not in the right place."

I opened my mouth to protest, but she held up her hand again to cut me off.

"Now, hear me out. You love liberty work, right? You still get inspired by it."

"Yes," I said cautiously.

"Great, well then, you're going to love the next stage. Now, no more questions yet. I'll get some homework together for you and look over my notes and figure out a lesson plan."

"Okay, but what are we doing?" I asked in confusion.

"You'll see," Oona said, rubbing her hands together. "You're going to love it."

I looked at her skeptically, but she just laughed and seemed so enthusiastic, that I didn't have the heart to argue.

"Why don't I give you a lesson on your little mare tomorrow morning so I can see where you two are at, and then I'll give you some homework for the chestnut, er, Red?"

"Okay, I mean, yes, thank you. I think."

That was the end of our very odd lesson and Oona didn't say another word as she left the arena. But for some reason, even though nothing much at all had happened during my ride, I felt lighter and more inspired than I had in a while.

I hummed under my breath as I pulled off Red's saddle and sweaty saddle-pad and carefully unbuckled the boots Oona had loaned me. I would have to take extra care to make sure those were cleaned properly.

"Come on, buddy," I said, "let's get you a shower and a snack."

I took an extra-long time with Red's bath, making sure that every last trace of sweat had been squeegeed from his coat and that he was carefully towel dried from head to toe before I led him back to his stall. I knew as soon as I slipped his halter off that it was a mistake: I should have taken him directly outside.

With a groan of satisfaction his knees buckled and he dropped down onto his thick bedding and rolled while I stood beside him clutching his empty halter, torn between anxiety at the thought of him maybe getting stuck on his back up against the walls and love over how adorable he was with his four hooves waving around in the air.

Luck was on my side because he didn't get stuck and a minute later, he popped to his feet, covered from head to toe in shavings, and gave a mighty shake. Then he stuck his face into his hay.

"Ridiculous horse," I told him affectionately but he didn't look up from his dinner.

Chapter Sixteen

When I got back to the house, Hilary's bedroom door was shut and she had some sort of weird Celtic music playing so loud that the door handle was vibrating.

I passed quickly without knocking, still too upset with her to even stop and tell her about my lesson with Oona. And that gave me a pang, too, because the old Hilary and I shared everything and could talk for hours together about every topic under the sun, especially about horses.

I took a shower that just bordered on ice-cold and changed into jeans and a t-shirt, pulling my damp hair back into a pony-tail.

I headed downstairs, still thinking about everything that had happened that afternoon.

"Hilary's not coming down for dinner, dear. Her stomach is a little off tonight," Mrs. Ahlberg said, "so it's just the three of us."

"Okay," I said, a bit relieved that I didn't have to see Hilary again until I'd had a chance to think about our earlier conversation. I'd pushed my hurt and confusion aside during my ride and I knew that I would need time by myself in order to process it all.

The food was amazing as always and I dug in, content to let Hilary's parents carry the conversation while I tasted a little bit of everything.

"Don't forget about picking up your uniform tomorrow afternoon, Astrid. Your fitting appointment is at noon," Mrs. Ahlberg said, just as I took a large bite of lasagna. "I almost forgot about it myself but I was speaking with Marion today and she asked me to remind you."

"Oh, right," I said, choking a little at the reminder of both school and Marion. Even though I'd decided to break off all communication with my parents I knew that my step-mom talked to the Ahlbergs once in a while and that she had had a hand in arranging for me to be enrolled in my old private school, Sacred Heart, this year.

I guessed it was too much to hope that both my parents would disappear completely; it had to be enough that they were thousands of miles away with no immediate plan to return. Although, there was always that lingering fear that my dad would change his mind and try and take me with them again.

"Hopefully, it's a simple fitting and they won't have to make any alterations," Hilary's mom said, still talking about my uniform. "I was certainly glad I didn't have to deal with that anymore when Hilary started homeschooling."

I sighed and looked down at my plate, pushing some glazed carrots around with the tines of my fork. I hadn't known exactly what size to order so I'd sort of guessed. I knew I'd changed a lot since the last time I'd had to wear a school uniform but some parts of my body were smaller and some parts had filled out more, and I was definitely taller. Marion had always handled stuff like that; in the past I'd preferred just to pretend it wasn't happening.

There had been one bad year where they'd had to add elastic inserts to all my skirts at the last minute because I'd expanded so much. The seamstress hadn't been very happy about all the extra work, either.

"It will be fine, dear, I'm sure that Hilary and I can go with you and we'll make a day of it and go for lunch afterward."

"Oh, okay, thanks," I said, thinking there was little chance of that happening now. There was no way Hilary wanted to spend the day with me. And maybe I didn't want to spend it with her, either.

The conversation shifted as the Ahlberg's talked excitedly about their very first bed and breakfast guests who were booked to stay in one of the water-view suites next week.

"I think we're as ready as we'll ever be," Hilary's mom said. "The room is prepped, the breakfast is planned, now all we need is our guests."

It was nice having the Ahlbergs all to myself for once; I could almost pretend they were my actual parents and I'd lived here all my life.

"So, Astrid, Nori's mom Annie came to see me the other day."

"She did?" I asked warily, caught off guard. "What about?"

"Well, it was mostly about *you,* actually."

"Oh," I said, staring down at my plate. Why on earth did the boarders think they had to interfere and treat me like a little kid?

I was perfectly capable to handle things myself.

"Yes, Astrid, she and some of the boarders are worried that you're working too hard at the barn. In fact, she said that you're pretty much doing all the work by yourself. Is this true?"

"Ah, um," I said, glancing up the stairs guiltily to where Hilary's music was still playing. "I don't mind taking care of the horses. And Hilary was injured…"

"We know that, dear, but we're concerned about you, too. You look exhausted and that's not what we wanted for you when we asked you to live here. You're supposed to be our guest, not a servant."

"But…" I paused, feeling heat crawl up my neck, "you took me in to live here when I had nowhere else to go. You took in Red and Caprice, too."

"Astrid," Hilary's mom laid a hand gently on my arm, "we love having you here. We asked you to live with us because we wanted to; you don't have to pay us back for that. I don't mind you working in the barn *part* time, and working off Red's board, but what you're doing right now is way too much. I think Hilary's taking advantage of your good nature. And that's not good for her *or* you."

I opened my mouth to protest, but she shook her head before I could even begin. "We've decided to hire a farmhand, maybe two, who can help in the stable and help us with the farm animals. We'll look for a part time housekeeper, too. We were foolish to think we could take on all of this ourselves.

"The bed and breakfast is going to be more than enough for us to handle and, unlike you two girls, we know when to ask for help."

She smiled at me to take the sting out of her words and patted my hand. "It's already decided, we'll be interviewing this week so we'll keep you posted. We want someone in place before you start school so you don't have to worry about anything. I've told Hilary already, although she wasn't exactly thrilled about us stepping in. I think you'll both agree that this is the best solution in the long-run."

I nodded, my irritation at Annie for interfering changing to relief. With even a little extra help I might be able to hold things together this year, once school started and once I was training seriously for archery again.

I was so relieved that it wasn't until I lay snug in bed with Caprice curled up beside me under the covers that I again remembered my argument with Hilary and all the hurt from earlier in the day came flooding back.

"It's not the end of the world, Caprice," I said to the little dog who was tucked in beside me with her head on my pillow. She opened one eye, yawned, and shut it again firmly.

She needs the money to keep the barn running, I reasoned, but it still didn't feel like a very good excuse. *She could have done something else*, the little voice in my head whispered back, *she's supposed to be your best friend. Is that how you would have treated someone you loved? Is that what you would have done to Rob?*

No, I acknowledged, *I would have never done that to anyone. I would have found another way.*

But that still left me with a hard decision to make. I picked up my phone and started to text Rob, ready to pour out everything to him, but then stopped myself. I didn't need him to make my decisions for me, I'd spent most of my existence letting other people run my life, now it was time to take care of things myself.

Well, most things. There was one thing I could definitely use his help with.

Hey, what are you doing around noon tomorrow? I texted.

His reply came back almost instantly. *Why? Are you planning to buy me lunch?*

If you're lucky. I need to borrow you for something awful.

Ha. He wrote back. *I'm all yours.*

I smiled and set my phone down. This was one thing I didn't want to do alone.

Chapter Seventeen

The next morning I woke up with my mind fully made up. I sprang out of bed before the alarm went off and threw on my clothes in record time. I pulled my hair back into a hasty ponytail and snuck outside into the half-light of dawn.

"Good morning, everyone," I whispered, quietly rolling back the stable door, not wanting to wake the drowsy horses too abruptly. I took my time feeding each horse, lingering beside them longer than I normally would have, petting them and running my fingers through their silky manes.

Now that there were so many horses to take care of by myself it was easy to be in a hurry to get the work over with and not really take the time to spend with the actual animals. It was these little moments that I loved best, when I could just quietly stand beside them and breathe in their essential *horsiness*. It made me remember that magical moment when I'd first seen Quarry and really, truly fell in love.

I can't put this off any longer, I thought, sliding Riverdance's stall door shut behind me. Taking a deep breath I headed outside and went down to inspect the paddocks.

I'd seen them when they'd first been constructed of course, but I hadn't had a reason to investigate them again until now.

Each paddock had a shelter, basically a three-sided stall, built up close to the exterior wall of the indoor arena. A narrow aisle-way, just wide enough to fit a person pushing a wheelbarrow, ran the entire length of the stalls so you could throw hay to the horses over their half-doors without having to go outside.

There was a medium-sized room at the far end for hay storage and a smaller area that had been made into a rough tack room built into the other end.

It was actually a really good design meant to minimize workload, and I liked that the horses could hang their heads into the aisle if they wanted, too. It made the place seem bigger somehow.

Each shelter was fitted with thick rubber mats and I imagined that they'd be quite cozy once they were filled with a deep bed of soft shavings. The paddock footing was heavy sand over crushed gravel so they would drain well when the monsoon rains fell in the spring and winter.

Since the half-doors into the aisle were too narrow to lead a horse through, each paddock had its own sturdy back gate to come and go from.

See, this is nice, I told myself, *it would be no big deal to move back here at all. I'll stock the little hay room for them so I don't have to go back and forth for feed every day, and I'll dump lots of shavings in their stalls so they'll have nice beds. It will be like having my own private barn.*

Pushing away any lingering doubts, I got to work.

It took me over an hour to move the many wheelbarrow loads

of shavings into my two stalls and ferry bale after bale into the little storage shed, but finally, everything looked perfect.

I broke open a bale and filled two mangers with hay before heading back to the main barn for what felt like my final time.

"Come on, Red," I said, in an overly bright voice, slipping on his halter and straightening his forelock a little. "Let's go see your new home."

He followed me out of his stall willingly enough and my heart dropped a little when I realized that it was for the last time. I unclipped him just inside his back paddock gate, walking beside him while he slowly sniffed everything, nibbling at the bits of grass that had managed to poke through the thick sand around the bottom of the fence posts.

He snorted softly as he went into his new stall, bedded so deeply that he had to wade through shavings up to his knees to get to his manger. He grabbed a mouthful of hay and marched outside again, his nose an inch off the ground as he inspected every last corner, snorting contentedly.

When I was satisfied that he was just going to quietly explore rather than do anything dramatic, I went back for Ellie.

She did nearly the same thing Red had, nosing about as she wandered around her new territory, grabbing a snack from her stall before coming outside to roll and explore again.

Within fifteen minutes they were both inside their new stalls, happily eating second-breakfast as if they'd lived there their whole lives.

It wasn't until I walked back up to the main barn and saw their now vacant stalls that I felt that pang of sadness again. It felt like this move, even though it was such a small thing, had driven a final wedge between me and Hilary. I wasn't angry with her anymore exactly, but I didn't think we could ever have the same friendship again, either.

I cleaned my old stalls and paddocks in record time, making sure everything looked pristine for the next boarders who'd be moving in.

I pulled out my phone and looked at the clock. I still had a little bit of time to spare before my lesson this morning. I'd completely forgotten to move my tack and brushes out yet so I had to pile everything into the wheelbarrow and push it quickly to the little barn.

There weren't any fancy tack lockers here. Just a few bridle racks on the wall and some wooden posts to hold saddles and pads.

I brushed Ellie carefully, making sure she was spotless from head to toe. She always seemed to have dirty knees and hocks from lying down outside so I had to spend extra time to get the grass stains out of her golden coat. But I managed to get back to the ring well before my lesson was due.

My session with Red yesterday had prepared me a little for what to expect from Oona and I'd planned on extra time so I could warm Ellie up the way I liked. I agreed with what Oona had said about finding exercises that excited and inspired the horses, but I still valued those first few minutes in the ring where we just sauntered around and hung out.

Sliding the big door back, I led the little mare into the cavernous indoor arena before shutting it quietly behind us.

Ellie and I had come a long way since my last lesson with Liza. At the time, I hadn't trusted her very much, not because she was naughty—which she wasn't—but because she was just a baby and I'd sort of expected her to act silly just because she was young. I also hadn't trusted *myself* very much to be capable of training a young animal.

But Ellie had such a solid, dependable personality that I'd quickly realized she wasn't going to start bucking or rearing or bolting out of the blue. And, I'd found out, that if I just rode her like I rode Red she responded very quickly to my aids. Very rarely did she get confused and, if she did, then I just needed to repeat things slowly and she'd figure out what I was asking.

The door grumbled as it rolled back again and Oona strode in, a travel mug of coffee clutched between her hands.

She stayed silent for a long time and I gathered up my reins a little so I could pick up some contact with Ellie's mouth and moved her into a slow warm-up trot.

"She's cute," Oona said finally. "this is the one you're training to sell?"

"Yes, she's my Aunt Lillian's horse and she's down here to be sold. She was actually Hilary's project until the accident. Now I'm riding her."

"Oh, your chestnut horse isn't a project, too, is he? You didn't say."

"No," I said quickly, "never."

I heard her laugh a little under her breath. "Good choice. You should keep that one; he's got some talent hidden away in there. This young lady will make someone happy, though. She looks pretty uncomplicated. What sort of lateral work has she done?"

"Um, leg-yields, some shoulder-in, spiral circles, that's about it."

"Okay, well, let's do some things to free up her body a little more. She moves forward willingly but doesn't have a lot of bend and, much like your chestnut, she finds it easier to travel on the forehand. That's the thing with these little quarter-horses, they have that big caboose behind, but without getting them to engage their hocks and lift their shoulders, they just drive their front-end right into the ground. Long-term, that's pretty hard on their joints."

"That's what Liza said, too."

"Don't worry about it. It's just something to always keep in the back of your mind. I'll give you some exercises to do to help her."

We covered most of the same routine we'd done with Red the day before and I was more conscious of keeping Ellie off the rail and not allowing things to get boring. Ellie wasn't as fit as Red so it wasn't long before her coat was damp and she was puffing a little.

"That's probably enough for her, Astrid. We don't want her to get sour. She'll do well in the winter series if you start her at Training level. If I remember it's a pretty casual show scene around here and it will be a good experience to take her out and get her some show miles. She should have no trouble finding a good home once she gets some exposure."

"I hope so. My aunt will be happy if she sells. I hate to see her go, though. She's really sweet."

"I know, it's hard not giving your heart to all of them, isn't it?"

"Yeah," I admitted, walking Ellie on a loose rein to cool her out.

"Oh, and Astrid?"

I turned around to look at Oona who was poised by the door, staring at me with a frown. "When you sell this horse, who gets the money from the sale?"

"Umm…" I frowned, wondering why I'd never thought of that before. "I'm not sure. She's Aunt Lillian's horse, but it was Hilary who took her on as a project. I'm not really training her; I just sort of took over when Hilary was hurt."

"Astrid, it's customary to work those details out *before* you take on a horse to train."

"Oh, but I'm just helping…"

"Look, you're putting the work into this horse. Make sure you get compensated somehow, okay? I've seen this scenario too many times and I know it always ends badly. My advice is to never mix business with friendship."

Great, I thought, *another complication. I never even thought of that.*

"I know I meant to have your lesson plan ready for you this morning, but I have to run to the mainland unexpectedly and I won't be back until tonight. If you're free tomorrow morning, you can come for a quick tea and I will have Red's homework ready for you."

"Okay," I agreed quickly. "I can come before archery." I was interested in whatever secret training thing Oona had in store for us, but I also was dying to see those paintings again. I'd been thinking about them ever since my first visit to the loft.

Chapter Eighteen

The problem of the uniform fitting had sort of fixed itself.

I'd been half-kidding when I'd asked Rob to come with me the night before, but in the cold light of day it seemed like a horrible idea. I didn't want him witnessing me being squashed into too-tight clothing like a squeeze pop. The thought was too mortifying.

As soon as my lesson was done, I'd called him and tried to cancel, but he wasn't having any of it.

"I haven't picked up my uniform yet, either," he said easily, "and I have to go shopping for a few other things, too. We can make it fun, Astrid, don't worry."

"Are you sure?" I'd asked doubtfully. "I thought guys hated shopping."

"Well, whether I like it or not, I still have to wear clothes from *somewhere*," he joked. "It won't kill us to spend an hour or two at the mall."

So, after I'd turned all the horses out and cleaned stalls and paddocks, I showered and threw on jeans and a tee shirt and braced myself for what horrors were about to come.

I was waiting anxiously by the front door when I heard the sound of tires crunching on gravel and I went outside expecting Rob's truck, but instead there was a little black Volkswagen Golf sputtering away in the driveway.

"I hope you don't mind if my sister drives us today," Rob said, getting out of the car and coming halfway to the door to meet me. "She's visiting for the week before her school starts and she offered to come along."

"Sure," I said, blushing furiously. Great, now there would be two people witnessing my shame. All I wanted was to turn around and go back inside, but I forced myself to keep walking to the car.

"Natalie, this is Astrid," Rob said as I slid into the back seat. "Astrid, my favourite sister, Natalie."

"Well, to be fair, I'm his *only* sister," Natalie said, turning around her seat so she could get a look at me. "It's very nice to meet you, Astrid. I've heard good things about you."

"Really?" I said, shrinking a little under her steady gaze. She had wide brown eyes that watched me curiously but not unkindly. A tiny diamond embedded on the side of her nose glittered in the sunlight. Her short, dark hair was streaked with thick, blood-red highlights, and she looked very much like a worldly city-person. All of a sudden it seemed incredibly important that she approve of me.

"Of course," she said, her mouth curving into a genuine smile. "Rob talks about you all the time."

"Okay, that's enough of that," Rob said, laughing. "You don't have to tell all my secrets."

"Never, you know too many of mine. Dad would kill me if

he ever found out half the stuff I got up to when I lived at home."

As they talked, I began to feel a little more optimistic. I'd known a bit about Natalie but I'd forgotten an important part; Rob's sister was in fashion school in Montreal and had won all sorts of student awards for her designs.

Maybe she'll give me some advice on how to pick out clothes that actually look good on me, I thought hopefully.

Natalie was quite a few years older than Rob and he'd told me that even though she rarely made it out here to the West Coast, they'd been really close when they were younger and she'd still lived at home, and they talked all the time on the phone. Besides his dad, she was the most important person in his life.

They bantered back and forth all the way to the familiar little yellow house right downtown that had been converted into a seamstress shop.

"Ah, memories," Natalie said, laughing. "I'm so glad I don't have to subject myself to this anymore, kids. Have a good time."

She settled down in the car with a novel and clearly did not intend to come with us for moral support.

I didn't blame her; I'd been coming here to pick up my uniforms since middle school and just the sight of it sent a shiver through me.

It wasn't like they'd been mean on purpose or anything but stripping down to my underwear in front of strangers, so they could figure out how to best camouflage my fat rolls had never been a high point in my life.

"We won't be long," Rob said reassuringly, and I wasn't sure if he was talking to me or her. He reached out to grab my hand and I held onto it gratefully, willing myself not to be such a big baby about all this. After all the awful things I'd been through this summer, I wasn't going to let a little old lady seamstress and a scratchy, uninspiring uniform intimidate me.

We were the only ones in the tiny waiting room; probably everyone else had picked up their stuff weeks ago when the notices first went out. Rob settled into a squishy wicker chair, picking up a rock-climbing magazine that sat on the low coffee table in front of us. I sat down right next to him, too nervous to read, and stared blankly at the wall, tapping my foot nervously.

"Robert?" A grey-haired woman said loudly from the doorway. It wasn't the same seamstress I'd had in the past but it could have been her sister. She smiled at Rob as soon as he looked up and beckoned him inside.

He was gone less than ten minutes and came back carrying a stack of thin white boxes stamped with the Sacred Heart logo.

"You're done already?" I said in astonishment.

"Yeah, easy-peasy. It's only four sets. What did you get?"

"I don't even remember," I said nervously. "I ordered them a while ago and I wasn't really paying attention when I did it. I hope I did everything right."

"Astrid?" the woman said sharply from the door. "It's your turn, young lady."

"Great," I muttered, wiping my hands anxiously on my jeans.

"Now, now, no need to be nervous," the lady said kindly as she shut the door firmly behind me. She took in my terrified expression and her face transformed from business-like to grandmotherly. "You're not the only one who's apprehensive at the beginning of the school year. Now, I have the measurements you gave me here but let me just check…" She whipped a tape measure out from one of her pockets and proceeded to wrap it around me in all sorts of configurations, tut-tutting under her breath.

I stood there, my cheeks flushing with heat, trying not to suck my stomach in.

"Perfect. Yes, I think these will fit just about right. Pop into the change room there and try the first one on. You've certainly shot up a few inches and sometimes that makes a big difference."

"All right," I said, escaping gratefully to the change room as fast as I could. This was so much better than having to stand half-dressed out in the main fitting area.

I held my breath as I tried on a navy polo shirt and grey plaid skirt first but, to my surprise, the skirt slid on and did up without any effort at all.

I can't believe it fits, I thought, staring at myself in the mirror. I mean, I didn't look like a super model or anything, it *was* a school uniform after all, but I just looked like a normal, athletic person in a plain, boring skirt and top.

Fine, well, that's the skirt but there's no way the pants will fit. I pulled them on slowly, waiting for the moment they'd snag on my thighs or get stuck on my hips, but they just slid on and did up like my jeans did at home.

"Are you all right in there?" the lady asked, knocking on the change room door.

"Yes," I said, coming out in a daze. "They fit."

"Well, that's lovely. Yes, the length looks good. Now show me the skirt."

I went back in to change into the skirt again and switched the polo up for the dress shirt.

"Perfect. I wish all my fittings were as easy as yours, dear. I think you have everything you need. Two pairs of skirt sets and two pairs of pants and one set for gym. You can always order more online if it's not enough now that we've established your size. Can I bill the credit card on file?"

"Er, yes," I said, still in a state of disbelief that this process had taken me less than a half an hour when in the past it would have taken hours. What was the difference now? Had we just always ordered the wrong sizes before? I hadn't been *that* much bigger than now. Could it have always been this painless if Marion and my father hadn't been involved?

Rob and I carried our stacks of boxes out to the car and stuffed them into the Golf's little hatchback, closing the lid carefully so we didn't squish them.

"How was it?" Natalie asked, sounding bored.

"Fantastic," I said, unable to control my happiness. "Everything fit. I mean, like, EVERYTHING. I didn't have to get re-measured or have elastics put in or have anyone stare at me like I was the weirdest, misshaped body to have ever walked in that room."

"That's what all shopping should be like." Natalie smiled at me kindly in the rear-view mirror. "When I get the chance to design my own lines, I'm going to make sure that everyone has a positive experience."

"That sounds great. Normally, I just shop online. I'm too scared to go to regular stores and try stuff on."

"But, why?" Rob asked, staring at me in confusion.

"Because… I…" My words turned to glue in my mouth. There was no way to make him understand. He was perfect, while I was…. *Perfectly normal*, a little voice in my head said firmly. *You are not a monster; you are a completely normal person who deserves to wear clothes just like anyone else.*

I caught Natalie's gaze in the mirror again and she sent me a small smile like she knew exactly what I was thinking.

"All right, you two. Here's the new plan. I'm taking you both out for lunch and then we're going to meet a friend of mine, deal?"

"But what about the mall?" Rob asked. "We still need to get regular clothes."

"Yes, yes, if you still want to go to the mall once we're done then I'll take you there afterward. First of all, let's get some food, I'm starving."

Right then I decided that I liked Natalie very much.

Chapter Nineteen

She took us to a little café attached to an art gallery in the old, cobblestoned quarter of town.

"What is this place?" Rob asked as he peered down at the painting on the table. All the tables had glass tops that had various prints pinned underneath them. Ours was a wooded scene painted in vibrant colours on what looked like silk.

"This is beautiful," I said, staring at the little stone house painted at the edge of a river near my elbow. "Oona would love this."

"Oona?" Rob asked in confusion. "She didn't strike me as very arty."

"Oh, but she is. I can't believe I didn't tell you about the paintings." And I launched into the whole story about what happened that night we went to the movies. In all the drama with Hilary, I'd completely forgotten to tell Rob about it.

You didn't tell him about moving the horses, either, I thought guiltily but I shrugged it away. I didn't need to ruin our day talking about that, not yet anyway.

When our food came it was another surprise. Apparently, the

restaurant specialized in was what was called "molecular gastronomy" art cuisine so it was a little bizarre. My French fries turned out to be mashed potatoes that had been whipped up into the shape of a baseball-sized sphere, battered and deep fried. To top it off, a ball of frozen butter had been entombed in the very center and it gushed out like lava when I cut the thing open which was a little alarming.

Rob's fish had been spiralized into curly little strips that were served in a champagne glass full of sauce and Natalie's veggie burger had been "deconstructed" which basically meant that lettuce, cheese and tomatoes were tossed around the plate surrounded by a burger patty that had been moulded somehow into the shape of a Mayan temple.

Despite how completely weird everything looked, it was actually pretty delicious food and we had fun laughing at it, and at each other's reactions to it, too.

"We have to order the blooming flowers for dessert," Natalie insisted, "it's the best part."

I had no idea what she was talking about but I wasn't about to say no to dessert.

A few minutes later, each of us was presented with shallow bowls that had one pale white dome sitting in the middle. It looked like it was maybe made out of white chocolate or meringue.

"Not yet," the waiter said as I lifted my fork, "you'll spoil the surprise."

He set down little pitchers of what looked like thick, hot syrup carefully beside our bowls. "Now, when you're ready, pour on the sauce."

"You go first," Rob told Natalie. "You're the oldest so you should be the Guinea pig."

"Gee thanks, well, wish me luck."

She poured the caramel-coloured sauce around the bottom of the bowl and we all leaned forward to see what would happen.

"Whoa," I said as her dome began to peel back miraculously like petals of a flower, unfolding one by one. When the last one was open, we were looking at a perfectly sculpted edible white chocolate flower with a realistic purple center.

"That's so beautiful," I said. I'd never seen anything like that before in my life.

Rob was next. Instead of folding open like a flower, his dome peeled back from one side and an actual puff of smoke spiraled up from the opening, making us all jump. We leaned forward to see a delicately carved chocolate dragon sitting inside, posed with one foreleg upraised as if he were about to take flight.

"Wow," Rob said, "that is amazing. This is too nice to eat."

"Your turn, Astrid."

I carefully picked up the little pitcher and poured the chocolatey sauce beside my dome. For a second, nothing happened, and then a purple crack zig-zagged across the surface, and then another and another, like it was an egg about to hatch. When nearly the whole surface was fractured the shell broke away to reveal a tiny chocolate bird on the inside.

"Oh, that was wonderful." I looked over to where a bearded man was watching expectantly from a door near the kitchen.

"I'm glad you like it," he said, catching my eye. "Seeing people enjoy my creations is the best part of my day." He saluted a little and then disappeared into the kitchen.

"His creations?"

"That was Chef Theodopholis," Natalie whispered, raising her eyebrows. "He's super famous but he's a bit of a hermit, too. From what I hear, he doesn't usually come out of the kitchen."

We ate the rest of our fantastic desserts in blissful silence, concentrating on the amazing flavours until finally it was time to leave.

"Thank you so much," I told Natalie, "that is one of the coolest things I've ever done. I've never had food like that before."

"Girl, we need to get you out more," Natalie said, laughing. "Rob, you need to step up your dating game a little."

"Uh, we're kind of busy with the horses most of the time," Rob said, rolling his eyes, "we were lucky to get to the movies last week."

"Hmm, I guess I'll just have to work on your cultural education whenever I'm in town then. Next stop, shopping." She didn't lead us back to the car but instead strode down the block with us trailing along behind hand in hand. I looked up at the old buildings happily, thinking how much better of a day this was than what I'd been expecting when I woke up this morning.

"Hey, Nat, the mall's the other way," Rob called to her retreating back but she ignored us completely. She peered in some of the shop doorways, frowning, as if she were looking for something she couldn't find.

"Oh, here it is!" she called, turning abruptly into a half-hidden doorway. She waved at us once and then disappeared.

"Guess we'd better follow her," Rob said, shrugging. "There's no stopping her when she gets an idea in her head."

We paused in front of a plain wooden door with a badly

peeling paint job that clearly needed touching up. The glass door had a simple word etched in it: "Clothier."

"What does that mean?" I asked.

"I guess someone who makes clothes. I'm not exactly sure what we're doing here, though."

We looked at each other and then Rob reached out and turned the handle, ushering me inside ahead of him.

"Oh, wow," I said, stopping inside the door so suddenly that Rob had to push past me to get inside.

The door hadn't led into a small shop at all. Instead we stood at the far end of a massive warehouse, so big that I couldn't begin to see where it began and ended. All around us stood rows of metal racking, stretching as far as the eye could see and all the racks were laden with miles and miles of clothing.

"Excuse me. Do you have an appointment? You can't come in without an appointment, Blaire won't like it."

A tall thin guy with glasses and a man-bun piled high on top of his head stared at us from where he'd been rummaging through a nearby stack of piled sweaters. He wore a black cropped tank top that left a good five inches of his abs exposed and a pair of artfully torn black jeans. He also had on thick, black eyeliner and orange lipstick.

I couldn't help but stare at him with my mouth open. I felt like I'd stepped into an alternate universe or something.

"Er," Rob said, "my sister Natalie…"

A series of high-pitched squealing noises cut through the stillness of the warehouse.

"Oh. My. Gosh. Natalie, where have you beeeeeen?!!"

There was more squealing and shrieking, and then Natalie

came around the corner with her arm slung over the shoulders of a tiny blonde woman, who looked like she was about ten years old even though she was clearly an adult. She had bleached blonde hair piled in spiky layers on her head, pale ghost-like make up, blood-red lipstick and about fifteen sets of earrings in each ear. As she got closer, I saw that she had one of those chin piercings, too.

"Blaire, you remember my little brother, Robbie."

"Oh, wow, Roberoo, you're all grown up. Seems a long time since we had to change your diapers."

"Hey, Blaire," Rob said, smiling at me weakly. "It's just Rob now, actually. This is my girlfriend, Astrid."

"Girlfriend? Are you old enough to have a—"

"Okay, Blaire, stop teasing him," Natalie said fondly, giving her friend a hug around the neck. "Astrid here needs our help."

"Oh? Why?" Blaire asked blankly, looking me up and down. "She looks fine to me."

"She hates shopping."

"Oh, now that *is* a tragedy."

I looked away, my cheeks suddenly burning. I didn't want anyone to pity me. Ever.

"What do you hate about it?" Blaire asked seriously.

"Um," I gulped, looking to Rob for help.

His mouth was pulling down in a frown and he put a hand on my arm protectively, shooting a glare at his sister.

"I guess... I guess it makes me nervous trying to find something I like with all those sales girls hovering around. I feel like they're judging me so I just try and grab something fast so I can disappear into the change room and then whatever I try on never fits and it's all so embarrassing." The words poured out before I could stop them and I felt my eyes prickle with tears.

"That's a pretty common experience," Blaire said quietly, not looking shocked at all. "That's why my friends and I started The Collective in the first place."

"The Collective?"

"Yes, this place." She looked around proudly and then fixed her gaze on me again. "We want buying clothes to be an empowering experience for everyone again, both men and women, people of all shapes and sizes. It should be about embracing our unique beauty, not about being ashamed."

"Oh." I had not expected that answer at all but I was definitely interested in what she had to say. "How does it work?"

"Easy. We take your measurements, figure out the styles you like, the colours that bring out the best in you, and find the kind of clothes that make you comfortable and happy. We have off-the-rack clothes, semi-custom, and fully custom designs, too."

She turned and laid a hand on Rob's shoulder. She was so small that she had to tilt her head way back to look up at him.

"Rob, your sister will take you to the men's side while Astrid and I work, my assistant Maizie is there and she'll help you find what you need. I'll bring Astrid back to you happy and unharmed, I promise."

"Are you sure, Astrid?" Rob asked, looking doubtful.

"Yes, it's okay," I said. "I trust Blaire. I'll see you soon."

As soon as he was gone, Blaire grabbed my arm and jumped up and down a little in excitement. "Ooh, Astrid, we are going to have soooo much fun. Just you wait."

And it *was* fun. She sat me down in a warm, comfortable

sitting room while the man with the lipstick, whose name turned out to be Aubrey, fussed over me and took my measurements, laughing and joking with me the whole time so I didn't feel awkward or nervous.

First, she brought over a whole bunch of colour swatches and the two of them took turns holding the fabric up against my face or under my chin and standing back and studying the effect.

They brought piles of clothes from some back room and draped them over me, tilting their heads and tut tutting when something didn't meet their approval. Finally, they brought another, smaller stack that I was actually allowed to try on. The clothes felt wonderful on my body, fabrics draping across my skin like they'd been custom made for me, but there wasn't a mirror in sight so I couldn't see how I actually looked.

They tossed the things into two piles, one to keep and one to go back on the racks.

"There," Blaire said finally, standing back in satisfaction. "Here are all the things I'd recommend for you. Now, I don't know what your budget is but try them on in front of the mirror there and pick out what you'd like. I'll make sure you get a good price."

"Thank you so much," I said, taking the gigantic armful of clothes into the change room. I tried everything on slowly, savouring the way each item made me look slightly different, as if a different part of my personality was revealed with every wardrobe change.

How will I pick just a couple of things? I thought, mentally going over my meager savings from working at camp. *I love them all.* I glanced down at my purse, thinking of my parents' credit card tucked away inside my wallet. I couldn't spend that money, could I? It wasn't really mine.

I thought back to all the mortifying years that I'd struggled with hating my clothes, my weight, and myself. How hard my dad had been on me, how he'd taught me to be ashamed of the way I looked and talked and acted. How he'd sent me to fat camp year after year, even though I'd begged not to go. How he'd nearly taken away everything I loved this past summer.

Oh, screw it, I thought, suddenly furious, *I'm sick of being scared of taking up space in this world. I'm sick of never standing up for myself. I refuse to live a small life anymore.*

"Did you love them?" Blaire asked excitedly as I strode out of the change room. "Did you pick out a few that spoke to you?"

"Yes," I said firmly, "I did. I'll take them all."

There was a brief moment of nausea when they were processing the card. I fought back my panic, wondering if a) it might decline, or b) that I'd made a very bad, expensive decision that my parents were going to make me pay for later. But my negative thoughts vanished when I was surrounded by piles of boxes and bags and I was, for the very first time in my entire life, in possession of clothes that I actually, a hundred percent, loved.

Rob had a much smaller stack but he was smiling, too, and we both thanked Blaire and Natalie a million times before leaving. Natalie went down the block and brought the car back to us because there was no way I could carry all that stuff on my own.

Overall it was the best, most fantastic non-horsey day I'd ever had and I felt like I'd been living someone else's movie-star life for the afternoon.

We were just leaving the outskirts of the city when another thought struck me. "Can we stop at the tack store?" I asked suddenly. "Red could really use some new boots."

If I was spending my parent's' money on designer clothes then I might as well get Red the boots he needed, too. It's not like my parents would really miss the money.

Rob helped me to ferry everything into the house and just as he was about to leave, he pulled me into a long kiss that made me curl my toes.

There was no sign of the Ahlbergs so I took my time carrying everything upstairs and arranging the boxes and bags in one corner of my room. My next chore was going to be to empty out my closet and dresser of all the things I didn't wear anymore and give them to Hilary's mom for the donation bin at their church.

That could wait, though. If I ran down to the barn now, I would be just in time to bring the horses in for dinner and take Red on a much-needed trail ride.

It was peaceful grooming the horses out in the little paddock area. It was like I had my own private barn. The sun was steadily marching its way toward the horizon, but the warm rays streamed into Red's stall, lighting him up until his coat shimmered like copper.

"You're so beautiful, Red," I told him, leading him by his reins out the gate and positioning him carefully right beside the fence so I could slip up onto his warm back. There was no need for a saddle tonight.

I rode him up the driveway, my legs swinging gently in time with his swaying hips and went straight up past the house to the ocean. I hadn't put his boots on so I didn't feel guilty riding Red out past the little waves and knee deep into the calm, quiet sea. Red moved forward steadily, barely making a splash, his hooves sinking only slightly into the firm sand.

"This is supposed to be very therapeutic for your legs," I told him, "expensive racehorses don't even get this kind of pampering so you must be pretty lucky."

Red flicked an ear back toward me and then suddenly stopped, his neck telescoping up and his ears pointing hard out toward the horizon where the sea was tinged with pink.

"What is it, boy?"

He snorted loudly as a round, black object bobbed to the surface of the water not fifteen feet away. It was followed by another and then another. Dozens of dark eyes regarded us solemnly.

"Seals," I said, hardly daring to breathe for fear they'd disappear. I felt delighted and a little nervous at the same time. I was pretty sure that seals were usually gentle unless they were threatened but maybe a big horse marching around in their territory would be enough to make them attack.

We both sat as still as stone. After a minute, Red relaxed and dropped his nose, lipping at the salty water. I felt like we were in a dream; the waves lapping around Red's knees and the seals bobbing gently on the sea as the sun went down. Now and then one would roll on its side, one front flipper extended to catch the last rays.

Red got bored before the seals did. He pawed a couple times in the water and then turned without me asking and splashed up onto the shore, stopping to shake like a dog once we'd reached the sand. Then he proceeded at a determined walk toward home.

Hilary was still sulking in her room when I finally got back and once again, she didn't come down for dinner. I waited around, hoping for an opportunity to tell her about the new arrangements I'd made for Red and Ellie, but she never showed up.

I didn't want us to be enemies. I wanted her to start acting human again so we could hang out and I could tell her about the way the light had looked on the ocean, about my lessons, and Oona's paintings and the surreal day of shopping that Rob and I had had. Those were exactly the type of stories that Hilary would appreciate.

I wanted my friend back again.

Chapter Twenty

The next morning I let myself sleep in exactly a half hour later than usual before heading down to the barn. Yesterday had been a blissful break from reality for me but now I was ready to get back into my routine. It was the last real day of archery camp and I still had to meet with Oona ahead of time.

"Morning, everyone," I called out, watching as their heads eagerly popped over the stall doors one by one. "Time for breakfast."

I waited for Red and Ellie to poke their heads out too before I remembered with a pang that they didn't live here anymore.

It's no big deal, I told myself, taking a deep breath, *they're perfectly fine outside.*

I gave all the inside horses their hay and then went into the tack room to mix grain and study the schedule Oona had set up on the whiteboard the night before. It was just Pender and Sadie riding from the barn that morning and then the rest were outside riders coming in. I hoped that Oona would be able to manage on her own without me showing everyone where to go and keeping the schedule running smoothly.

Okay, so Riverdance and Rabbit can stay in. I'll turn everyone else out as soon as they're done with breakfast, I thought, stirring grain into the beet pulp. *Meantime, I can clean Red and Ellie's paddocks now while they're eating.*

I dumped grain into all the tubs and then picked up Red and Ellie's grain buckets and eagerly went outside to see how my two had passed their first night.

They were both waiting for me at their gates, ears pricked expectantly in my direction.

"Hold on, guys, I'm coming," I said, leaning over to give Ellie a quick kiss on the nose as I went by. "I'll meet you in your stalls."

I skirted around the paddocks to the narrow, covered aisle that ran in front of the semi-detached stalls and tossed extra-large flakes of hay over the doors into their mangers. Red nickered excitedly when he saw how much hay I'd given him.

"Don't get used to it," I told him, dumping his grain into his feed tub, "this is just a little bit extra to celebrate your first real day in your new home."

Their stalls were clean, but I fluffed the bedding and scooped their paddocks while they ate. Then I filled their water buckets and, when I was positive that they'd had enough breakfast, I led them both side by side out to the pasture.

"Oh good, Astrid, you're here," Oona said, coming down the loft steps just as I was reaching for Sox's halter. "Come on up when you're finished. I'll put on the tea."

I turned the rest of the horses out in record time and was up the stairs before the water had even boiled.

"Well, that was quick." Oona laughed as I went straight over to look at the newest paintings. The one of Furioso was gone and a large bay horse had taken his place, this one with his head arched doing some sort of Spanish walk. But the rider wasn't on the horse's back. He was on the ground, holding the reins lightly in one hand, his other hand resting gently on the horse's shoulder.

"That's beautiful," I said.

"I thought you'd like it. I set it out just for you. It will give you some idea of what our plan is this winter."

"Painting lessons?" I asked hopefully, but she just laughed.

"Maybe when you're not so busy. I was thinking more about getting you started with some work in-hand."

"Oh, like ground work? I've done a bit of that back at the ranch. Justin gave me lessons on how to lead Folly without her trampling me."

Oona laughed and smiled up at me. "Well, that sounds like a valuable skill to have. You'll find what I have to teach you much different, though. Here, I made a list of videos for you to watch first so you can have an idea of what I mean."

She handed me a piece of thick paper that looked like it had been torn out of one of her sketch books. Along one side in cramped, slanted writing was a list that I could hardly read.

"Thanks, I'll watch them tonight." I said, shoving the list into my pocket.

I took the tea cup she handed me and blew across the top, still studying the paintings. There was a new one I liked of a large grey horse cantering on the beach. I didn't know where she found the time to get so many finished so fast.

"We'll start our next lesson with free-lunging since you enjoy it so much," Oona said suddenly and I turned to face her in surprise. I'd thought she'd said she didn't believe in playing with horses.

"Okay, that would be great," I said, "and then what?"

Oona raised both eyebrows as she stared at me over her half-empty tea cup. "Work your way through the videos on the list," she said, one side of her mouth pulling upward into another smile. "Then you'll be able to ask me better questions."

"Fine, fine," I grumbled, looking at my watch. It was time to go and get ready for archery. I went over to the sink to rinse out my cup and put it in the dish rack. "Thank you," I said, glancing over at the paintings and back at Oona. "For the tea and for wanting to teach me."

"Anytime," she said, "have fun with the videos."

Chapter Twenty-one

Nori was bubbling over with enthusiasm over our last official day of archery camp. We still had the field trip coming up on the weekend but after that it meant that the summer was officially over and school would start in only a week.

We were so caught up in the fun of the day, the final cake for dessert, the silly prizes for categories like most improved and least likely to shoot themselves in the foot, that it never crossed my mind to tell Nori that I'd moved Red and Ellie. If I'd have remembered, I probably could have avoided, or at least lessened, the outburst that followed back at the barn.

All the horses were out in the pasture when we got home so Nori and Annie brought Maverick and Norman in themselves while I led the other horses in one by one.

I brought my two in last and put them in their paddocks so they could have dinner; my plan was to ride one or, if I was lucky, both of them after the rest of my chores were finished.

I was just hanging up Pender's freshly cleaned bridle that she'd carelessly left in a messy heap on her tack trunk when the yelling began.

"What. The. Hell. Astrid?" Nori bellowed when she threw open the door. "Why are Red and Ellie not in the barn?"

"Nori, calm down," I said reasonably, which of course is the silliest thing to say to someone who is freaking out.

"I wondered why they were out so I went to visit them and all your stuff is there in that gross, dingy tack room. "What's going on?"

She stared wildly around the room, her eyes flicking to my empty saddle rack and the blank spot on my old locker where I'd unscrewed my name plate.

"Nori! Language," her mother said sternly, coming up behind her. "What on earth is all the shouting about?"

"That stupid Hilary has made Astrid move," Nori guessed with uncanny accuracy, "I *knew* there was something up when I heard her on the phone the other day. She's been skulking around here looking guilty all week."

"Nori," her mother said firmly, "that is enough rudeness out of you. We don't talk about other people like that."

"But—"

Annie held up her hand for silence and turned to me, taking a deep breath to calm herself. "Now, Astrid, can you tell me what is going on here?"

"It's really nothing," I said, gulping nervously. "Hilary needed some space in the barn for boarders, so I moved Red and Ellie. It's not a big deal at all."

"But—" Nori started then closed her mouth again when Annie sent her meaningful glare.

"Did you volunteer or did she ask you to move?"

"Well," I hesitated, not willing to completely lie but not

wanting to make it sound dramatic, either. "I guess Hilary sort of suggested it first. But I agree that it makes sense for me to move. She's so worried about money and I want to do what I can to help."

"You already do a lot to help around here, Astrid," Annie said firmly. "I don't think there's any question of that." She looked down as the Fitbit on her wrist made a little jingling sound. "Right, I have a lesson to get ready for but I think we should discuss this later."

I looked up to see that Nori had already disappeared. I relaxed a little, glad that her temper tantrum was over, at least for now. She would calm down once she'd ridden and spent time with Maverick.

I decided to keep myself out of the way for a while and went down to spend some time with my horses.

They both needed their manes trimmed and the fur around their fetlocks cleaned up; even though it was roasting out, their coats had already started changing for winter. They were beginning to look a little scruffy.

"Spa day today, you two," I told them. "We can't let our standards fall just because we're not in the fancy barn anymore."

I started with Red, brushing and massaging him first, and then combing out his beautiful tail hair by hair until every strand fell like a waterfall down past his hocks. I was so caught up that it wasn't until there was a loud thump on the other side of the wall that I looked up again, brought abruptly out of my daydream.

"Hello?" I said. But there was no answer. "Caprice, is that you?"

There was a slight clawing sound on Red's door, and I opened it and let the little dog run inside.

"What were you doing out there, puppy?" I asked suspiciously. "Were you getting into trouble?"

She wagged her tail happily and buried her nose deeply into Red's clean shavings right up past her eyeballs. She inhaled loudly, snuffling after some scent, and then pulled her head up covered with about a thousand pieces of shavings clinging to her fur. That was the thing with poodles…if you didn't keep their coat trimmed up then they were magnets for all sorts of debris.

"Great," I said, leaning down to brush the worst of it off her face. Just then, there was another slight bumping sound on the other side of the wall. Then there was a snorting noise that was definitely the sound of a horse in a place where a horse shouldn't be.

I put down Red's brushes and went into the aisle, looking both ways cautiously, but there was nothing amiss except the tack room door was slightly open.

I went to the stall beside Red's and peered over the doorway, jumping back as Maverick met me at the half-door with a sour expression on his face.

"Ack," I yelped, "What are you *doing* in here?"

He flattened his ears in my direction and turned back to his pile of hay, wrinkling his nose at me until I went away.

"Nori?" I said, opening the tack room door and there she was, lifting her saddle onto one of the bare wooden racks. She turned to me and crossed her arms over her chest protectively.

"I'm not leaving," was all she said.

"Why is Maverick here?"

"We're moving in. If Hilary's going to kick you out of the big barn then I'm going with you."

"But she didn't—"

"Whatever, the point is that if Red and Ellie are here then so is Maverick." A smile suddenly danced around her lips. "Besides, it will be so much more fun. It will be like having our own little barn here full of cool people while all the old, boring people can have the big barn. And I bet we could paint the tack room black and silver so it will be all edgy and we can have parties and only invite people who will do what we say. It will be great."

I choked a little, both at being called cool for probably the first time in my whole life, and at Nori's terrifying idea of renovating the tack room for parties.

"You're not going to try and make me leave, are you?" she asked, narrowing her eyes at me.

"No," I sighed, "you can stay, as long as your mom's okay with it. But no parties, and no edgy black and silver paint in the tack room. Horses like things peaceful and that's the atmosphere we're going to create here, okay?"

"Fine. But, for the record, Maverick *doesn't* like things peaceful."

I laughed. "You're probably right. He'd probably really enjoy the black paint. Maybe just dress up his saddle pads or something instead."

"Fine," she said again, sighing dramatically. "whatever you say...roomie."

Chapter Twenty-two

By the time she left, Nori was quite happy with the new arrangements. She'd reorganized our little tack room until it suited her and had asked her mother nicely if they could build proper lockers for our things.

"As long as Hilary says it's okay," Annie answered, not surprised at all that her daughter had moved Maverick over here while she was busy having a lesson on Norman. I doubted much surprised her about Nori anymore.

The upshot was that I felt better and better about the move. The horses were happy and, once we had a chance to paint the tack room a nice, neutral colour like taupe, and set up lockers, it was going to feel like home in there. It was exciting to have a project again.

The only thing left to do was tell Hilary. I'd had some idea that I'd casually bring it up some time before bed, but she surprised me during evening feed by showing up without warning. I was in Norman's stall dumping his grain into his feed tub while he stood behind me waiting politely.

"Astrid," Hilary called, "are you there? We need to talk about Ellie. I'm sure we can figure out…"

She stopped and I heard her marching down the aisle. I briefly wondered if I could just stay hidden until she went away.

"Astrid?" Her voice rose up a few notches.

I sighed and left the safety of Norman's stall, latching the door carefully behind me. I hated confrontations and I'd already had enough drama from Nori that day.

Hilary stood staring into Red's open doorway, her arms crossed over her chest and her lower lip trembling.

"You *moved* them," she said, her face draining of all colour. "You didn't have to do that."

"It's fine, Hilary," I said, trying to sound casual, "they have a really nice set-up back there and they're happy. The paddocks are big and they have each other for company."

"I never asked you to—"

"Well, you kind of did. Don't worry, I really don't mind anymore. You have boarders who want to come and it was the logical choice for Red and Ellie to move."

She shook her head, looking forlorn. "It wasn't supposed to be like this, Astrid..." She frowned at Maverick's empty stall. "Where is Nori's horse?"

"Oh, well, she moved him to be with my two."

"Moved him? She didn't ask my permission."

I stiffened at her suddenly commanding tone. "I don't think Nori ever asks permission. Annie said she was going to call you tonight. I guess she forgot."

"Well, that's annoying. It's *my* barn. I should know what's going on here at all times."

I raised my eyebrows but said nothing. How was she

supposed to know what went on here if she never stepped foot inside anymore?

"I don't see why you mind," I said finally. "Now you have three spots to lease out in this barn. I would have thought you'd be happy with the extra money."

"Well, I'm not happy right now. Nori's going to be paying less, of course, and I have to find someone to replace her on short notice. This is super inconvenient. You have no idea how hard it is to run this place, Astrid. I worry about money all the time. I watch the hay and the bedding go steadily down every single day and I can't help wishing the horses ate less or that we weren't so generous with the shavings."

I stared at her, waiting for my sympathy to kick in, but all I felt was irritation. When would she stop whining and start actually appreciating everything she had? I couldn't bring myself to say that, though, no matter how annoying she was.

Hilary walked down the aisle and stood in front of Jerry's doorway, staring blankly inside.

"I don't even have time to ride my own horse," she said gloomily.

"Oh, give it up," I snapped, my temper finally flaring. "You can somehow find the time to send a million texts to Darius every day, to go out to the movies, and to hide in your room sulking all day, but you can't bother to walk five minutes down to the barn to see your horse. Actually, you don't even have to walk, you can ride the golf cart. It couldn't be easier, Hilary, you're just making excuses because you're scared."

She lifted her head to glare at me, obviously too angry to even speak.

"Jerry misses you," I said finally, waving an arm at his stall.

"Can't you see that? He depends on you, he's your responsibility, and you're totally bailing on him."

"I'm not bailing on him," she hissed. "He's *my* horse, not yours, and I know what he needs. He gets fed and goes out on pasture, and Rob rides him. He doesn't need anything else."

"He needs *you*," I said fiercely, "you're his human and he has no idea why you abandoned him. You hardly even look at him anymore and it's not fair."

My words came out almost a yell and afterward, we both just stared at each other in silence, that giant chasm opening up further between us.

"That's ridiculous," she said finally, her lower lip trembling. "You have no idea what you're talking about."

"It's not ridiculous. I don't know what happened to you, but you've turned into a spoiled *princess*."

She opened her mouth to say something back but a creak on the stairs made us both look up.

"Are you quite done here, ladies?" Oona said, standing barefoot on a middle step with a paintbrush in one hand. There was a smudge of blue on her cheek and her hair was pulled back in a messy bun on top of her head.

Hilary blinked at her in astonishment and I realized that she hadn't spent enough time at the barn to ever see the other, artistic, side of Oona.

"Um, yes," she gulped. "Sorry if we disturbed you."

"It's pretty hard to concentrate with all the yelling," Oona said with a shrug. "Is there a problem here?"

"No," Hilary and I both muttered at the same time, not looking at one another.

"Well, I trust you can finish your chores quietly then and not disrupt the horses again. Oh, and Hilary?"

"Yes," Hilary said, her voice coming out small and yet defiant.

"Have Jerry tacked up for nine o'clock tomorrow. I'll give you a lesson."

"No...no thank you. I don't want a lesson." Hilary stammered, "I'm still injured..."

"If you want me to stay here, you do. It's your choice. I can't work in a place where the whole team isn't committed to taking care of the horses. This is not optional."

Hilary drew herself up and glared furiously at Oona. "Well, this is my barn and nobody gets to tell me what to do."

"Suit yourself," Oona said calmly. "I'll start looking for somewhere else to go in the morning."

Hilary opened her mouth to argue, but then changed her mind and spun on her heel striding out of the barn. Not limping at all.

"Ah, youth," Oona laughed softly, poised in her doorway. "I don't miss the drama and the tears at all."

"Hey," I said, "I'm the same age as her and I don't throw tantrums..."

"Well, you're an old soul, Astrid. Now what's going on with you and the princess?"

"Oh, she's not a princess," I said. "I shouldn't have said that. She used to be so much fun and we were best friends. She's never, ever acted spoiled in all the time I've known her, but she changed so much when she got the farm. It's like she's playing this role of someone she thinks she should be or something."

"People change all the time, even if it's only temporarily, especially when their world changes dramatically in some way. I wouldn't take it personally. I think your friend is still in there somewhere, she's just gotten a little lost."

"Will you really leave if she doesn't ride Jerry?"

"Yes, but I don't think it will come to that."

"I don't know, she's pretty stubborn."

"Well, you just let me handle that. I dealt with my share of little entitled lords and ladies at my last position so I'm pretty sure I can manage one mildly-sulky teenager."

I hoped for everyone's sake that she was right.

Chapter Twenty-three

I stayed down at the barn hanging out with Ellie and Red until it was time for night feed and it wasn't until the temperature began to drop that I headed back home.

Nobody was around when I got back to the house. Someone had left the hall light on, and I locked the front door behind me and climbed slowly upstairs, avoiding the step that creaked. I'd had no idea it was this late, but I was still jacked up after my argument with Hilary and I knew sleep was hours away.

"Should we watch some videos, girl?" I asked Caprice, who had sprawled herself out across my entire pillow.

She blinked sleepily and yawned, rolling over and nudging at the covers until she'd burrowed underneath.

I grabbed my laptop and crawled into bed, scooting the little poodle over slightly to make some room for myself.

I looked at the list I'd put on my nightstand and tried to decipher the cramped handwriting.

I think this first one is someone's name. I typed the Latin- or French-sounding name into my search engine and sat up a little more when a whole list of videos popped up.

I clicked randomly on the first one and settled under the covers to watch.

First, it was just a horse galloping around at liberty, swirling its head and clearly loving just tearing around the ring like a maniac. Subtitles popped up at the bottom but unfortunately, they were in a language that I didn't recognize.

From one corner a man stepped out, dressed in weird old-fashioned yellow breeches and carrying a dressage whip in one hand.

The horse swerved toward him, galloping hard directly toward the man, only to skid to a stop a few feet away from him, popping up on its hind legs before coming to a complete stand still. The man didn't flinch, just waited a beat and then reached up to stroke the horse who now stood motionless, sides heaving from his run.

I watched closely as the man ran his fingers lightly across the horse's shoulder. At that touch, the horse arched his neck and began trotting slowly alongside the man as he walked, never moving from the trainer's side even though he was completely loose.

The man stopped and, with no signal that I could see, the horse rocked back a little on his haunches and did a few steps of piaffe before moving forward into that slow, suspended trot again. They did that a few more times before moving to the wall, and the horse, without the trainer doing anything more but adjusting his own posture slightly, moved into a shoulder-in, first three track and then four and then back to straight again, all the while keeping a slight inside bend.

What is this? I thought, sitting up straight. *I thought Oona didn't believe in playing with the horses. Is it some sort of circus trick?*

I leaned closer, studying the screen intently. How was he getting the horse to bend his body like that? Was he just cuing the horse in a voice so low that the microphone didn't pick it up? I couldn't tell.

Just like that, it ended and a bunch of words I couldn't read popped up, probably a full explanation for whatever it was I'd just watched.

Too bad I can't actually understand anything, I thought, *that might have been helpful.*

Still, I was intrigued. I looked down to find the next thing on my list.

Once again, the video was in a guttural language I didn't understand.

Seriously, am I going to have to learn like ten different languages for this?

I kept watching, though. This one was an older, grainy video of a class of four or five happy, blonde pig-tailed girls who looked like they were a few years younger than I was. Each girl had a lovely, fine-boned pony beside them, and I felt a surge of jealousy. What might my life have been like if I'd started riding at such a young age? If I'd gone to live with Aunt Lillian as a child like she'd wanted me to then I might have spent my whole young life just like this.

But maybe I wouldn't appreciate horses properly if I'd always had them, I thought, *maybe I'd be acting just as spoiled as Hilary right now.*

I turned my focus back to the video. The girls started out just walking beside their ponies on the left rein. They lightly held the inside rein a few inches from the horse's bits and their right hands held the outside rein just below their ponies' withers.

The ponies didn't seem to mind this strange position at all, most of them stretched gently into the light contact, dropping their noses and mouthing the bits softly. They were much better behaved than I was sure Sox would have been.

Before anything interesting could happen, the camera jiggled and the video ended.

Well, that was weird, I thought. *What were they even doing?*

I looked down at the list in my hand and sighed; so far, these videos were giving me more questions than answers.

"All right, Caprice, let's try this one," I said, carefully typing in the next name.

This one looked more promising right from the beginning.

A tiny woman worked beside a gigantic bay warmblood, her body at his shoulder while he trotted around her. She was in the same position that the little girls had been with their ponies; one hand on the inside rein near the bit and the other hand just below the horse's withers.

The horse's face was full of concentration as his pace slowed and his weight shifted backward to his hindquarters. For a few steps, his trot became a piaffe and then he moved forward again into a trot. They continued on, transitioning from trot to walk to halt and back up again, adjusting the speed and tempo each time.

Neat, I thought, leaning forward so I could see better. *She made that look easy. Is that what Oona wants me to do with Red? I could totally do that.*

The woman looked up at the horse's face with an expression

of such pride and devotion and the horse responded right away, leaning over to rest his nose against her shoulder in a position of complete trust.

I set the laptop on the desk beside my bed, suddenly feeling uncomfortable, like I was watching a personal moment that wasn't meant for anyone but the two of them. Which was silly of me since she'd posted it on the internet for millions of people to watch.

When was the last time Red and I had done something like that? I wondered, thinking back over my summer. It had certainly been before that awful night when I'd run away. Had I even done any ring work at all since then? Not until my first lesson with Oona maybe. I couldn't remember.

I shivered and pushed down under the covers, staring at the dark ceiling overhead for a long time, my mind swirling with possibilities.

Chapter Twenty-four

Oona was probably the only one *not* astonished when Hilary showed up at the barn after morning chores, dressed to kill in new vibrant, purple full-seats with scroll work on the butt and a matching shirt.

I thought Oona might argue about the colour scheme but she didn't say a word.

"Um, do you want me to help you get him ready?" I offered but Hilary brushed past me, not bothering to answer so I left her alone to get Jerry brushed and tacked up by herself.

I hovered around the barn during their lesson, just dying to know what was happening in there and ducked into Riverdance's stall when they came out of the ring.

They were talking together, voices too low for me to overhear, but when I peeked out, I saw that Jerry's neck was covered in dried sweat so I guessed that they'd at least managed to get some work done.

"How was it?" I asked tentatively as Hilary passed but she didn't acknowledge me at all, just headed to the wash rack outside.

Well, at least she's taking care of him, I thought, stung that she'd ignored me.

I finished turning the rest of the horses out into the pasture and headed back up the driveway by myself. When I got back to the house there was a strange red car in the driveway where the guest parking was.

I went inside cautiously but the house was quiet. I found both of Hilary's parents in the kitchen drinking coffee together and laughing together in whispers.

"What's going on?" I asked quietly.

"Our guests arrived two days early," Mr. Ahlberg said. "They're already in their room and said they don't want to be disturbed and they don't want meals at all for their entire stay, they just want to eat at restaurants."

"So much for our carefully planned menu," Hilary's mom said, laughing.

"Come on, Astrid, let's have some of this cake to celebrate. Our new business has officially started."

Mr. Ahlberg set a beautifully iced chocolate cake on the table and handed out forks.

The cake was delicious, as was everything he made, and I closed my eyes as I took the first bite.

"Well, this looks cozy," Hilary said from the doorway. "Was nobody planning to invite me?"

"Of course, darling, sit down, I'll get you a fork."

Hilary resisted for a second, but the cake was too good to turn down. She sat on the opposite side of the table from me and refused to look in my direction.

"How was your lesson, darling?" Mrs. Ahlberg asked.

"Good, actually," Hilary said tentatively, her mouth curving into a smile. "I have another one booked for tomorrow. Oona is an...interesting teacher. I learned some new things and Jerry behaved himself really well. I didn't fall off, so that's really all I was hoping for.

Fall off? I looked up in surprise. Hilary was a brilliant rider. Why was she even thinking like that?

"Your mother was telling me that there's some auditions coming up for a musical next month. She said it was West Side Story." Mr. Ahlberg said.

Hilary looked up quickly and sent her mother an irritated glare. "Yes, it is, but I'm not doing any auditions."

"Oh, why not? I thought that was your favourite musical."

"It is...I mean, it was. But I'm too busy for that stuff anymore."

She dropped her fork on the table and stood up, pushing back her chair. "Sorry, I've got to go and shower. I have lots of work to do."

I didn't miss the worried look her parents sent each other the second she was gone.

Chapter Twenty-five

It wasn't a regular horse trailer that pulled up the driveway the next morning; it was a slick black Mercedes horse van with silvered scroll work on the sides. A little black sports car followed so closely behind it looked like it was attached to the rear bumper.

"Hello," the window of the van rolled down and a dark-haired man in his twenties hung his head out the window, smiling broadly. He glanced over at me but his eyes lit up when he saw Hilary, still dressed in her breeches after her lesson. "Okay to park anywhere?"

"Yes, out front is fine," Hilary said. "'You can unload him here. Is the van staying?"

"No, *she* keeps it at home in a special garage." He pointed a thumb backward toward the little sports car. "Doesn't want a tree to fall on it or anything." He laughed at his own joke but managed to instantly look serious when the car door opened and a tall, painfully-thin woman stepped out.

"John, why are we standing around talking when there is a horse to be unloaded?"

"Right, just figuring out where to park, Mrs. Robinson. We'll unload him here."

"Here? Is it safe? It looks too close to the barn to me. Have you even checked the footing?"

"Doing that right now," John sang out, sending Hilary a wink and jumping down out of the horse van.

The woman came toward us, her arms clutched over her thin chest and her mouth pulled down into a frown. Her pale faced was deeply lined and her brown hair had been raked back into a tight bun.

"Hello, Hilary," she said abruptly. "I hope everything is ready for Baloo. I want to make sure everything is perfect before we unload him. I brought some of his old bedding from his stall. He's very sensitive to change and I want him to have a smooth transition to his new home."

"Sure," Hilary said, gulping. "Come on inside. There's a space ready for you in the tack room, too. We can help you get settled." She looked over at me and frowned, either because she was still mad at me or because she remembered that Linda was taking over my old spot. "Um, this is Astrid, she keeps her horse here too, and she's the one who looks after most of the—"

"Oh, are you the groom?" Linda said, reaching out to clutch at my arm with her bony fingers, an intense look on her face.

"Um, well, we all help out..." I started to say but she'd latched onto me and practically dragged me into the barn.

"I have to tell you all about Baloo," she said. "He has very special needs and I want to make sure he's happy at all times. First, he likes a deeply bedded stall."

"Uh huh," I said, looking over my shoulder desperately for Hilary to help.

"He needs his water changed three times a day. He won't drink it if it's not fresh. He hates loud music so I hope there isn't a radio in the barn."

"Well, we don't usually—"

"He's very sensitive to chemicals and any sort of commercial products. I do hope you only use natural organic products here. No bug spray. Ever. I make his own special blend."

"Um, okay—"

"He can't have a commercially produced salt lick. Only the ones that are mined by hand from the Himalayans. I hope you don't mind that I've arranged to have a camera installed so I can watch him at all times."

Finally, I detached myself from her grip, rubbing my arm and stepping back quickly before she could latch onto me again. "Okay, well, you can talk to Hilary about that. Here's his stall and I can show you where your tack—"

She whipped out a twisted green rope made out of what looked like hay from one pocket and a lighter out of the other. With one deft move she lit the rope on fire and began to wave it in the air.

"Oh, you can't smoke in here," I said in alarm. "It's a fire hazard."

"This isn't smoking, it's smudging," she said, walking into Baloo's open stall and waving the smoldering stick rhythmically back and forth. "I'm getting rid of any bad energy."

"What?" I said in astonishment. "This was my horse Red's old stall. I cleaned it out totally. There's nothing bad in here."

"No, of course not," she said quickly, "smudging just balances anything cosmic that might be out of alignment. There, all done. Inhale deeply and you might be able to feel it yourself."

"Hmm," I said, a little grumpily, eyeing the still-smoldering greenery. It did smell okay I guess, woodsy and kind of relaxing, but I the only thing I sensed is that Hilary had brought a certified crazy lady to keep her horse here.

Chapter Twenty-six

It took Linda forever to go away and stop bothering us once Baloo was unloaded and happily eating lunch in his stall. He was a big dark bay warmblood with a thin neck that looked like it had been put on upside-down and a hollow back that definitely could have used a massage and a visit from the chiropractor. He had a wide blaze and two white socks. He probably could have been very flashy if it wasn't for the haunted, vacant look in his eye.

Linda flitted around, alternating between harassing Baloo every two seconds to see if he was handling the move okay to ferrying her stuff to the tack room from the van, to following me around giving me advice on everything that was wrong with the barn.

"We'll have to have a wash-rack indoors for winter," she said, trailing behind me as I fed the horses lunch. "That's non-negotiable, and I can see from here that there's a bit of dust in the hay; you'll need a steamer. That's non-negotiable."

I quickly discovered that non-negotiable was her favourite phrase and that she used it for everything.

She probably uses it when she orders pizza, too, I thought, trying in vain to tune her endless chatter out, *extra cheese is non-negotiable*.

Finally, by some miracle, she actually left but not without letting me know that she'd be back that night to check on him.

"Good grief, Baloo," I said to him as I passed by, "I don't know how you put up with that."

He raised his head and snorted, glancing at me disinterestedly before going back to his hay.

I was grateful when Rob's truck finally chugged up the driveway. I was looking forward to spending the rest of my day hanging out with him in peace. I went to the tack room to quickly soak that night's beet pulp before our ride.

"Astrid?" he called as soon as he got inside the barn, "why are Red and Ellie in the back…" His voice trailed off and I knew he must have seen Baloo's big head sticking over Red's stall door. "What the heck?"

He pushed open the tack room door and stood there not saying anything.

"Rob, it's fine," I said, wondering how many more times I was going to have to say that this week. I ran water over the beet pulp and swirled it around. "Hilary needed the spot in the barn for boarders so I moved out to the paddocks. It's not a big deal."

He came over and leaned against the counter beside the sink. Not moving until I turned to look at him. "You didn't tell me on the phone last night."

"I…I couldn't," I said. "I feel stupid that this bothers me. I really isn't a big deal and the horses are happy there."

"But it *does* bother you?"

I shrugged. "Yeah, it does but that's my problem. I'm just being silly."

"Why couldn't the new boarders go back there?"

"Linda, Baloo's owner, would only board here if she could be in the barn. And that would have left Ellie out there by herself so I moved Red, too."

I glanced over at Rob and saw that he was looking down at the floor, a deep scowl on his face.

"Rob, I'm okay with this now, honestly. I get it. I'm not paying board and Hilary's really scared about money right now. It made sense for it to be me who moved."

"Astrid, she's not paying anyone to clean the barn or do all the things you do with the horses. You more than pay your own way."

"Yeah, but I live in their house and eat all their food. Her parents drive me to archery. They wouldn't take money from my dad and Marion when they offered to pay for me to stay here; working hard is the only way I have of sort of paying my way."

Rob sighed heavily and put an arm around my shoulder. "I actually get that. I would probably feel the same way if I were in your shoes. But that doesn't mean it's right. The Ahlberg's love you; they wanted to help, and they're not hurting for money. They want you to be happy."

"I know," I said, leaning into him gratefully. "But let's not talk about this anymore. Let's go ride."

Chapter Twenty-seven

The night before our archery field trip the heatwave broke with a vengeance. It hadn't rained a drop in almost a month, but that night and the morning that followed it seemed to be doing it's best to make up for the drought.

"I don't know whether to put you all out or not," I said to the horses who were staring gloomily at the buckets of rain pouring down outside. In the end, I put their rain coats on and left them in. The Ahlberg's would be at church today so there'd be nobody around if the weather really took a turn for the worse. One day without pasture probably wouldn't hurt.

"Are you sure you girls want to do this?" Annie said when we got to the range, staring through the rain that poured down over her windshield.

"It's okay, Mom," Nori insisted, "it's just a tiny bit of rain. We won't melt."

"All right, if you say so. Call me if you want to come home early."

"We won't," Nori said as we slammed the car doors and

ducked out into the rain-drenched parking lot.

We were the first ones there and we huddled in the doorway, keeping our gear far away from the cascades of water pouring off the roof.

"All right, everyone," Earl called to those of us who'd assembled. Not everyone had come, tromping around in the woods in the middle of a rainstorm wasn't everybody's idea of a great time. "Onto the bus."

We piled onto the half-sized bus that Earl had rented for the occasion, our raincoats dripping puddles all over the seats.

I had mixed feelings about the trip. Rain didn't bother me very much, but the course was set deep in the woods and I knew from experience that we were about to get very, very wet. The hills and steep banks would have turned slick and muddy from last night's rainfall.

Still, I'd set my mind to just have a good time when we pulled up in front of the range.

"What the heck?" Earl said, pulling the bus to a stop just outside the clubhouse.

I stood up to look and saw that the gate that usually hung open was closed tight. A handmade sign was tied to the padlock. Earl pulled the creaking bus door open and ducked outside into the pouring rain.

"Sorry, kids," he said as he got back onto the bus and shook the water from his hair. "Looks like a big chunk of the bank washed away in the storm last night and they're not letting anyone in until they have a chance to assess it. They don't want to risk a landslide. Looks like we'll have to cancel."

There was a chorus of disappointed groans.

"Don't worry," Earl said, "we'll try again in a few weeks once the weather dries out a bit."

"But I want to go today," a little girl from Miranda's group said, her voice rising plaintively.

"Wait, let's go the farm," Nori said suddenly, turning to me excitedly. "We said we were going to do it eventually. Why not now?"

"But, I didn't ask the Ahlberg's yet," I protested, looking around at their suddenly expectant faces.

"So, call them. It's not like we're doing anything else."

"Maybe Earl doesn't want—"

"Hey, I'm okay with it if you are," Earl interrupted, "I'm interested in seeing these horses Nori's always talking about in action."

"Fine." I sighed, fished my phone out of my pocket and wiped off the damp screen which somehow had bits of hay stuck to the surface. I went to dial Hilary's number and then hesitated. She still wasn't really talking to me and it was possible that she'd say no to us visiting just because she was angry.

I dialed Mrs. Ahlberg instead.

"Well, that sounds lovely, sweetie, what a great idea. I'm sorry we'll miss it. Have fun, though, and be safe."

"Okay, thanks," I said incredulously, amazed that I'd gotten permission so easily. Hilary would have grilled me for half an hour before going along with anything like this.

"We're good to go," I told Earl, turning my ringer off and shoving my phone back in my pocket.

The first thing I saw when we reached the farm was Rob's trailer and I silently cheered when I remembered that he'd said he would come over to ride and would also school Ellie in the indoor. I knew that he'd be more than happy to help.

"This is so neat," one of the boys said, as we piled out of the bus. The rain had actually let up for the most part, although dark grey clouds still billowed overhead.

"Yeah, if you can get past the horse stink," Miranda muttered, but everyone ignored her.

I was glad to see that there weren't any other vehicles besides Oona's in the parking lot. Apparently, the weather had scared off all the boarders, too.

"Nori, can you take everyone to meet the horses?" I asked. "I'm going to get Rob and we'll figure out a plan."

Rob was cantering around on Artimax when I came in and he looked up in surprise and brought the little horse to a halt in front of me.

"Whoa, you look soaked. What are you doing here?"

"The range was closed and we had to cancel our field trip. Want to help me on a little project?"

"That sounds dangerous," Rob said, laughing. "What do you want me to do?"

It didn't take long to figure out a plan.

Nori and I grabbed our brushes and led Red and Maverick up to the indoor so everyone could meet them and get a chance to learn how to groom them and see how to tack them up.

Even though they'd seen it before, I brought out my horse bow and the special quiver I used when I was shooting from horseback so the kids could see how different it was from a regular recurve or a competition recurve. I wished we had some targets set up in the indoor; it would be much nicer to just stay dry in there.

"Well, everyone, should we go on a hike?" I asked, moving to the door of the barn and looking up at the sky.

It was a unanimous yes and we led them down the trail, cutting in the back way through the pasture on the right to take the shortcut to our makeshift range.

I showed them the targets and explained how we'd made them, and then had everyone stand back while Nori and I did a demonstration. We did it at a walk and trot first to make sure the ground wasn't too slippery, but the trail was made of sand and the water had drained away a long time ago so we were safe at higher speeds.

Red and I were comfortable cantering the whole course by now, and so was Rob. Nori just cantered to each target, stopped Maverick so she could shoot, and cantered on again. She even managed to hit each target and was beaming when everyone cheered for all of us.

After that, I showed everyone how to use the horse bow and they took turns shooting from the ground, laughing at the strange feel of the bow.

"Does anyone want to be led on the horses at a walk to try?" I asked.

"I'd do it," Miranda said in a nasty voice, "but I don't want to stink like a filthy barnyard for the rest of the day. Nobody wants that, do they, kids?"

"I do!" A little boy from Miranda's group piped up. "Me too, me too," they all said, swarming around us excitedly.

We let the older kids go first, fitting them with whichever one of our three helmets fit them best. I carefully explained how to make their shots without endangering the horses and led them cautiously from one target to the other.

The little kids were next and we moved the horses a little closer to the targets so at least they had a chance of hitting something. They all loved it and the hardest part was getting them off once they'd shot. Everyone wanted to keep going.

"That was the best day ever," Nori said, beaming with happiness as we finally waved the bus down the driveway. Rob's dad had already come to pick him up. "Thanks so much for doing this, Astrid."

"No problem—" I started to say but she surprised me by squeezing me into a tight hug and then letting me go just as quickly, turning back to fiddle with Maverick's bridle to cover her embarrassment.

"Come on, let's put these guys away and go up to the house for hot chocolate, your mom won't be here for another hour."

The horses were tucked in their stalls with hay and extra carrots, and by the contented looks on their faces, I guessed they'd enjoyed themselves, too.

"Maverick was so good, wasn't he?" Nori said as we trekked up to the house.

"He was, I think he actually had a good time. He didn't seem to mind the little kids at all."

When we got inside, I put the kettle on for hot chocolate and then ran upstairs to change. Mrs. Ahlberg took one look at the sopping wet Nori and appeared a few minutes later with a pair of fluffy socks and a warm fleece top.

"We can't have you getting sick," she said, handing them to her. "Go get changed and then you can warm up with a nice cup of hot chocolate and a slice of chocolate cake."

Nori was all prepared to argue until she heard the word *cake* and then she obediently followed Mrs. Ahlberg's orders. Sort of like Maverick did when he thought there were treats involved.

We sat there and drank and filled our faces until Annie showed up to pick up Nori.

Chapter Twenty-eight

"Wow, Astrid, that outfit almost makes me wish I was going to school with you," Hilary said. "Almost."

"Not too awful?" I asked, smoothing down the plaid skirt self-consciously.

"Of course not, you look great."

"Thanks," I said, busying myself getting breakfast. Darius was scheduled to come back into town this weekend and Hilary had miraculously decided yesterday that she was speaking to me again. It was amazing how that worked.

Even though she was probably just using me to get her alone-time with Darius, it was still preferable to the silent treatment. She had been acting a little better since she'd started taking regular lessons on Jerry, although she still didn't spend any extra time hanging out at the barn like she'd used to. And she still had Rob schooling him a couple times a week.

"Good luck today," she said sincerely. "Don't worry, I'll take care of everyone here."

I didn't have much choice. The Ahlbergs hadn't had any luck hiring anyone yet and it wasn't like I could put off going to school for a week. I had to trust that Hilary and Oona would take care of everyone on their own.

A car horn honked outside and I grabbed the rest of my stuff and headed for the door.

"Are you ready for this?" Rob asked, nudging my shoulder companionably as I hopped in the truck beside him.

"Yeah, I think so. As ready as I'll ever be."

"Don't worry, it will be fine. At least we have lunch together and History."

"Yeah." Although Rob and I got along in almost every way, our chosen subjects in school differed wildly. He was more of a math and science guy and I was more of an English and history girl. We'd already had to pick our core subjects so I knew we only had one class together so far. We still had our electives to pick out though.

Despite the heavy morning traffic we reached school quickly and my heart dropped when I saw the familiar building. There were not a ton of good memories for me here. "All right, you two, have a good day," Rob's dad said, "make me proud. Astrid, you keep an eye on this guy for me."

"Thanks, Dad," Rob said with a laugh, "we'll try not to get into too much trouble."

The big limestone frontage of Sacred Heart looked exactly like it had the last time I'd seen it; imposing and familiar at the same time.

It might not have changed, but I sure had. I felt like a completely different person walking through these front doors, like I'd lived a whole lifetime in the year I'd been away.

"You okay?" Rob asked, glancing over at me as we reached to top of the stairs.

"Yes," I said, taking a deep breath. "Let's do this."

We pushed open the big front doors together and headed straight to the big auditorium where everyone was supposed to gather on the first morning. It was already packed but we found two seats together at the edge of the room and squeezed in.

"Astrid!" I turned to see Susan Ling bouncing toward me, her long silky hair hanging like a waterfall almost down to her waist. I'd known Susan and her brother Thomas since childhood. Since their dad had worked for my dad's company we'd always been thrown together at various functions. Susan had usually been decent to me but she did have a bit of an edge.

"You look great," she trilled, her eyes flickering toward Rob and then back to me, "you're so fit and tanned."

"I'm outside all the time," I said with a laugh, feeling my muscles relax. Susan was a little unpredictable but overall, she'd never been mean to me, not really.

"Well, it shows," she said, looking at Rob again curiously. "I'm sorry, I'm not sure if we've met. I'm Susan."

"Yes, we've gone to school together since middle school," Rob said with a wink, "so we've met."

"Oh," her hand fluttered to her chest and she tilted her head to one side. "Good grief, I recognize you now. You've sure aged well, you've filled out in all the right places. Good catch, Astrid."

"Um, thanks?" I said, not sure if I should laugh or be offended.

"Well, I'd better go, it was so nice seeing you both, though. I hope I can interview you both later for the school paper."

She leaned down to pull me into another quick hug and then was gone, leaving only the lingering scent of her perfume behind.

"She hasn't changed a bit," Rob said, shaking his head. "But she's right about one thing; I'm definitely a good catch."

I elbowed him and rolled my eyes just as the lights dimmed and our principal climbed the stairs to the center of stage, waving a hand for silence.

I paid attention for about the first five minutes and then my thoughts drifted back to the barn and I wondered what Red was doing and if Hilary would keep her end of the bargain and turn all the horses out properly. And whether Portia would break out again and how Ellie would do at the upcoming schooling show. Of course I wanted her to do well, but maybe if she had a meltdown and messed up completely then nobody would want to buy her and she could stay with me for just one more season.

There was scattered laughter and applause in the auditorium and I shook my head in an effort to focus. I'd missed probably the one interesting thing in the presentation, though, because for the rest of the hour it was just a series of overly long welcoming speeches put on by what felt like every single staff member of Sacred Heart.

"Well, that's interesting news," Rob said as soon as the lights went on and we started to file out.

"Um, which part?"

"The part about some extracurricular stuff counting toward school credits. They talked about doing it a couple years ago, so I'm glad it's finally happened. The public high schools in the area have been doing it for a while so it's about time Sacred Heart got with the program."

"Wait, what? What sort of extracurricular activities?"

He shot me a strange look. "Weren't you listening? I thought you would have been all over that."

"Er, I must have missed that part."

"If you're competing in some sort of program outside of school, like music or sports, then it can count toward your school credits and you can leave early or duck out for competitions and stuff as long as you've organized it ahead of time."

"Oh," I said, wondering what that would mean for me.

"You have to get your coach to sign off on it and everything. I'm not sure if they'll include horses, but they'll definitely include archery since you're on the school team and everything. You are signing up for the team again, right?"

"I think so," I said, "I mean, I didn't talk to Earl about it yet…"

"Well, what are you waiting for?"

Yes, what *was* I waiting for? I should have had this organized a month ago, when I knew for sure that I'd actually be going to this school. The old me would have been chomping at the bit to be part of a team again. What was wrong with me? I felt like I'd been moving in a fog lately.

"Hey"—Rob nudged my arm—"earth to Astrid."

I shook my head to clear it and smiled up at him. "Yes, you're right. I'm joining the team. Definitely. Although I'm not sure if they'll want me when I'm shooting like this."

"Good, well, let's go to the office and convince them that dressage is a legitimate sport, too."

In the end, there was no problem signing up, although there were still a lot of details to be worked out. It was just like subbing out one of our regular courses two days a week and inserting something we actually enjoyed doing instead. We got to leave early on those days if our coach signed off on it and were given credits for it just like taking a normal elective like gym or music. The only tricky part was figuring out if we could actually organize lessons for that time.

"Yours shouldn't be a problem once your archery practice schedule is up. The whole team will probably do the same days. I'm not so sure if Oona would be available at that time, though."

"I bet she would be. She's actually more nice and helpful than I thought. We should ask her."

The rest of the half-day was just a sea of tweaking our class schedules and figuring out where our homerooms would be and what sort of electives to choose. The anthropology course I'd wanted had been cancelled since not enough people had signed up, so I had to try and get into something equally interesting quickly before everything was filled up.

I managed to sub out statistics and world economics for the more daunting pre-calculus that I'd originally been put into. I did not want to spend another five hours on homework every night after school.

Rob, of course, took every advanced math and science course he could get his hands on and probably only signed up for any electives at all because he was forced to. For someone who said he didn't want to go on to university he was sure taking on a huge course load.

"Come on, we have to have at least one more class together," I said, giving him a poke in the ribs as he poured over the schedule. "Oh, here, how about cooking? I know you love to eat."

"Cooking?" he said flatly, and then shook his head and smiled. "Actually, that's a good idea. I have to take *something* fluffy, I guess."

"Wow, I had no idea you were such a snob. Maybe I don't want to take any classes with you."

"I'm not a snob," he said laughing. "I just want to be strategic in my choices."

"Okay, I'm not sure why, though. I thought you wanted to train horses for a living."

He glanced around furtively as if I'd said something forbidden. "Well, I'm not sure what will happen," he whispered, "but, just in case I *do* decide to go to university I want to be prepared. But, you are right about one thing; I do love food."

By the end of the half-day, we had our classes mostly sorted and had figured out that at least we'd have the same homeroom in the mornings even if we didn't have much together for the rest of the day. I didn't mind that much; I was used to doing my own thing in school and taking classes that interested me rather than what my friends were taking. I hadn't actually had that many friends back when I'd gone to school here so it hadn't seemed important before now.

I'd been lucky that my dad and Marion had never actually cared about school. I mean, I had to bring home top grades and everything but, for people who tried to control every *other* aspect of my life right down to the food I ate and the clothes I wore, they'd left me pretty much alone when it came to choosing classes and things.

My dad had an ingrained mistrust of any sort of higher education and had never encouraged me to think about college or university. He'd focused all his intense micromanaging on my archery career instead, and Marion had just gone along with him. I guess they figured that I was the school's problem once I was inside the building.

While I was waiting for Rob to get out of his meeting with the career counsellor, I'd taken myself on a tour of the whole building, trying to remember where everything was.

Hello, friend, I thought, reaching the vast, glassed-in library where I'd spent so many hours hiding and studying. There were already some kids inside at the kiosks, bent over heavy texts with concentrated looks on their faces. I'd holed up here over many a lunch hour, avoiding the shouting and chaos of the cafeteria.

Not this year, though, I told myself. I'd learned a lot about making friends and being brave when I'd spent the last year at public school when I'd lived with Aunt Lillian. This year I planned to be a different person entirely. If I spent time in the library it would be because I *wanted* to, not because I was hiding from life.

I wandered down to the small, indoor greenhouse where I would be taking my Horticulture class this year and paused in the open doorway, inhaling deeply. I'd never bothered to visit this area before, but I'd spent part of the summer helping Hilary's mom in the garden and it turned out that I really liked working with plants so I'd signed up for it this term just to give it a try.

The doors to the gym were open and some guys had already started an impromptu basketball game and the sounds of squeaking shoes on the court and yelling filled the hallway.

My heart thudded a little bit as I headed that way, the same direction as our archery range. Sacred Heart was all about academics but they also spared no expense to have winning sports teams. When I'd last been a student here our archery team was virtually unbeatable and part of that was probably because we had our own indoor range big enough that we could shoot full Olympic distances.

Some of the basketball players turned to look when I came in and I gave them a nervous little wave, not really recognizing anyone, and slipped into the small door to the right.

The room was empty but a few unstrung bows lay on a table near the door, and there was a white plastic bucket full of battered arrows nearby. I closed the door carefully behind me, feeling that old thrill of excitement of being on a range again. The place felt full of possibilities.

I glanced at the targets set up at the far end of the range and then back to the bows again. They were probably the school's practice bows, they didn't look nice enough to belong to anyone, and I was sure that nobody would mind if I just shot a few rounds.

I hesitated and then strode forward, picking up one of the battered wooden bows and stringing it quickly before I could change my mind.

There was a thumping sound behind me and I looked over my shoulder to see that there were faces pressed up against the glass in the door leading to the gym. The basketball players…

Yuck, they'd been watching me the whole time. I shook my head angrily and tossed the rest of the arrows back in the bucket and unstrung the bow quickly, just dying to get out of there.

The door opened and sound poured in, wrecking the peaceful quiet of the range.

"Hey," one of them said in a booming voice. "You're that girl, aren't you?"

I looked up to see a tall, dark-haired boy standing in the doorway. There was some cat-calling, yodeling sounds from the gym, and the guy rolled his eyes and shut the door firmly behind him.

"Sorry, ignore them. You're the archery girl that won all that stuff, though, right?"

I glanced at him warily, not loving being trapped in here alone with a stranger while all his friends waited outside. "I used to compete a lot," I said neutrally.

He nodded, not moving from the doorway. "Yeah, my little sister told me all about you. She's crazy about learning archery."

"She should join the team then," I said, relaxing my guard a little.

"Well, that's the thing. Last year was her first year at this school and she was really excited about joining, but that girl who runs it said she wasn't good enough. Peyton came home crying. But this year, she heard that you'd be back and she got all excited like you were someone famous or something."

"Oh, gosh," I said, blushing. "I'm really not that good."

"That's not what Peyton said. Anyway, I just thought I'd check with you to see if maybe she could try out again. She practices all the time at home, but my parents won't spend money for lessons or anything outside of school, they can barely pay our school fees. Isn't there any way she could join?"

"Well, of course she can," I said frowning, "anyone can. It's supposed to be about learning."

"Yeah, that's what I thought. But that stupid cow who says

she's president of the club said they'd only take a few of the best archers, people who are already competing. She said they didn't want to bring the tone of the club down."

"Wow, that's awful. Who would say something like that?"

"I dunno." He shrugged. "Some snarky redhead. Mindy? Marsha?"

Miranda, I thought, my heart sinking. Of course she'd be involved in archery here, too.

"Yeah, I know her," I said warily.

"Anyway, can you try and help Peyton? Can you keep an eye out for her?"

"Yes," I said slowly, "of course I will."

"Great, she's too scared of getting embarrassed again to come out unless she's sure, though. Can you call her and let her know when it's safe?"

"Um, I guess…"

"Here, give me your phone. I'll give you my number."

It seemed rude to say no so I slowly pulled out my phone and handed it over, watching while he punched in the numbers. My phone beeped once as if there was a text coming in and then fell silent. He glanced up at me with a smile, hit one more button and held out the phone.

"There, I'm Preston, by the way."

"Astrid," I said weakly, taking my phone back from him. Our fingers brushed lightly and I noticed that his were calloused with work like mine. I wondered what he did when he wasn't playing basketball.

"I know who you are," he said with a wink and headed back out into the jeering and whooping crowd of boys.

I waited until they were definitely gone and the gym was silent before heading out myself. I found Rob waiting for me out in the hallway, a strange look on his face.

"Where were you?" he said. "I've been done for ages."

"I thought you were going to text me."

"I did, like three times."

I glanced down at my phone but there weren't any new messages from him. "No, nothing," I said handing it to him so he could see. "It was a weird phone glitch, I guess. But you'll never guess what just happened."

I filled him in on what Preston had told me about Miranda. "I don't know where my head was when I agreed to come back to this school. Of course Miranda is running everything now; it was her dream job to be able to boss people around. Preston seemed really upset about the way she'd treated his sister."

"Huh," Rob scowled, "I remember that guy; I can't imagine him being protective over his little sister."

"Well, he seemed nice enough. He asked me to help her."

"Fine, so how are you planning to stop Miranda's reign of terror then?"

"Well, technically, she can't keep people from being on the team. It's not like cheerleading where there are only so many spots. Anyone should be able to join and compete, and there's no such thing as bringing down the tone of the club by not being good enough. That's not what archery is about at all. Earl would lose it if he found out she was acting like that."

"Are you going to tell him?"

"No, not unless I absolutely have to. What I am going to do is go to that first meeting, though. I guess my days of being able to avoid Miranda are over."

Rob was strangely quiet on the way home, and no matter what I said I didn't seem to be able to draw him into conversation.

I hope he's not mad at me, I thought, but there was no way to ask him with his dad sitting right there. Maybe he was just thinking about his classes.

Still, he walked with me up to the front door, carrying my backpack for me and gave me a hug goodbye, although he didn't say anything.

"See you tomorrow," I called but he just waved.

Well, that was strange, I thought, feeling uncomfortable. It wasn't like Rob to not want to talk with me.

I pushed my uneasiness aside when Caprice came bounding to the door, yapping up a storm in her excitement to see me.

"I've only been gone a few hours." I laughed, picking her up and giving her a hug while she tried unsuccessfully to lick my face. That was one of the few of Marion's germaphobe traits that had rubbed off on me; warm farm-dog saliva on my skin was the grossest thing ever.

Chapter Twenty-nine

By some miracle, Hilary had actually cleaned the stalls and paddocks herself, even Red and Ellie's, which she really didn't have to do.

"Don't worry about it," she said when I thanked her. "It's your first day back at school. I wanted to do something nice."

Which left me wondering about what would happen the other four days of the school week but I decided not to question it.

The sky was still overcast but at least it wasn't pouring. I'd decided to take Ellie for a quick ride since I'd been spending most of my time lately with Red. She had her schooling show coming up in a couple weeks and the least I could do was keep her exercised in between Rob's schooling sessions.

"Hey guys," I called, quickly tossing hay into their stalls. They came inside one by one, nickering eagerly for dinner.

I looked up suddenly, feeling like there was someone watching me and was surprised to see Oona in the far stall, the one on the other side of Red.

"Oh, you scared me. What are you doing here?" I said,

putting a hand over my thudding heart.

"Sorry, I thought you saw me. I was just checking out this paddock; it's nice and roomy, isn't it?"

"Yes," I said slowly, "it is. Why? Are you thinking of getting a horse?"

"Not really. It was just a thought, but it's probably not the right time. Come on up for tea after your ride and we can talk about a plan for Red if you like."

"Sure," I said, "I shouldn't be too long." I knew Rob would be riding Ellie tomorrow after school and again on the weekend. My job was just to keep her lightly exercised in the meantime, something I was very good at. The show was two weekends from now we had to make every ride count in order to have her fit and ready.

She amiably walked up the driveway and I headed her into the sandy trail that led around the upper pasture. It wasn't as scenic as the ocean trail but it was flat and good for trotting and cantering after days of rain.

Ellie obediently did whatever I asked, her ears pricked with interest as she cantered through the dripping forest. She was a fun, easy ride, but there wasn't the same feeling of brilliance as when I was riding Red. He sort of injected his funny personality in everything he did while she was just sweet and obedient.

We did some gentle leg yields and shoulder-ins and I asked her to turn a few steps on her haunches in both directions when we reached the place where we had to turn to go back to the barn.

"You're such a good girl, Ellie," I told her, reaching down to scratch her withers.

We walked and trotted back to the barn on a loose rein. She

was speckled with rain water but cool when we got back so I toweled her off until she was dry and put on her rain sheet.

"Have a good dinner, girl," I told her, checking to make sure her manger was still full of hay. I went over to give Red a scratch behind the ears and then ran upstairs to Oona's place and knocked on the door.

"Come on in," she said, meeting me at the door. She handed me a steaming mug of tea and stood back as I went straight to the paintings.

Wow, I thought, looking at her art in amazement. She must have been the fastest painter on the planet since I didn't recognize a single one of the new paintings stacked up on easels around the room.

"These are so amazing," I said, whispering as if we were in a library. These ones were all of racehorses, some standing proudly, the rest frozen mid-stride, leaping out of the painting. "They look so alive," I said in awe. I could almost hear the thunder of their hooves, the cries of the jockeys, and the roar of the crowd. "How do you make it seem like there's light shining out of the canvas like that?"

"A whole bunch of techniques mashed together, I guess," she said, shrugging.

"Huh." I bent down so I could study the nearest painting, that of a proud bay horse in blue silks charging across the finish line, in detail. The closer I got, the more the picture blurred, and up close I could see that the whole thing was made up of a thousand multi-coloured tiny dots. Even the grass growing on the far side of the track wasn't really green; it was made of a million pixels of colour that made this particular green look like living grass, undulating in the wind. "But how did you know which colours to use or where to even put them? How did you learn all this stuff?"

"Astrid, drink your tea," she said in exasperation. "Not everything needs an explanation. Art is there for you to enjoy, you're supposed to be thinking about the experience, not the technique."

"Okay, fine." I sighed and obediently took a sip of tea, cupping the mug between both hands as I moved from painting to painting again.

"It's called pointillism," Oona said finally from her place at the table and I turned to look at her questioningly over my shoulder. "The painting style, that's what it's called. And I went to school in Scotland, at the Glasgow School of Art. That's where I got my degree."

"But you teach riding."

"Yes," she said, staring at me as if I were the densest person on the planet. "And I paint. It is perfectly possible to do two things in life at the same time."

"But you're so talented, you could sell your work all over the world."

"Yes, that's what I do," she said, raising an eyebrow. "You'll have to google it when you get home. I love to teach and I love to paint. Now that we have that cleared up, let's talk about your horse. What did you learn from the videos?"

"Not a lot," I confessed, "but it did get my interest."

"Good, that's all I wanted you to see. I wanted you to understand that true dressage endeavors to keep the horse's joy and personality intact, and the rider's too, for that matter. You don't have to give anything up to ride well or compete. Except time and money, of course."

"Okay," I said thoughtfully, mulling it over.

"I wanted you to know that we're not at cross purposes, that training Red up through the levels is the same path as the one where you do liberty and gallop through the woods. Or at least it should be."

"Oh," I said, setting my cup down and watching her carefully. What she'd said made perfect sense and it laid to rest one of the worries I'd been harbouring about schooling Red too much.

"Anyway, if you have time tonight, I'd love to show you a few things."

"Sure," I said, now very interested. "I didn't ride Red yet, so I can get him if you like. It would only take me a few minutes to tack him up."

"Just his halter is fine for tonight."

I gulped the rest of my tea down, washed my cup, and put it in dish rack. I sent one last look at the bay horse poised mid-race, ears pinned, neck stretched, mane flying, and then followed Oona rapidly downstairs.

That night, I lay in bed and tried to process all the things that had happened that day. Starting back to school had worried me more than I'd let on and it had been a relief to get the first day over with and know that it wasn't going to be an absolutely awful year.

The lure of an archery team hadn't hurt, either.

Then there was the strange way Rob was acting at the end of

the day, but I decided to put off thinking about that until later.

Finally, there'd been my fantastic lesson with Oona and that was something I really *did* want to share with Rob.

It had started out with just me showing Oona how I normally free-lunged, letting Red gallop around the indoor to blow off steam and then gradually stepping in to play with him. Using my body language to encourage him to change directions and transition up and down as I played with him.

"Nice," Oona had said, watching Red curve around me in a tight arc. "Now turn your body slightly so you're facing the same direction as him, so he's moving beside you instead of around you. But keep an eye on him, let him know that you're still connected."

Nodding, I tried to do what she said and suddenly, it wasn't Red moving around me, it was us cantering together, me making a smaller circle inside his larger one. We drifted closer until I put my hand out, brushing my fingers against his shoulder, both of us moving in sync.

"And so it begins," Oona said with a smile as Red and I both dropped to a walk and then stopped together. "Astrid, you're really a natural at this."

"Not really," I said, side-stepping her compliment. "Justin, one of the cowboys at the ranch, showed me a lot of this stuff. He was really talented."

"A-ha, is that the same Justin that Liza goes on about non-stop?"

"Yes." I broke into a grin. "They're completely perfect for each other."

"Well, I had no idea that I would be working with such an advanced student," she teased, smiling at me. "Go put his halter on and I'll show you a few more things."

She'd had me lead Red along the rail while she explained about what we would be trying to accomplish.

"It's sort of like yoga for horses, we're going to help him isolate the different parts of his body in order to help him balance. And we're going to strengthen his hindquarters so he's doing more lifting and less pushing."

"I didn't know there was anything wrong with his balance," I said, frowning. He'd been an agile cow-horse once; if anyone was balanced it was him.

"Well, there's nothing *wrong* with a regular human who doesn't do yoga, either, is there? But building that strength slowly, over time, allows them to do what they'd never thought was possible before. I promise you that he's going to love all his lessons, especially once we bring out the treats."

"Oh, he'll be all over that," I said, laughing.

She had us do a simple exercise where we'd just walk three steps, then halt, then back up three steps. At first, we did it slowly, but gradually she had us pick up speed but at the same time keep the transitions smooth, like we were doing a dance. One-two-three, One-two-three. After a minute of confusion, Red actually liked it and it was like we were flowing together across the arena.

"That's enough for him today," Oona said, "it doesn't seem like hard work but it's actually a good work-out for both of you. Let him process that tonight and we'll do more tomorrow."

Chapter Thirty

I was brushing Red when the first text from Nori came in.

Tuesday nights! Was all it said. I shrugged and stuffed my phone back in my pocket. This was Red's time and I didn't want to waste it trying to figure out cryptic texts from Nori.

Two seconds later, it pinged, and then another time. I tried to ignore it but finally fished my phone out again. This time it was a row of pictures.

Is she at the range? I thought, squinting down at the screen. Yes, it was definitely the notice board that hung outside of Earl's office.

The first picture was a close-up of a poster listing a bunch of dates. *Those are dates of the Winter Archery series. What on earth is she up to?*

The next one was a picture of a typed page that said Winter Series Training at the top and Nori had zoomed in on the Tuesday afternoon scheduled.

Then she sent me about four hundred question marks in a row.

What are you doing at the range? I typed quickly to put her out of her misery.

What do you think? Mom's here signing me up for lessons. And guess what? You and I are entering the Winter Series together. Earl let me go in the older group with you if mom agreed to drive you home afterward. Isn't that awesome?

Oh no, I thought, my heart dropping. Why did people seriously feel the need to interfere with my life all the time? I wasn't anywhere close to ready to sign up for any public competitions yet.

Don't worry, she wrote, as if guessing my spiraling thoughts, *that's why we're doing the lessons first. Don't fight this, Astrid, it's for your own good.*

I stared down at the phone not sure how to respond.

Come on, Astrid, don't make me shoot with the little kids. She added a dozen smiley angel faces.

Fine, I typed back, *but you're responsible if I mortify myself in front of hundreds of strangers.*

Don't worry, I will kill anyone who laughs. You're the best.

That is one scary child, I thought, shaking my head. *But I guess I'm in this now whether I like it or not.*

Chapter Thirty-one

The next few days of school were completely uneventful. The first week was always just about getting organized and figuring out schedules and there was very little actual learning going on. Although I did come home with an armload of new text books every day.

Rob's strange moodiness had passed and he was back to his old self again, happier now that his course load was locked in and he didn't have to make any more decisions for the moment.

I saw Miranda in passing a few times, but she was always stalking somewhere purposefully with a scowl on her face and she never so much as glanced at me.

Between Hilary and I, we managed to get the barn chores done, although sometimes the cleaning had to wait until the end of the day when school ended. I knew that wasn't going to cut it for very long with the boarders, though. Linda especially was neurotically paranoid about Baloo ever having a dirty stall and for a couple days after installing her horse's personal security camera, she'd call Hilary every time he dropped manure in his stall as if she expected us to drop everything and rush to his side.

The problem was solved by the end of the week when Hilary's dad proudly produced a short, stooped man wearing green pants with suspenders and a plaid shirt.

"Girls, this is Alfred, say hello to the newest member of our team. His wife Hannah is going to be helping us with some of the housekeeping; she's in town shopping with Linea right now."

We stared at the newcomer in astonishment and finally, the elderly man stuck out his hand and grasped ours tightly, one at a time.

"Nice to meet you," we said politely, but I could tell Hilary was barely containing her irritation. This wasn't exactly the sexy stable boy she'd been envisioning, or the twelve-year-old girl who'd work for nothing just to be around horses. This man was old. How was he supposed to lift heavy wheelbarrows and things when he looked ready for a retirement home?

"Alfred here used to work at the racetrack in Vancouver. He's just moved over here to be closer to his grandkids. Oona told him about the job and recommended him, actually."

"Oh, that was nice of her," Hilary said in a controlled voice.

"Yes, it was," Mr. Ahlberg said, glancing at his daughter. "It's good to find someone local who has experience with both horses and farming. We were lucky to find him. Should we go show him the barn now?"

"Sure." Hilary sighed resignedly. "Why not?"

"So you worked at the racetrack?" I asked politely as we trotted to keep up with him. "What did you do there?"

"Oh, a bit of everything over the years. Mucker, hand-walker, exercise rider, jockey, groom, assistant trainer. I guess the assistant trainer part is what I did the most."

"Did you ever ride in any big races?"

"No, not myself. But I helped to train and condition quite a few famous horses. To tell you the truth, I never much cared for the riding part; I always liked feeding and conditioning them until they felt like they could do anything. There's an art to that, you know."

We nodded wordlessly and even Hilary looked a little impressed.

"How do you know Oona, though?"

"Oh, we met at the track a long time ago. I knew her father, you see, and he used to bring Oona to see the horses when she was little. He'd leave her with us at the barn while he went and did a little gambling and a little socializing.

"Anyway, Oona didn't mind, she was crazy about the horses and she'd ask for rides on anything. It was a shame when the family moved to the island; I was looking forward to helping her with her career at the track. She would have made a fantastic jockey."

"Oh, I was always way too tall for that," Oona said, coming out of the barn just in time to overhear the last part. "It's good to see you, Alfred."

"You too, princess," he said, pulling her into a tight hug, "I can't wait to see your painting of Pants. Is it finished?"

Pants? I thought with a laugh. *Who would name a horse Pants?*

"I have about five of them done. You can take your pick."

"Good, Hanna wants something nice to hang in our new condo. She'll be thrilled."

If his job hadn't been a sure thing before, it certainly was once he stepped into the barn and caught sight of Sadie and Pender tacking up for their trail ride.

"Well, if it isn't The Rabbit," he said in astonishment, striding up and patting Rabbit's long neck fondly, "good to see you, fellow."

Of course, that won Pender over instantly and we stood in the aisle listening to them reminisce about Rabbit's fast, but not very accurate, career. Apparently, he'd been a great runner if you could get him out in front right away. But if he came from behind then he just basically bulldozed his way through the other horses, knocking them over left and right no matter what his jockey did. That sounded like a very Rabbit-like thing to do, actually. Pender had bought him straight from the track after he'd been permanently banned from racing.

"It was hard work to train him," she said, "but it was the best decision I ever made. Claudia loved him too, she was always so patient and kind with him."

There was a moment of silence as we all thought back to our time with Claudia.

"Well, I guess we should carry on," Mr. Ahlberg said finally and we followed them on a tour of the rest of the farm.

By the time our tour was over, I was pretty much Alfred's biggest fan. He obviously loved horses as much as I did; he went up to every single one of them in the pasture and spoke to them in the soft, comforting tones that they loved.

He stayed to help feed dinner that night and clearly knew his stuff, he was even familiar with the weird supplements that Linda had Baloo on although he did do a bit of eye-rolling.

His wife Hannah was just as nice. She was round in the soft, comfortable way that people never made fun of old people for. In fact, it probably made them *more* likable because it hinted that they might like to bake pies and things for others.

She had a broad, smiling face criss-crossed with lines that spoke to a lifetime in the outdoors. Linea clearly adored her and I felt like, between Hannah and Alfred, I'd just inherited the fairy-tale grandparents I'd never had.

Hilary, of course, was not quite sold on the whole idea, but when Hannah unexpectedly wrapped her in a warm, grandmotherly hug as she was passing her in the kitchen and told her not to worry so much because everything would work out, I saw tears in Hilary's eyes.

After that, she never complained about them again.

Chapter Thirty-two

It felt weird just heading off to school without even feeding the horses, but it was Alfred's first full day and Hilary was in charge of showing him how everything worked. She'd gotten up before I had and was already down at the barn by the time I was eating my breakfast.

As we left, I had Rob's dad drive as slowly as possible so I could peer out the window and confirm that Red and Ellie were indeed eating their hay peacefully.

Stop worrying, I told myself, *they'll be fine.*

The moment I got home from school, I ran down to the barn to check on them to find that they were just finishing the last remnants of their lunch.

Okay, that's fine, even if lunch was fed a bit late, they still look happy.

I'd just pulled out my brushes when there was the sound of footsteps in the aisle.

"Astrid, that stupid sheep is sleeping in the indoor again," Hilary said, barging into my tack room with Linda in tow. "Linda wants to ride, but her horse is scared of that dumb animal. Can you get her out?"

"Fine, fine," I grumbled, wondering how I had somehow become the sheep herder around here. It's not like they were mine, after all. And how did Portia keep getting out anyway?

"This is very unprofessional," Linda complained as she followed me closely back to the barn, nearly stepping on my heels. "I can't be in a barn where there are farm animals present. This is non-negotiable."

Ignoring them both, I crossed the grass to the larger barn with both of them bobbing in my wake. I marched down the aisle, noting with satisfaction that at least everything looked clean and the horses were happy.

"Come on, Portia," I called, stepping into the ring. For some reason known only to Portia, she liked lying down in the soft footing of both the indoor and the big outdoor sand ring. If she could sneak into either of them when nobody was looking then she would.

She lay there now, quietly chewing her cud and staring at me disinterestedly. "Come on, girl," I said again, reaching into my pocket to pull out a treat.

That did it; instantly, she was on her feet, lumbering toward me, her round sides swaying from side to side. I frowned and tilted my head to study her.

"Hey Hilary, she's looking pretty big. Is she due to lamb soon or something?"

"I have no idea, ask Dad. She always looks fat to me."

"Hmm," I said, walking slowly so the sheep could keep up with me. She took the treat out of my hand but when I started moving again, she looked back at the indoor longingly.

"Can't she move any faster?" Linda asked sharply. "I don't have all day."

"Usually she can," I said, frowning. "I don't know what's wrong with her."

"Well, lock her up somewhere for now and I'll ask Dad to look at her tonight," Hilary said impatiently. "I wish he'd get rid of them all."

I rolled my eyes but didn't bother to answer. Hilary's nature had improved a lot since she'd started taking lessons with Oona. She was spending more time at the barn and I'd even caught her down at the pasture a few times just hanging out talking to Jerry. But she still had her cranky moments and this was clearly one of them.

I didn't think that Portia would be able to follow me all the way back down the hill to the pasture. But maybe I could lure her across the barnyard to one of the empty paddocks.

"Come on, girl, you can do it," I said encouragingly. She waddled after me slowly but put on the brakes when I opened one of the paddock gates and tried to lead her through.

"It's okay, Portia. You're just going to have a sleepover." But she wasn't having any of it. She stayed rooted to the ground and it wasn't like she had a halter or anything to pull her in with. I gave her a tentative push from behind but she just leaned into me, refusing to move.

Red came to the front of his stall, watching us curiously and then marched over to see what all the fuss was about. As soon as she saw him, Portia walked right up to his gate and then turned to look at me.

"Okay, fine, sorry, Red," I said, swinging the gate open just enough to let Portia lumber inside. "I guess you get a roommate tonight."

He looked at me mildly, reaching over to touch Portia gently with his nose before turning to walk slowly into his stall. It honestly looked like he was waiting for her to catch up. She followed him happily and as soon as she was inside, I saw her drop down into his shavings right beside the hay. Red didn't look like he minded at all.

Chapter Thirty-three

By that time, it looked like everyone who had a horse there showed up at the barn at the same time and my hopes for a peaceful ride alone in the ring were dashed.

Annie came with both her kids, and Sadie and Pender showed up together in Sadie's new little bronze-coloured Porsche Boxster. She'd bought it for herself as a mid-life crisis present and, even though it was a convertible and the weather was getting colder, she was driving it around like mad before the snows came and she had to put it away in storage for the winter.

"I think it will just be a trail ride for you and me, Ellie," I told her, "it's getting pretty crowded here."

I pulled Ellie's light sheet off and started working a round rubber curry comb through her thickening hair. Both she and Red were getting woollier by the day; winter was definitely on its way.

Suddenly, I heard the sound of someone yelling and when I looked out Linda came storming out of the barn, pulling a reluctant Baloo along at the end of his reins. Her face looked like a thundercloud and she stomped over to the big sand ring and threw open the gate abruptly, making the big horse throw up his head.

"Wow, I wonder what that's all about," Nori said, appearing over the half-door of Ellie's stall.

"No idea, she seems a little intense, though."

"Yeah, no kidding. Are you okay if we come with you on a trail ride?"

"Of course, I just started getting ready."

We brushed the horses in companionable silence before tacking up and heading down the driveway.

"Let's try the lower trails," Nori said, "we haven't really checked out the trails down at the bottom of the property yet."

It was true, the trails leading to the ocean were so nice that we never really wanted to try anywhere else.

We headed left, ambling past the sand ring on the way down toward the lower pastures.

"What is she doing?" Nori asked in horror as we came to the edge of the sand ring where Linda was trotting Baloo aggressively across the diagonal. She had pretty big spurs on and she thumped her heels into his sides with nearly every step he took. That would have been disturbing enough on its own but she also had a death-grip on the reins so his head was cranked in so hard that his nose nearly touched his chest. I wasn't sure what sort of bit he was wearing but he didn't look comfortable at all.

The veins in his face and neck bulged and he was covered in sweat, his eyes rolling backward in distress.

"I have no idea," I said, horrified. "I've never seen anything like that."

Linda rode Baloo down the long side in a ground-covering

trot, tilting his nose left and then right with every step, his head swinging like a pendulum from side to side in an exaggerated see-sawing action.

"She's hurting him," Nori said, and I glanced over to see her face clouded with anger. She held Maverick's reins in one hand and had the other placed protectively on his neck.

Baloo certainly didn't look happy. His neck was bent so tightly that he could barely breathe and we heard him grunting under his breath as he passed by. He switched his tail back and forth erratically with every step.

"Maybe we should go get Oona," I said. "This doesn't seem right."

Before I could move, Linda pulled Baloo to an abrupt halt right in front of us and patted his neck enthusiastically, her mouth curved in a triumphant smile.

"Wasn't that wonderful, girls?" she said, her eyes alight. "He's finally starting to submit. I can really feel how much suppler he is."

"It looked awful," Nori said bluntly, never one to waste words. "What were you doing to him?"

"He was doing his exercises," Linda said in a suddenly hard voice, her eyes narrowing. "It's like yoga for horses. I don't expect you to understand."

"My mom does yoga every single day," Nori said, clenching her fists, "and it doesn't look like *that*. You were hurting him."

Linda smile fell away completely. "You clearly know nothing about dressage," she snapped. "And I think you should mind your own business. I've had years of experience with this sort of thing. Baloo is a highly-trained horse, but they can be explosive and they need discipline. I think I know a little bit more about it than you do."

"Fine," Nori said nudging Maverick away. "And that's exactly why I hate dressage. Go ahead and ruin your horse, see if I care."

"Why, that little brat," Linda said, glaring after her as I turned Ellie to follow. "See, this is why I didn't want to ride at a stable that allowed children. They're completely irrational."

I looked at her pinched expression and then down at her sweating horse who was hanging his head, gratefully stretching out his neck muscles in relief.

"Actually, I agree with her, he looks miserable," I said over my shoulder, not looking back.

I felt a twinge of guilt and hoped that Linda wasn't going to go marching straight to Hilary and complain. Hilary would kill me if I lost a boarder.

But when we got back after our ride Linda was gone and Baloo was calmly eating his hay in his stall.

Hilary didn't say anything about it at dinner so I figured that I was in the clear.

I will find a time to tell Oona about it, though, I promised myself. *I won't be able to stand watching her school that poor horse like that all the time.*

By the time we got back, Portia looked much like her old playful self again and she marched up to bunt Red with her nose when we arrived back at the paddock.

I'll let Hilary's dad know just in case, I thought, *he might want to call the vet just in case.*

That night Mr.Ahlberg came down to the barn to check on her but couldn't see anything wrong.

"She looks fine to me, Astrid," he said, giving the sheep a scratch behind the ears. "Although she could stand to lose a few pounds. It's strange she doesn't want to stay with her flock, though. I'll see if I can find anything about that in my sheep book. Maybe she thinks she's a horse."

The next morning she followed Red out to the pasture as if she didn't have a care in the world and I told myself to stop worrying so much. Everything was fine.

Chapter Thirty-four

It was just dumb luck that I survived my first archery club meeting unscathed.

I'd been dreading it more than looking forward to it because of how little I wanted to spend time with Miranda.

But in the second week of school when all the clubs were starting up again, Pheobe Marsh who sat next to Miranda in biology came down with the measles and had to be hospitalized.

It sent the entire school into a panic, which meant that everyone who hadn't already been vaccinated had to stay home until the contamination situation was under control. And, because Miranda was unvaccinated and had spent so much time sitting beside Pheobe, it meant that she had to go into quarantine. Which was pretty much the best news I'd had since school started.

For once, being raised by a paranoid germaphobe like Marion had finally paid off: I'd been vaccinated for practically everything a person could get. I was sure I could hop on a plane to a malaria-infested swamp without a care in the world.

Miranda, who was livid that she couldn't be there, had left a nervous-looking girl named Francis in charge with strict orders to report back everything that went on. But I had hardly walked in the door before Francis shoved her clipboard into my hand with a terrified squeak.

"I don't know what I'm doing at all," she said." I've only been to one sanctioned shoot and it did not go well for me. I hate stress."

"First of all," I said, smiling to put her at ease, "it's not supposed to be stressful. We're here to have fun."

They all looked at each other blankly.

I gazed around the room, noticing how few people there were compared to the last time I was part of the school team. There were only a couple of people that I recognized at all.

A small dark-haired girl that I thought must be Peyton stood staring at me wide-eyed, bracing herself as if she expected me to throw her out of the room.

"So, you all probably know about the new program the school is running, where you get credits toward sports if you're competing."

Most of them nodded and a few actually looked interested. "I don't know how many of you use a real coach. I do recognize a few of you from the range. My coach Earl has a winter training program going right now if anyone wants to join. It's to get people ready for the Winter Series."

"How much is it?" Peyton asked uncertainly. "I'd like to go but…" she broke off and shrugged.

"I'm not sure exactly, but I can find out. What I was thinking, though, is that maybe I can ask him if he would do a special afternoon for us, maybe one day a week. Maybe he would do a group rate for us."

I looked at Peyton questioningly and she nodded.

At the end, we had about ten people sign up for the archery team which was about a third of the size that it had been in my last year at Sacred Heart. It wasn't fantastic but it was a start; I was hoping that once word got out that our club was under new, although maybe temporary, management that other people would want to join.

I had to find a way to make it seem fun again.

We decided to confine most practices to in-school times and the lunch hour so that nobody had to stay late after school. I hoped that most of them would join our Tuesday night classes with Earl to prep for the winter series and that maybe there would be one afternoon a week where everyone could leave early to go to the range.

It was strange, I'd gone from not knowing if I'd get to practice at the range at all this winter to having so many opportunities that I didn't even know what to do with them. My schedule was full to the brim without even counting the time that I wanted to spend with the horses. I was extra-glad now that I'd asked Rob to show Ellie for me and that I'd held off on entering Red in the winter dressage shows; I was barely going to have time to breathe as it was.

Having the indoor to ride in saved me a little, though; as the days shortened and winter marched steadily toward us it was so nice to be able to ride after it got dark. Otherwise, I would only have been able to ride on weekends.

Red and I had fallen into a routine where I would free-lunge if there wasn't anyone else working in the ring, practice his ground work just like Oona had showed me, and then finish with a short ride.

Our groundwork had progressed from the walk-halt-back dance to light lateral work like leg-yields and shoulder-in. It was interesting to see how the movements looked from the ground and to see what sort of position their body was supposed to be in. Seeing things from the ground really helped me to visualize the movement when I was back in the saddle. We took things very slow and Red just accepted our strange new way of training in that good natured way he had.

Rob would often trailer over after dinner and I'd either ride with him or just sit in the small sitting area at edge of the ring and work on my own homework while he schooled Ellie, Jerry or his own horses.

Sometimes Sadie or Pender joined us, but Linda preferred to ride in the daytime when, in her own words, there weren't so many children around to distract Baloo.

Chapter Thirty-five

Even though I'd had a few pretty spectacular lessons on Ellie by the time the deadline arrived for the fall schooling show entries, it was decided between Oona, Rob, and I that Rob should still be the one to show her.

"It's on Sunday, so at least I can go along to help," I told him. It would be fun to be on the sidelines, actually; I'd get to enjoy the show without any stress.

"You'll definitely have to come," Pender agreed, sidling into the tack room behind us. "I've entered Rabbit and I'll need you there to keep both of us calm."

I laughed and shook my head. "You don't need me. You and Rabbit are doing great together."

"Yes, but I'd lose my head if it wasn't attached to my body. No, it's decided. You're to come along as a groom, and I'm going to pay you for it."

"Oh, no, Pender. I'm happy to help," I protested.

"I know you are. But it's my way of showing you how much I appreciate everything you do around here."

There was no point arguing with her since she'd made her

mind up and by the time the day was over, she'd convinced Sadie and Annie to go along and Annie decided to take Callie, too. Nori refused flat out to have anything to do with it, even to help groom. And Linda, it turned out, had signed up Baloo a long time ago.

Hilary had assumed all along that Rob would leap at the chance to show Jerry and had already paid his entries. As if Rob didn't have enough on his plate already.

Because nobody but Rob had been schooling with any real consistency over the summer, most of the boarders decided to drop down a level in their tests in order to pick up some decent scores.

I wasn't sure if it was exactly an ethical thing to do since none of the riders were exactly beginners, but Pender argued that they hadn't shown in so long that it was basically like starting over again.

"I have no idea what Rabbit will do after all this time," she said, "if we actually manage to make it around the ring without him leaping out or eating the flowers then I'll go up a level next time."

And since it wasn't *me* out there riding, I couldn't very well argue.

Luckily, the fairgrounds weren't very far away so we could take the horses in stages. Hilary didn't have her own trailer, of course, none of us except Linda did and she refused to let any horse but Baloo get inside it.

"I can't risk it being damaged," she said firmly, "and Baloo wouldn't like it if his trailer smelled like a strange horse. It might put him off his game."

Even Pender and Sadie didn't have their own trailers.

"I guess I should think about getting one," Sadie said thoughtfully, "it's not very safe that we don't have one on the property. What if we needed to evacuate for a fire or earthquake? Or what if we needed to take one of the horses to the vet?"

The upshot was that everyone chipped in to pay Rob's dad to ferry the horses back and forth. He tried to wave away the money, of course, but in the end, Pender made him take it.

"It's the least we can do for being such pests," she said, "take it at least to cover the fuel and we'll think of a better way to repay you later."

Because there were so many horses going at various times, and the whole point had been to get the young horses some show-time exposure, it was easier to just get stalls for the day.

Ellie, Possum, Rabbit, Sox, and Norman were all doing Training level tests, which would run early in the morning.

Rob had decided to leave Artimax at home, but he was riding Ferdi and Jerry both at Second. Sadie was riding two Fourth-level tests on Riverdance.

Linda was somehow aiming to get through a Third-level test, which I thought was very ambitious of her since Baloo had a habit of bolting in a panic whenever she even thought of asking for a half-pass.

We'd arrived there with the young horses first so we could get everything ready and have them settled in their stalls so they had a chance to relax. Hilary's parents drove right up in front of the barn just as we'd gotten the tack room set up, and Mr. Ahlberg opened the hatch and pulled out baskets of food.

"Help yourself to breakfast, everyone. I made way too much,

as usual," Mr. Ahlberg said. "Apparently, guests these days hardly touch their food and just want to stay in bed all day. They leave good reviews, though, so I must be doing something right."

This was our third series of bed and breakfasters, and it turned out that most guests in general rarely wanted to interact with us much once they'd checked in and learned what they needed to know about the area.

They had their own entrance, their own patio overlooking the ocean and gourmet coffee and snacks already in their room. There wasn't much point in leaving at all.

Hilary's mom had worried at first that there wouldn't be enough work for Hannah to do everyday, but Hannah had made herself so useful in the kitchen and garden, and had pretty much taken over the chickens, the quail, and the bees that pretty soon nobody could imagine life without her.

We laid all the food out on a nearby picnic table and dug into the piles of crepes and fruit and croissants and drank the fresh-brewed coffee.

Other competitors shot us envious looks as they passed by, and I could see them looking around wondering where the crepe food truck was hidden.

"Come over and help yourself," Mr. Ahlberg called to some especially hungry looking girls in pigtails wearing grass-stained breeches. And pretty soon we'd attracted a small herd of children to the table. I wasn't sure what parents told kids these days about accepting food from strangers but apparently that didn't apply to free crepes at a horse show.

It was much different being the person on the ground at a horse show. In the first place, it wasn't as relaxing as I'd thought it would be. I groomed, I braided as best I could until Nori pushed me aside in exasperation and did most of the horses herself. I kept the stalls clean and the hay and water buckets full. I ran around finding lost things like numbers, saddle pads and gloves. I kept track of the schedule and constantly reminded everyone when they were supposed to meet Oona at the warm up ring and when to get in there and ride their tests. I made sure everyone stayed fed and hydrated and gave the riders and horses a last minute polish right before they rode their tests.

I called tests for Pender and Annie and held Mister Sox while Callie had to run to the outhouses two minutes before she was supposed to go into the ring. Luckily, she had signed up to ride two tests because in the first one Sox refused to go into the ring without someone leading him, and when he got there, he pretty much just made up his own test, circling when he felt like it no matter what Callie did, and stopping to scratch his nose on his knee for what felt like forever.

By their second attempt, though, they both had their act together and they managed to walk, trot and canter somewhat accurately through their test, and Callie came out of the ring all smiles, leaning down and hugging Sox tightly around his neck.

Norman was obedient as always, and Rabbit surprised everyone by not only behaving perfectly well but also getting high marks for his willingness and expression.

"Okay, Astrid, you were right," Pender said grinning at me from ear to ear and accepting the water bottle I handed her, "next time we go up a level. One more step toward Grand Prix."

"All right, girl, you're next," I whispered to Ellie, running a hand down her neck. "Don't be nervous and listen to Rob."

She flicked an ear toward me and then turned back to calmly watch the horse just coming out of the ring. She looked like this was her hundredth show this year not her first; nothing at all had phased her so far.

"Wish us luck," Rob said, and I stepped back to let them go in.

I went and leaned over the white railed fence, watching them with my heart in my mouth. There was absolutely no reason to be nervous, but that was my project out there all alone in the ring embarking on her very first showing adventure. I took out my phone and took a few pictures to send to Aunt Lillian.

"Hey, is that your horse?" a small voice said next to my elbow. A younger girl, maybe around Nori's age, looked up at me, smiling tentatively. A man who was most likely her father stood a few feet away pretending not to listen.

"Yes, that's Ellie, this is her first show."

She nodded and turned to watch Ellie in the ring. "She's so pretty. My parents said I could get a horse this year."

"Oh," I said, looking over at her, feeling a flicker of something that might have been jealousy. I pushed it away firmly. "Ellie's a very sweet horse, but she's green; she's just a baby still."

"I know, I saw her picture on the poster. I've been riding for a long time even though I don't have my own horse yet. My coach lets me ride her horses and she said that a project horse would be okay as long as it doesn't buck or anything."

"Ellie would never buck," I said, looking over at her eager face. "But, wait, what poster did you see her on?"

"Um, there's a few of them. Some on the barns and some on

the outhouse doors. I took the number down, but do you think we could come see her?"

"Sure, whatever," I said, "I'll be right back."

Leaving the girl behind, I headed toward the closest outhouse as fast as I could. I looked at the poster taped to it in amazement. It was Ellie all right and beneath her picture and a flattering description was Hilary's phone number.

I almost pulled it down, but in the end, I stopped myself. Ellie *was* for sale after all; technically, Hilary hadn't done anything wrong but she hadn't even consulted me before putting up the posters. She hadn't asked me for help with the ad; she didn't even know anything about Ellie at all so how was she supposed to tell prospective buyers about her?

By the time I got back, Ellie was just finishing up, looking as happy and relaxed coming out as she had going in. I stood back pushing down my jealousy, watching the little girl and her father push forward to congratulate Rob and pet Ellie on the neck.

Rob smiled down at them easily and I could see him answering their questions. He looked up and smiled at me and I forced myself to smile back even though inside a part of me was dying.

The rest of the afternoon passed in a blur and the only embarrassing part was when Linda was not only excused from the ring when Baloo kept rearing and refusing to go forward but was also told off by the judge for riding at a level way too high for her, and also for riding Baloo in a double bridle when clearly neither she nor her horse could use it properly.

Linda had refused to speak to any of us afterward and had left the showgrounds with Baloo shortly afterward. Part of me felt bad for her, even though she was sort of an awful person. Maybe this would be her wake-up call to treat Baloo better, but I sort of doubted it.

Rob and Jerry had done very well and Hilary was beside herself with excitement when she went to pick up his ribbon at the show office.

"Maybe you'll be out here yourself next time," Oona said as she plucked the ribbon gently from Hilary's fingers and handed it to Rob. "You have a fantastic horse and I know the two of you could do great things together."

Hilary's expression wavered between anger, irritation, and laughter, and finally she gave in and smiled.

"Yeah, maybe," she said, looking a little wistful.

When we were packing up the final remnants of another gourmet lunch Rob told us about the little girl, Brianna, who'd been interested in Ellie.

"She rides at a mainly hunter barn but wants to try dressage, too. I know of her coach and she's got a good reputation. Brianna's dad said it's a nice place with lots of turnout."

"That's nice," I said abruptly, not wanting to even think about Ellie leaving right then.

"Oh, that reminds me, Astrid," Hilary said, coming out of the make-shift tack room with her arms full of dirty saddle pads, "I'm sorry I didn't tell you about putting up Ellie's poster. I didn't think about making some up until last night and then I whipped them up after you were in bed. I forgot to tell you this morning."

"Um, it's okay, I guess," I said, caught off guard by her apology.

"It would be nice if she sold, though," Hilary went on, ruining our moment, "I could really use her space in the barn."

Rob looked up and caught my gaze, rolling his eyes and making a funny face behind Hilary's back to make me laugh. And right then I knew everything would turn out okay.

All in all, it was a successful day and we all came home tired but happy. Well, everyone but Linda that was.

Chapter Thirty-six

Despite Hilary's dire predictions that the remaining stalls in the barn would never be rented in this economy, and the fact that she charged over six hundred dollars for a spot, the last two spots were snapped up in quick succession.

The rainy season was upon us and apparently there were plenty of people leaping at the chance to have an indoor to ride in.

There was quite a bit of excited speculation when the older barn ladies discovered that one of the new boarders was a middle-aged man named Owen with a lanky chestnut Saddlebred.

Men who rode were like a rare species in the horse world and it felt like all the boarders showed up at the same time to watch the poor guy arrive.

He had an older half-ton truck towing a small, serviceable silver trailer that was just big enough for one horse.

"Hello," he said shyly, looking a little overwhelmed at the size of the welcoming committee. He was an older guy with grey hair and a mustache and wore a pair of gold-rimmed glasses. He seemed nice enough but I had no idea what all the fuss was about.

His chestnut was long-backed and long-necked, but she was the prettiest colour. Her russet coat was lighter than Red's and her mane was so light it was almost white.

She had a narrow blaze and wide eyes rimmed with white that gave her a permanently startled expression.

"She's beautiful," I said honestly, eyeing the horse up from a safe distance. She looked like a lot of horse at that moment, standing up on her toes, her nostrils flared and her tail flagged up over her back like a banner. When she stood at attention her neck shot up impossibly high, every muscle rigid and trembling.

But, at a soft word from her owner, she walked, or pranced, next to him obediently to her stall in the barn, snorting all the way. I really hoped she'd calm down quite a bit before I ever had to handle her.

"She's just excited," the man said from inside the stall, smiling at me kindly. "She'll settle down."

"What's her name?"

"Well, her registered name is Bianca's Fine Time Rebel Without a Cause." He looked up and winked when he saw the expression on my face. "But I just call her Bee."

The next tenant arrived that same afternoon and she didn't inspire nearly the same level of interest in the boarders as Owen and Bianca had.

Just after lunch, when Rob and I had finished cooling out and loading up Artimax and Ferdi, a small red pickup rolled slowly up the driveway and crawled to a stop in front of the barn.

A girl hopped out and waved to us tentatively, turning to pull her saddle off the seat beside her and throw the strap of a canvas grooming tote over her shoulder.

"Hey," she said as she drew closer, looking from me to Rob nervously. She shifted the saddle higher up onto her arm and gulped.

"Hi, are you Marcy?"

"Yeah, sorry I'm early. The shipper called and said he's on his way with Oreo so I thought I'd better get down here to meet him."

"No problem, I'm Astrid and this is Rob. Here, let me take your stuff."

"Oh, thanks. I have lots more in the truck. It feels like I brought my whole tack room from Alberta."

"Wow, that's a long way to come."

"Yeah, well, I'm here for university. I tried leaving Oreo back home, but it was awful not having him with me. I've had him since he was a baby."

Rob had to go so I gave him a quick kiss goodbye and waved him and his dad down the driveway.

Then I helped Marcy carry her stuff inside and took her on a brief tour of the farm, glad to see that she seemed impressed with the pastures full of happy horses.

She had curly red hair and had a handful of freckles scattered across her nose and cheeks. Her expression was open and friendly, and I found myself liking her right away.

I liked her even more when her buddy Oreo finally arrived. I somehow thought he'd be a little painted pony, but instead he was a massive tricoloured Warmblood cross with great splashes of white, black, and brown across his body. For all his size, he was really gentle, and he whinnied happily the second he caught sight of Marcy.

"Hey handsome, don't worry, you're home now."

She looked him over carefully to make sure he hadn't been injured on the trip and then walked him around the yard a few times to stretch his legs before taking him to his stall in the barn.

Oreo didn't bat an eye at anything. Marcy had said they'd done a lot of competitions in the past so he was used to travelling to strange barns.

He went out and inspected his paddock, and then came right back inside and got to work demolishing his lunch.

Chapter Thirty-seven

My archery practice sessions had gotten much better over the last month. I still wasn't as confident as I had been before, that winning magic hadn't returned to me yet, but with hard work I'd been able to recover a little of my skills.

Miranda had missed three whole weeks of school; she'd had to stay quarantined at home even though she'd never developed any measles symptoms. I probably should have felt bad for her but I was just grateful and happy that she wasn't in my life.

By the time she came back, our schedule was already set up and there wasn't room for her on Tuesday nights so she'd had to move to Mondays. Our school archery team was already going strong without her and there wasn't much she could change or grumble about by the time she showed up for meetings.

I was feeling pretty good by the time the first fun competition of the Winter Series came around and it was a shock and a disappointment when I completely tanked and came in fifth from the bottom. Deep down I must have thought that something magical would happen when I got there and somehow win the whole thing. I stared at the score sheet in disbelief, struggling not to cry.

"I'm sorry, honey," Annie said sympathetically when we got out to the car. She laid a gentle hand on my shoulder. "I know you're disappointed."

"I shouldn't be," I said, holding back tears with great difficulty. "Earl said I couldn't expect to walk in and just shoot like I used to. But it still feels awful. I just lost it out there. I froze."

"It happens," Annie said. "It happens to all athletes. It's really more of a mental game than a physical game, isn't it?"

"I guess so." I sniffled and looked away, not wanting to meet her kind gaze. "But I feel like I let myself down, and Earl down. And I hate the thought of facing Miranda at school tomorrow. She's going to be thrilled that I've lost my winning streak. She's been waiting for this for years."

"Well," Annie said thoughtfully, "from what I hear, Miranda works very hard to make sure she comes out on top."

"Yeah, she was always going to the gym and drinking these vile smoothies to try and be the best. She'd get so mad that I'd beat her when I barely even exercised at all."

"Natural talent is a gift, Astrid, but you still have to nurture it. Miranda might not have that natural talent so she had to make up for it with hard work and determination, much like Nori, I suspect. It shows a lot of self-discipline, too."

"But I work hard, too," I protested. "I feel like I do nothing *but* work."

"Of course you do," Annie said quickly, "you're one of the most hard-working people I know. But, Astrid, there's a difference between working hard and working smart."

"But I practice all the—"

"I know you do," Annie interrupted, "But if you're goal is to be the best archer you can be, if you're serious about one day trying out for the Olympics, then I'm afraid you're going to have to make some lifestyle changes."

"I'm not giving up riding," I said quickly, biting my lip.

"Of course you shouldn't, that's not what I meant. Horses are a part of your life, and mine too, actually; I couldn't give up Norman, either. But you can ride and take care of one or two horses rather than a whole barn full of them. You can work less at the bed and breakfast. You can stop riding Rob's horses, too. Then you'd have time to do some cross-training. I said before that I was here to help when you wanted to put together a fitness program. No charge, I owe you for being so kind to Nori."

I stared at her, my mind whirling, not quite knowing what to say.

"You think on it, Astrid. Maybe do some research on what sort of cross-training programs top athletes are using. Then you can decide if you want to get serious or not; it's a big lifestyle commitment."

Chapter Thirty-eight

Over the next few days I thought about what Annie had said but I didn't expect part of the solution to arrive so soon and to be so horrible.

My phone rang when Rob and I were at lunch but the cafeteria was so loud I could hardly hear it.

"Hilary, hang on. It's crazy in here," I said, stepping quickly out into the hallway. "What's wrong? Is Red okay?"

"Yes, it's Ellie. I mean, she's fine, I just got a call from someone who wants to try her out. Isn't that great?"

"Uh, yeah, that's great," I said, leaning against the wall for support. I'd known this day would come but did it have to be so soon? "How did they find out about her?"

"They saw her at that schooling show you did. Apparently, they loved her. The girl said that she talked to you and that you said she could try her."

"Oh, yeah, there was that girl, Brianna, and her dad there. I didn't know they were serious, though. They did seem okay, I guess."

"Well, the dad was nice on the phone, anyway. They want to

come out this afternoon to meet her, though. Is that all right?"

"But I won't be there," I protested, feeling a surge of protectiveness. I couldn't let some stranger ride Ellie without me being there.

"Don't worry, Oona said she'd ride her first for them as long as I asked you first. It is okay, isn't it? It sounds like a good home."

"Yes, I guess so," I said, feeling sick to my stomach.

"They just want to try her; it might not lead to anything. I'll take video for you if you like so you can see how the girl rides and I'll tell you every detail of their visit when you get home."

"All right," I said reluctantly. Of course it would be fine, Oona wouldn't let Ellie get hurt, but I still felt queasy.

I said goodbye and slowly went back inside the cafeteria to tell Rob.

Even though we weren't supposed to, I kept my phone on for the rest of the day, checking it every thirty seconds or so to see if there was anything from Hilary.

Finally, during Economics I felt it vibrate and, when the teacher was looking away, I fished it out.

She was so good, Hilary wrote. *They loved her! They made an offer and want to take her right away. I told them yes, I hope that's okay.*

I looked down at the screen, my eyes blurring with tears. So much for us all sitting down and making a decision together. *What does Oona think?* I typed.

No idea, she's cranky today. I think she liked them, though.

Okay, I typed and then shoved my phone into my backpack, feeling nauseous.

Well, that's it then, I thought, *it's over. She'll get her vet check done and she'll probably be gone next week.*

Chapter Thirty-nine

Nori and I had archery practice that night so I didn't even get to go home right away, and even though I loved the range there was nothing more I wanted at that moment then to go home and spend what little time Ellie and I had left together.

At least my distraction seemed to help my shooting somehow. Maybe because I didn't care about hitting anything just then.

"Wow, good job, Astrid," Earl said. "Whatever you're doing, keep it up."

I smiled but I couldn't even enjoy his praise.

The ride home seemed to take forever but finally, I was there.

"Thanks for the ride," I called over my shoulder to Annie and Nori, "see you tomorrow."

"Bye," Nori shouted from her open window, "make sure to give Maverick a carrot for me."

"I will." I laughed and put my gear in the barn aisle, waving as their car pulled away and heading to the main tack room for a handful of carrots. I grabbed extra ones for Ellie since she'd been so good and hurried out to the back paddocks to see my crew.

"Hey guys," I called, swinging open the door into the small covered aisle way that ran the length of the stalls. Red and Maverick poked their heads out right away but there was no sign of Ellie.

"Here, girl," I walked toward the stall, a sinking feeling in my chest.

Oh no, I thought, looking over the half-door into her stall. It was completely empty, swept free of shavings and all traces of hay carefully raked out. She was gone.

I sat down hard on the wooden floor, my back up against the wall, fighting the choking feeling in my chest. Why hadn't anyone told me she was gone? How could they have just taken her without doing a vet check or without us taking the time to go see their farm or check them out at all?

I hadn't even gotten to say goodbye. What had she thought when complete strangers just loaded her up in a trailer and took her away? She must be so confused and lonely.

Why on earth hadn't Hilary told me this had happened?

A feeling of rage welled up in my chest and suddenly, I hated her more than I'd ever hated anyone in my life, even my dad when he was at his most obnoxious.

Red nickered anxiously under his breath and I lifted my head to see him standing there watching me closely, his face full of concern.

"Don't worry, buddy, you're never going anywhere."

I pulled myself up and went to the hay room, grabbing two flakes for each of them and tossing it into their stalls. Red didn't eat, though, he just stood there looking at me, ignoring his food until I let myself into his stall, wrapped my arms around his neck and let myself cry.

I stood there for a long time until I felt a sharp nudge against my leg and looked down to find Portia there looking up at me. Even though the other sheep had been locked back up in their winter paddock, Portia still somehow found a way to regularly escape and make her way down to the barn. It happened so often that the boarders had taken to shoving her in here with Red whenever she was causing trouble in the barnyard.

I laughed through my tears and reached down to scratch her behind the ears, thinking how much nicer animals were than people.

I was feeling a bit better by the time I got to the house, but that hadn't lessened my anger at Hilary at all and when I found her alone in the kitchen, I let her know exactly how I felt.

"But, Astrid, I thought you'd be happy. I *texted* you," Hilary protested, taking in my tear-stained face with a look of horror. "I said they wanted to take her right away and you wrote back *okay*."

"Oh my gosh, Hilary, that's not what I *meant*. I thought they liked her and were going to do a vet check and everything, not steal her away before I could even say *goodbye*."

"I'm sorry, but what was I supposed to do? They made an offer on her. I wasn't about to turn it down. You sound just like Oona. She knew you'd be mad."

"Of course she did. Anyone with half a brain would realize that taking someone's horse without asking them might make a person mad. Use your head and stop being so stupid, Hilary."

I stopped, putting a hand over my mouth. Those were the exact words my dad had used on me countless times. I hated it when I found myself acting like him, even in a small way.

"Sorry," I said woodenly, "I shouldn't have said that. But what you did was really bad, Hilary, and I don't know when I can forgive you for it."

"They said you could visit any time," Hilary called as I stomped up the stairs. "They're really nice people, Astrid. Honestly. I'm sorry!"

I went to my room and slammed the door loudly before I could hear any more. I flopped face-first down onto my bed, feeling tears well up again.

They *were* nice people, I remembered, the girl had really seemed to like Ellie. But she was so young and I didn't even know much about her coach. What if she couldn't handle a green horse? What if she ruined her?

I forced myself to take a deep breath and calm down.

My phone pinged and I looked at it half-heartedly. *Oh, my gosh, Hilary, why can't you just leave me alone?* I thought, tossing the phone to the side without reading the message. It pinged again and then another time and I finally snatched it back and looked at the screen.

Astrid, I am so, so sorry, she wrote. *I never meant to hurt you and I hope you can forgive me. I would have never sent her to a bad home. See, look how happy she looks.*

A photo popped up of Ellie in our ring with the little girl, Brianna, on her back. The girl had her arms wrapped around Ellie's neck and her dad was standing nearby smiling proudly. Ellie did look really content.

Okay, fine, I thought, *maybe it is a good home, but that still doesn't make what Hilary did okay.*

Despite myself, I did feel a little less sad, though. Tomorrow,

I would get their contact information and see when I could come and visit. Maybe it would make me feel better if I could see that she was truly happy in her new home.

Chapter Forty

"Where do you think Oona goes when she disappears to the mainland on her days off?" Hilary asked a week later, taking another spoonful of the homemade chocolate peanut butter ice cream she'd just created. Her dad loved kitchen gadgets and he'd just brought home a full-sized, industrial ice cream maker.

Hilary had insisted that he show her how to use it and had brought me a bowl as a peace offering. I still hadn't really forgiven her, but it was nice that she was at least trying.

"I'm not sure but I think it's the racetrack," I said, thinking of the beautiful new paintings in her loft upstairs; the flashy bay with the arrogant eyes, the soulful chestnut galloping full out with her ears flattened in concentration.

"Really? I wonder why. Do you think she has a gambling problem?"

I snorted with laughter, nearly spitting out my ice cream, and then shrugged.

"I don't think so. I bet she just loves watching the horses run."

"Weird," Hilary said, clearly not getting it. She definitely liked her horses to be controlled and steady, she didn't really approve of the wilder side of their nature.

Later that afternoon, Hilary tried to wheedle it out of Oona directly.

"Oona," Hilary said casually, hanging up her bridle on the washing rack. "I was wondering why you go to the mainland so often—"

"I bought a horse," Oona interrupted, not looking up, "he's coming tomorrow."

"What!" we both said loudly, and Oona looked up, her face crinkling into a smile.

"It happened pretty fast. He's a racehorse…well, he was until yesterday. I happened to be there when they made the decision to retire him. He had a few issues with the starting gate and he's not that fast, so they decided not to keep working with him."

"Is he one of the ones you painted?" I asked, thinking of the canvasses full of beautiful horses.

Oona nodded. "Yes, he's the bay in the one I'm working on now. I haven't decided on a name yet and I'm not even mentioning what his registered name is."

"Oh, come on," Hilary wheedled, "tell us."

"Nope, not happening. It doesn't fit him at all anyway. He deserves an elegant name like my old horse Furioso had."

I looked up with interest, surprised that she'd said his name out loud. Oona rarely talked about her past and it was only because she painted him so much that I knew that Furioso had been her horse to ride back in Belgium but that she hadn't owned him. When she'd left so abruptly, she'd had to leave him behind, they hadn't even given her the option of buying him.

"You know we'll find out anyway," Hilary said, laughing. "We'll just read his lip tattoo and trace him."

"If you can get close enough to him to read his tattoo then you deserve to know his name." Oona raised an eyebrow. "He's a bit of a handful."

Chapter Forty-one

The trailer pulled up first thing Saturday morning when I was still mixing grain in the feed room. Red and Maverick must have seen it first from their paddocks because Maverick let out an unexpected neigh in greeting, which set the rest of the horses in this barn off, too.

Rabbit flew out of his stall with a scrabble of hooves, banging his hip hard on his way out the door. The rest of them took off too, and the air was full of the sound of running, snorting and bucking.

"Come on, you guys," I called into the now-empty barn, "you see trailers come and go all the time. What's the big deal about this one?"

"They know this one is special," Oona said, clomping down the stairs in her boots. Her face was flushed with excitement and she looked like a little kid on Christmas morning.

"I got his stall and paddock ready for him," I said, "there's already hay and fresh water in there for him."

"You're always so organized, Astrid," she said, pulling on my ponytail affectionately as she went by. "Come on, let's go meet him."

The man getting out of the sparkling white truck was round, short, and balding but he had a big smile on his face and laughing eyes that made him look much younger than he was.

"This horse is a good one," was the first thing he said. "He has plenty of spunk, not like these tame ponies everyone prances around on. This is a horse with fire in his heart."

Oh, great, I thought, my heart sinking as I heard the sound of angry hooves pounding rhythmically against the trailer wall. *Feeding him and cleaning his paddock should be fun.*

"He'll settle down," Oona told me reassuringly, "give him time. He's just excited."

"Feisty," the man said with satisfaction, dropping the ramp and limping up into the trailer. "Whoa there, son!" He laughed, ignoring the snorts and thudding hooves. "Now don't you bite me, don't you do it."

He was still laughing as he came down the ramp again, bumping along in the wake of a massive bay horse with four white socks and a huge blaze. He wore a leather halter and had a brass chain running over his nose back through his mouth which was gaping open in protest.

As soon as he caught sight of the barn, his eyes bulged and he opened his mouth and bellowed at the horses in challenge, striking out one front foot angrily.

"Wow," I said, edging backward as the animal clattered toward us.

"Told you," Oona said breathlessly, stepping forward fearlessly to take the lead. "He's fantastic."

That was definitely not what I'd been thinking.

"You just lead the way," the man said, when the horse snorted loudly at Oona's approach. "He's used to me now, but it took us a few minutes to decide who was boss. I'm still not sure who won." He broke out into more laughter, completely ignoring the horse who took turns rearing, prancing, shaking his head from side to side like a fish on a hook and striking out in all directions with his front feet.

The man glanced back and saw my horrified expression. "Now, don't judge him too quickly," he said, slapping the horse affectionately on the neck. "This boy is all show, he has a good heart underneath all this fire and fury."

He reached the open paddock and led his charge inside. "Don't kick me, son," he said as the horse tried to wheel around and break away. He led him back to the gate and made sure to step outside before carefully unbuckling the animal's halter.

The second the halter fell free the horse squealed and wheeled away, charging toward Red with his mouth open.

I screamed, putting a hand over my mouth as I watched that creature bear down on my sweet horse like an avenging angel.

Red stood a few feet away from his side of the fence looking at the newcomer in astonishment. When the horse hit the fence with a resounding crack, Red's ears flicked forward and he rocked back slightly, and then stood stone still, just watching.

On the far side of him, Maverick looked equally unimpressed. He curled his nose at the newcomer and flattened his ears sullenly against his head.

The horse wheeled around again and repeated his charge, this time rearing up and waving his front hooves dramatically in the air.

Red didn't even flinch. He just stood there with a bemused

expression on his face as if he couldn't quite understand what the newcomer was trying to say.

The horse dropped his front feet to the ground and snorted loudly, trotting up and down the fence line with his head in the air and his black tail fanning straight up.

Red reached down and scratched his nose on his foreleg in a bored sort of way and then turned his back on the newcomer and sauntered back into his shelter to finish his dinner.

Oona's horse neighed in outrage, watching Red walk away as if he could hardly believe it was happening. He reared again, but this time his heart was hardly in it and, after trotting around his paddock a few more times, he disappeared back into his own shelter to root around in his manger.

"See," the man guffawed loudly, "all show. That boy wouldn't hurt a fly. You got yourself a good horse there."

"Thanks," Oona said breathlessly, "I can't wait to get started with him."

They walked back up to the truck to sort out the paperwork and I slipped into Red's paddock to make sure he hadn't been traumatized by his new neighbour.

He looked up mildly when I came into his stall, not disturbed in the slightest by the thumps and whuffling sounds coming from the shelter next to his. It sounded like a warthog was foraging around in there.

Oona and I ferried what little stuff that had come with him to the tack room and then she reluctantly had to leave to teach an early morning lesson.

"Wow, he's quite something," Hilary said, coming in and staring cautiously over the horse's half door while I was busy organizing Oona's things in the tack room. "Here, quick, hand me his halter before she comes back."

I handed her the leather halter in confusion but she held it up to the light, wiping furiously at the name plate.

"Ha," she said, putting a hand over her mouth to keep from laughing out loud. "Yep, that is awful."

She pushed it into my hands and I looked down, trying not to laugh, too. "Captain Thunderpants," I whispered, snickering under my breath.

"All right, all right," Oona said, coming in and snatching the halter from my hands. "Now you know. Girls, meet Pants."

Chapter Forty-two

"And you're a hundred percent certain you girls will be okay on your own? I could ask Alfred and Hannah to stay with you." Mrs. Ahlberg said, looking at us skeptically.

"Yes, Mom, we're fine. I promise. It's only three nights and we can always call you if there's a problem."

"Well, I really wish the timing had have been better. I had no idea Oona would be going away at the same time. I just don't feel comfortable—"

"Come on, honey," Hilary's dad said, leading his wife out the door, "they'll be fine. They're responsible girls and we'll have our cell phones on us. But we have to go now or we'll miss our plane."

"All right, but I don't like it."

"Go, Mom, have a great time. We'll only be alone at night after all. Alfred and Hanna will be here in the daytime and all the boarders will be around, too. It's Christmas break, I bet everyone's going to be spending every second of their free time with the horses."

"I suppose you're right. I asked Annie to check in on you, too."

"Oh great," Hilary said, rolling her eyes, "thanks a lot."

"Bye, Astrid, you keep an eye on everything for us, okay?"

I nodded, feeling Hilary stiffen beside me in irritation, and let both the Ahlberg's pull me into a final hug.

They'd had a spot at the small business owners conference in Vegas booked for months and it was just bad timing that Oona had decided to go away and visit family for a few days at the same time over Christmas break.

Today was my final day of school before the holidays began and I couldn't wait. Our second archery shoot was coming up next weekend and I felt much more ready to face it.

I had followed a little bit of Annie's advice. I stuck to just riding Red and Artimax, I was trying to make sure that I ate a little bit healthier, and I'd agreed to join her gym in the new year and let her tailor some sort of fitness plan for me. I wasn't quite sure what she had in store but she'd assured me over and over that I wouldn't regret my decision.

I had much more energy now that I wasn't exhausted by so many barn chores and I'd found my strength and stamina returning a little; my archery was improving slowly day by day.

I was looking forward to the three glorious weeks of vacation stretching out in front of me. Soon it would be Christmas, too.

"There's Rob," I said, grabbing my backpack. "I have to go, see you tonight, Hilary."

We might as well have stayed home that day for all the work anyone got done. Everyone was too excited about the upcoming holiday to pay attention and when the first snow of the season started to fall outside the window, it basically became a party inside.

"Man, am I'm ready to hit the ski hill," Preston said as he passed me in the cafeteria. "Good luck at the shoot next weekend, Astrid, that's all Peyton's talking about."

"Are you coming to watch?" I asked and Rob sent me a sidelong glance.

"Nope, I'm staying up at Mt. Washington with my dad the whole time. It's his turn to do Christmas. Peyton's staying with mom, though."

"Well, have fun," I said as he sauntered away.

"I really don't like that guy," Rob muttered.

"How come?" I asked slowly, studying his surly expression with confusion. Usually Rob liked everyone.

"We used to play soccer together," Rob said, shrugging. "He wasn't very nice then and I doubt he's changed much now. I wouldn't trust him, Astrid."

"Well, I'm pretty sure he feels the same about you, actually. But that's why we're in school, right? To learn to get along in with people we dislike, and have nothing in common with, so we don't grow up to be sociopaths."

Rob choked on his sandwich and looked up at me, laughing. "That's probably true. Where did you hear that?"

I shrugged. "Dunno, I'm just wise beyond my years. Oona says I'm an old soul."

Rob responded to that by bouncing a crust of bread off my nose.

Chapter Forty-three

By the time I got home, the snow was falling in flakes so thick we could hardly see.

"Catch you later," Rob said. "I'll text you tonight to see if we're still bringing the horses over tomorrow. I don't know if we'll get the trailer out in this snow."

"Well, you should still come over even without the horses," I told him, "we can just make snowmen or watch movies or something."

He grinned at me and I stood there waving until their truck disappeared down the driveway.

Holiday time, I squealed to myself, practically dancing up the walkway to the house. Maybe Hilary would get over her fear and come trail riding in the snow with us. The world looked like a fairy-tale right now.

"Hey, Hilary. I'm home!" I called out, dropping my backpack by the front door, but it was only Caprice who came to meet me.

I reached down to cuddle her and then flicked on the light switch. But nothing happened. I flicked it again but the house was silent and dark, and cold.

"Hello?" I called again. Still no answer. I pulled out my phone, glad to see it was fully charged, and sent Hilary a text.

Hey, where are you? The power is out, I think.

It only took a second for her to respond.

What do you mean the power's out? I'm with Darius but I'll be home soon. We're just hanging out. What do you want me to bring for dinner?

Pizza, I wrote back, *should I text your parents about the power?*

Not yet, wait until I get home. Maybe it will come back on by itself. And don't tell them about Darius, okay? They don't know he's back in town yet. I said he'd be back after Christmas.

I stared down at my phone, grinding my teeth in frustration. I seriously hated lying for her.

Fine, I wrote finally, *I'm going to feed the horses. Where are the flashlights?*

Umm, I have no idea. Maybe the pantry? See you soon.

Great, I thought, stuffing my phone into my pocket and hurrying upstairs. There was still daylight left to see by so at least I could get the chores done and hopefully find some flashlights before it got dark. The light on my phone would drain the battery in no time.

Caprice was beyond excited about the snow and ran around barking, stuffing her face into the drifts and stopping to roll every few feet.

I paused at the sheep paddock to see how they were doing but they were all, sensibly, inside their shelter, hiding from the storm. Alfred had filled their huge manger with three bales worth of hay a couple of days ago, so I knew they'd have enough to see them through the night.

When I reached the barn the door was open a couple of feet and snow had drifted inside the entry way.

"That's weird," I said, grabbing a broom and sweeping the snow back outside where it belonged. "Who would leave the door open?"

It was probably Hilary when she fed lunch, rushing to get away to see Darius now that he was back for the winter. I wondered what he'd do now that he was back from tour.

The light barely filtered into the barn through the open stall doors as I made my way to the hay room. All the horses were inside, looking at me expectantly.

"Are you ready for dinner?" I asked, frowning at them in the dim light. They weren't acting quite like their usual selves; there was a strange tension in the air that I didn't understand. There was a soft thud from inside the hay room and all their heads swung toward it in unison, ears pricked.

"Hello?" I said cautiously, my heart suddenly thumping in my chest. I crept toward the hay room door, just noticing at the last minute that it was open, too, and peered into the darkness.

There was another thump and the sound of breathing, and I pushed the door open all the way, letting what little light there was left pour inside.

"Portia, what are you doing here?" I said, putting my hand on my chest to calm my shuddering heartbeat.

She barely glanced up when I came in. She was lying on her side and breathing heavily, her eyes half-closed.

"Portia?"

She lifted her head and looked at me, and then let her nose flop back down on the nest of loose hay she'd burrowed into.

"Are you okay?" I crept over to her side and knelt down, carefully laying a hand on her shoulder. She sighed when I touched her, and then suddenly her whole body stiffened and she let out a little bleating noise, her fat sides rippling suddenly with effort.

"Oh my gosh, Portia, are you having your lambs?"

I'd never seen anything but foals born before but the symptoms were definitely similar. I pulled out my phone with shaking hands and dialed Hilary. It rang and rang and then went to voicemail.

"Hilary, it's me, I think Portia's lambing and I'm not sure if she's in trouble or not. The power still isn't back on, please call me."

I hung up, tapping my phone against hand while I thought hard. There was an emergency first aid kit in the tack room. The least I could do was pull it out and see if there was anything useful in it.

At first glance, there wasn't really anything I could use right away, just bandages and a stethoscope and a thermometer. This certainly didn't help when I had no idea what a sheep's heart rate or temperature was supposed to be. What I really needed was someone to tell me what to do.

I was just about to pick up the kit and take it to where Portia was lying when a red bag that had been stuffed to the back of the cupboard caught my eye.

"Yes," I said, kneeling down and fishing it out. I swept the dust off and unzipped it, silently congratulating myself. It was one of the earthquake kits Hilary's dad had insisted in stocking all over the property. It had seemed stupid at the time; all the earthquakes I'd ever felt had been little tremors that had hardly shaken the buildings at all, but right now I couldn't have been happier.

Flashlight, batteries, snacks, a wind-up radio, bottled water, an emergency blanket. I piled all the things to one side and dropped the batteries one by one into the stem of the flashlight, hoping I was putting them in the right way.

A few seconds later the strong beam of light cut through the growing darkness and I breathed a sigh of relief. Somehow, that ray of light made everything seem better.

I looked down at my phone again, wondering what to do. There was no message from Hilary and I really wasn't sure what to do next. I texted her one more time and waited but still, nothing.

Finally, I pushed the number for Hilary's mom.

"Astrid, are you and Hilary okay?" Linea said sounding worried.

"Yes, and I'm so sorry to bother you," I said, gulping. "But I think Portia is lambing. She somehow made it to the hay barn. I'm not sure what to do."

"Lambing...oh dear. Hang on, I'll get Ronald." There was the sound of muffled voices.

"She should be okay, Astrid," Mr. Ahlberg's voice came on the line, sounding rushed. There was the sound of laughter and clinking glasses behind him and I was pretty sure I'd disturbed their dinner. "Sheep are very good at doing things for themselves. Can you and Hilary get her back to her own barn?"

"Um, I don't think so. She's lying down on her side and she looks exhausted."

"Hmm, darn it. This is bad timing. She's earlier than she's supposed to be. Okay, here's what you're going to do. Go back to the house, to my office and get the guide to sheep book. It's on the shelf somewhere. I think it's next to the beekeeping books. I wrote the vet's number on the inside of the book so you can give him a call if you're worried. But she should be okay, Astrid. They're very self-sufficient and this isn't her first lambing."

"Um, okay," I said, looking down at Portia's heaving sides and her outstretched nose. She didn't look good at all to me.

"Just leave a message if anything changes and call the vet if you're worried at all. Can I speak to Hilary for a moment?"

"Um," I stalled, thinking fast, "she's, um, in the bathroom right now."

"Okay, well, I'll give you girls a call later tonight to check how things are going. Sorry, the speeches are starting so I have to go but call us if you need to."

"Okay," I said weakly but the line had already gone dead.

Moving softly so as not to disturb her, I tiptoed around, getting the hay for the horses' supper, and then went out to Red's barn to do the same for those horses.

Portia groaned a little when I got back and I winced in sympathy, wishing there was some way to help her. I knew I needed to go up to the house and get the sheep book, but at the same time I didn't want to leave her alone. I wasn't sure what to do.

Get moving, I told myself firmly, *she needs your help.*

I finally ran through the snow up to the house, Caprice springing happily by my side. The house felt even colder when I got inside and it was creepy moving around the rooms in the dark. Even though I had the flashlight, it cast strange, looming shadows everywhere and the house didn't feel safe and familiar at all.

I dashed up the stairs and into the office, shining my light across the bookshelves. *Raising chickens, Growing Mushrooms, Farming on a Small Acreage, Beekeeping,* there … *Caring for Sheep!*

I grabbed the book and flipped it open to the first page, melting with relief when I saw the vet's name and number written clearly on the front page.

My hands shook as I dialed and I held my breath as I waited, willing anyone to pick up the phone. It rang and rang, and I was certain it was about to go to voicemail when suddenly, a woman's voice answered.

"Oh, I'm sorry," she said when I'd quickly explained about Portia. "The doctor is out on an emergency call right now and I'm not sure how long he'll be. I'll pass on the message as soon as I hear from him, though; you hang in there."

"Okay," I said in a small voice, "but I'm not sure what to do."

"I wish I could help you. I'm his sister, though, not a vet. I normally do the accounting, but I'm just filling in for the receptionist because she's sick today. I don't know a thing about sheep. I'll make sure he gets to you next, though."

I sat there in the darkness, my mind whirling, trying to figure out my next move. I would grab a blanket so I didn't freeze to death and go sit with Portia until the vet called.

But the thought of sitting down there alone, in the dark, with Portia possibly dying beside me was too much. I didn't want to do this all by myself.

Rob, I thought suddenly, dialing his number.

He answered right away, listening as I fumbled out my story. "I'm coming over," he said, as soon as I explained the situation.

"It's okay...you don't have to."

"You wouldn't have called me if you didn't want help, Astrid," he said patiently. "We'll be there in fifteen minutes."

I felt so much better once I knew that help was on its way. It wasn't logical; Rob probably knew just about as much as I did about sheep, which was nothing, but there was something comforting about having someone in your life who would drop everything to help out.

I gathered some extra blankets and snacks and headed back down to the barn.

Portia looked exactly the same as when I left her and I sat down carefully a few feet away so as not to disturb her, leaning my back against the stack of hay.

With the sheep book open on my lap I shone the flashlight at the page and began reading the chapter on sheep births as fast as I could.

***

"Well, I'm no expert on animals but she seems pretty comfortable now," Rob's dad said as he knelt down next to Portia.

The ewe was sitting up now, with her front legs tucked neatly under her body, quietly chewing her cud with a far-off look on her face. "How did she make it down here anyway?"

"I have no idea. The books said that sheep often like to separate themselves from the flock to give birth. They like to go somewhere quiet. The hay room is one of Portia's favourite places to sneak into. Maybe she thought she'd be safe here."

"That sounds reasonable. Well, if you kids don't need my help here then I'll go sit in the truck and finish up some paperwork."

"Dad, you don't have to stay. I know you have work left to do."

"Rob, what if it becomes an emergency and she needs to go to the vet? Time might be important."

"Hilary has a desk set up in a corner of the tack room," I said, "would that work?"

"Maybe, if there was light or heat in here," he said, winking at me. "I think I'll choose my warm truck, thank you."

I went out into the aisleway to try calling Hilary again, but it just went to her voicemail. I didn't know whether to be angry with her or just worried. She'd said they were on their way back, what if the car had flipped over in the snow or something?

"Astrid," Rob said, coming up behind me anxiously in the aisle. "I think something's happening."

We both crept to the hay room door and peered inside.

Portia was flat out with her feet kicked sideways in the air, her breathing came fast now, and every so often she made a sad little bleating noise.

Poor Portia, I thought, reaching out and grabbing Rob's hand. I wished hard that there was something we could do for her.

But, just when I could hardly stand it any longer and had nearly made up my mind to call the vet again, she suddenly gave a giant heave and scrambled to her feet, and then like magic, a little black and white lamb slid out and landed in a pile of hay.

Before I could move, Portia made a little bleating sound and whipped around to sniff her new baby, and then lovingly began washing it with her tongue while it sat up and took its very first breath of life.

"Oh, welcome to the world, little one," I said, and felt Rob's arm wrap around my waist. I leaned into him, so glad that it had been him here with me.

And, as if adding to the miracle, the lights suddenly flickered and then came on full-force.

"Yay," I said, extremely thankful that I did not have to sleep in a freezing, dark house all by myself.

Portia made a satisfied little bleating noise and the baby struggled to stand while she washed his head and neck and worked her way down over his shoulders, cleaning all the afterbirth off until we could see that he was mostly white with just a few black spots. He had his mother's two big eye patches, though, and a funny group of speckles at the end of his nose.

"You're beautiful," I told him as he pushed his little hind end in the air only to have his mother knock him over with her washing. He only stayed down for a second before he was up again, standing on wobbly legs and starting to search for her udder.

Rob and I stood breathlessly with our hands clasped, waiting for him to take that first important drink that would be packed full of nutrients that would make sure a lamb survived. As soon as he found the milk, his little tail began to wag and he closed his eyes, sucking noisily while his mom continued to clean him.

"I should go get my dad," Rob said finally, breaking the spell of silence that had fallen over us as we watched this miracle of new life unfold. He squeezed my hand and disappeared.

"Well, you two did a great job," Mr. Harris said, laying a hand on my shoulder. "That's big, healthy lamb, and the mama looks mighty proud of herself, too."

As if agreeing with him, Portia let out a loud *Baa* and bunted her baby a few steps toward us, nearly knocking the little guy over.

"Easy there," I said, kneeling down and reaching out to steady him. His soft fur was still damp beneath my fingers, curly with cowlicks where his mom had washed him. He looked straight at me with a pair of large brown, trusting eyes, and then stuck his nose under my arm, looking for shelter. Instantly, I was in love, and I wrapped my arms around him, feeling his little heart beat next to mine. I stayed like that for a minute and then carefully directed him back to his mom.

Rob came in and set a bucket of water next to Portia which she stuck her nose in and drank greedily. Her round sides were sunken in and hollow-looking, all that space the baby had taken up suddenly hanging.

"There's alfalfa up at the sheep barn," I said. "I'll go up and get some and bring it down to her. I don't want to risk moving her tonight."

"Why don't we just throw a bale in the back of the truck," Rob's dad said, "she might be here a few days.

With three of us helping, it was easy to grab a bale of hay and set her and her baby up properly in a corner of the hay room.

"Hilary's going to have a fit when she sees this," I said, stifling back a laugh. "This is not her idea of a fancy dressage barn. And Linda is going to lose her mind."

"Well, they can both stuff it," Rob said, grinning at me. "Who wouldn't want to board at a barn that has baby lambs in the tack room?"

"It's pretty late, you two," Rob's dad said, and suddenly I realized how tired I was. "So we'd better get home. Are you going to be okay by yourself here, Astrid? Did you want to come to our house so you don't have to be here alone?"

It was tempting but I knew I'd want to come down and check on Portia and her lamb one more time during the night. "Thanks, but I'll be okay. Hopefully Hilary is back soon."

I had almost forgotten about Hilary in all the excitement over the lamb but now my worry came creeping back. She hadn't answered any of my texts or phone calls. But she'd pulled stuff like this before when she was off with Darius. It was possible that she was just sneaking around with him and not telling me anything because she thought I'd rat her out to her parents.

Together, we gave all the horses a last flake of hay and then, with a final hug and kiss from Rob, I was alone again but, thankfully, not in the dark.

"Goodnight, Portia. Goodnight, lamb," I whispered to them. They were curled up together side by side, the little lamb tucked in behind his mom, his eyes drifting closed.

I backed out into the aisle and then slipped out of the barn, stifling a yawn, as I slid the big outer door shut.

Chapter Forty-four

All the earlier adrenaline of the evening faded and left me feeling bone-tired but in a good way, as if I'd accomplished something big. Which was silly because it was Portia who'd done all the work, although I'd probably worried enough for both of us.

I tilted my head back as I walked up to the house, looking at the half-starred sky. Part of the canopy overhead was crystal clear with a million pin points of light dancing away but ahead, in the direction of the house, a whole bank of clouds darkened the sky, not letting any light through at all.

Hilary, where are you? I thought again, reaching down to check my phone for the millionth time. I'd sent texts to both her parents letting them know the good news about Portia but I hadn't said anything at all about Hilary being missing.

Caprice met me at the front door, pushing past me to run outside and leap off the porch into the snow with a happy yelp. I flicked the hall light on and kicked off my boots, leaving the front door open an inch for her as I padded to the kitchen and flicked on the lights there. It was just a relief to have power at all. The house was still cold, though; I guessed it would take a while for the temperature to come up again.

Caprice bounded back inside with a clatter of claws on the hardwood floor and I went back to shut and lock the front door.

Inside, I put on the kettle to make myself a hot chocolate and went around the kitchen assembling myself a double-decker cheese sandwich with mayonnaise and extra tomatoes which was probably *not* on Annie's list of healthy things an athlete should eat. I hadn't realized how starving I was until just that moment.

When the clock reached eleven and I still hadn't heard from Hilary, I knew that I couldn't put off sending her parents a message any longer. I felt awful but what if something had really happened to her on the way home? I didn't even have Darius's cell number.

Suddenly a streak of light flashed across the wall and tires crunched through the snow on the driveway. I moved to the window and saw with relief that it was the compact sports car that Darius drove when he was home, zig-zagging a little as it tried to gain traction on the snowy driveway.

I saw Hilary get out and slam the passenger-side door, stomping up the driveway toward the house with Darius trailing in her wake. He reached out to grab her hand and she snatched it away, turning on him with a snarl.

What on earth is going on? I thought in astonishment. I quickly went and unlocked the front door and swung it open just as Hilary whooshed inside. She dropped a gigantic backpack in the front entry way and marched toward the stairs without looking back.

"Hilary, be reasonable," Darius said stopping in front of me as I blocked the doorway.

"No, go away," she shouted over her shoulder. "I don't ever want to see you again. Lock him out, Astrid."

I narrowed my eyes at her retreating back. She was definitely mad but she didn't seem hurt at all. She seemed more like she did when she was working herself up to a fit of temper. Hilary did have a flair for being dramatic.

Darius on the other hand looked devastated.

"What's going on?" I asked slowly, looking at his pale, anxious face.

"Talk sense into her, Astrid," he said, "she won't listen to me."

"Why, what's going on?"

"She wanted me to run away with her," Darius said, his voice dropping. "She had some plan about going to California to be an actress."

"Fine, make me sound ridiculous," she snapped from where she'd stopped on the third stair. "I just wanted to go on a little road trip, that's all. Is it too much to ask that I wanted a little adventure in my life?"

"Your parents would kill me if I took you in the night. They'd call the police, I'd be accused of kidnapping, they'd never let us see each other again."

"They might try," she said, her eyes glinting, "but they couldn't stop us...it would be like Romeo and Juliette..."

Um, I'm pretty sure that they both died at the end of that play, I thought, but I didn't say it out loud.

"I don't want to fight with your family Hilary; they're nice people."

"So you're saying you don't want to fight for me, then. That you're just willing to give up."

"No, you're talking nonsense. There's nothing to give up. Hilary, I love you."

"No, if you loved me, you'd take me away like I asked."

"You're not being reasonable."

"Get out," she said, turning around and marching up the stairs. "Astrid, shut the door. I don't want to see him."

She ran the rest of the way up the stairs and I heard her bedroom door slam once, then two more times for emphasis.

Darius and I looked at each other with wide eyes.

"I'm sorry, Darius," I said. "But I guess you'd better go."

I stepped toward him unhappily, not liking the heartbroken look on his face. Darius had been through so much in his life. He really didn't deserve to be treated like this.

"Astrid, I don't want her family to be mad at me. I want to make a future with her, not steal her away in the night like a criminal. When I tried to explain she got mad at me and said I didn't love her and made me bring her home. I really don't understand any of what just happened."

"Um, yeah," I said, sighing. "I think I get the idea; I'll try and talk to her for you, though."

After Darius left, I marched upstairs and banged on Hilary's door.

"Go away," she yelled, but I pushed it open anyway and stepped inside.

"Sit up," I ordered and went over and sat down hard on her bed.

She glared at me but pushed herself upright, crossing her arms over her chest.

"Look, Hilary, I'm the last person to give relationship advice, but you are being really mean to Darius right now. He's a good person and playing with his heart is not a fun game. I know you want drama in your life, but this is not the way to get it. He really loves you and if you throw that away just because you're bored or unhappy then you are truly the stupidest person in the world."

"Get out," she said, gritting her teeth together, but I just shook my head.

"No. I'm not leaving until you apologize to me for bailing on me like a million times this summer and for being an awful friend."

She opened her mouth but I held up my hand.

"I'm not finished. You apologize to me and then you apologize to Darius for acting like a spoilt brat tonight. Then you apologize to your parents for lying to them all those times and for also acting like an entitled princess whenever you don't get your own way."

"But—"

"Wait, I'm not done. Then, lastly, you need to apologize to yourself."

"Myself?" she asked in confusion, momentarily distracted from her outrage.

"Yes, for trying to stuff yourself into this role of a running a business when clearly it is not you at all. Or at least not yet. Just let Oona run the damn barn so you can get back to doing the things you love like acting, dancing, and having actual fun with your horse and yes, spending way too much time drooling over Darius. The way you're doing things now clearly isn't making you happy."

"But my parents—"

"Will be happy when you stop going around being awful and making everyone else miserable. Honestly, Hilary, you're the only one who can't see that."

"Oh," was all she said, looking more surprised than angry. "Why didn't you say all this before?"

"Well, I sort of did but maybe I didn't say it loud enough or something. Anyway, I hope you're hearing it now. I hate this version of Hilary; I want the old one back."

"Me too," she said and started laughing at the same time she burst into tears.

"Good, now get dressed so you can come down and see our new family member. I've been pretty busy while you were out breaking Darius's heart."

Chapter Forty-five

Sometime in the night, Hilary sent a very long, apologetic email to Darius and the next morning he showed up for breakfast, his face all smiles. That meant I had to call Rob over too, and the four of us spent all day together just hanging out while the snow fell.

We drank hot chocolate and watched cheesy Christmas movies, watched the snow fall in soft flakes outside. It was honestly the best day I'd spent with Hilary in ages, and when she showed us a flyer for an upcoming play she was thinking of auditioning for, I knew she was well on her way to being back to her old self again.

After lunch we went out and gathered pine and cedar bows from all around the property and decorated both barns for Christmas. Darius admired Portia and her new lamb, and he and Hilary spent an hour in Jerry's stall just brushing him together and talking.

Both Rob and Darius stayed until well after dinner when they finally had to go, and the house felt sort of empty without them.

"This was a good day, wasn't it?" I said to Hilary, looking over at her fondly.

"The very best," she said, smiling back at me. "I wouldn't change a thing. And, Astrid?"

"Yeah?"

"Thanks so much for being here for me, even through all that. I'm so sorry I was so horrible to you and to everyone. I know I've made a lot of mistakes."

And having my best friend back was one of the best parts of my day.

Chapter Forty-Six

But the next day the holiday feeling ended when I went to check on Portia and she wouldn't get up at all. She would eat and drink if I brought hay and water to her, but she wouldn't stand unless I helped her up, and even then, she looked uncomfortable.

When it came to the point where she wouldn't let the little lamb nurse anymore, I knew it was time to call the vet.

He pulled into the driveway and slid to a quick stop, spraying snow and gravel against the barn, sending the horses flying out of their stalls into their paddocks.

He didn't say much in the way of greeting, and he examined Portia and the lamb quickly before standing up and shaking his head.

"Will she be okay?" I asked nervously, trying to decipher the expression on his face.

"She'll live," he said brusquely, "but she shouldn't be bred again. She hardly has any milk and she's not in the best condition. She looks on the older side and I don't think she'll survive another lambing. Otherwise, she's fine."

"Oh, good," I said, full of relief. I reached out to scratch

Portia under her chin, and she leaned into my hand, closing her eyes happily.

"Yup." The vet brushed a few bits of hay off his overalls. "I've given her an anti-inflammatory and some antibiotics that should help her udder. You'll have to keep an eye on the lamb, and if she won't nurse him after an hour or so you'll have to bottle feed him. You get a bottle and the powder to mix up at the feed store. At least he's already had some milk off her so he got a good dose of colostrum. He should do fine."

"Okay, I'll keep an eye on him," I assured him.

"Good. Better get her processed as soon as this lamb is weaned, before the ram can breed her again. It's best not to put these things off."

"Wait, what do you mean? I thought you said she'd be all right."

"Yes, but her purpose is to have lambs. If she can't do that then she's best as sausages."

"Oh, but I couldn't. She's—"

"You'd be surprised how tasty older mutton can be when it's mixed with the right spices. Delicious. Now, I'll be on my way."

"But—"

He stopped halfway into his truck and turned to look at me impatiently. "Look, do it now before you get too attached. If she gets bred again, she'll die for sure. And it won't be pretty. Do the right thing and get her processed."

He slammed the door before I could say anything else, revved the engine, and sped away.

Tears stung my eyes and I went back to where Portia lay curled up in the straw with her lamb tucked trustingly beside her.

She *baahed* quietly under her breath when she saw me, blinking in the morning light.

"It's okay, girl," I said quietly. "Don't listen to him. You're not going to be sausages. We'll figure something out. But first I need to do some research."

Chapter Forty-seven

I was busy on my laptop when Hilary's parents came in the front door.

"We're home, girls," Mr. Ahlberg called, setting their luggage down in the hallway. "Did anything interesting happen while we were away?"

Hilary was sitting on the couch across from me and we both just looked at each other and started laughing. Some things just couldn't be explained.

"Astrid, there's a letter for you, dear," Hilary's mom said, coming in the front door after her husband and stamping snow off her boots. "We stopped at the post office on the way home."

"A letter? For me?" I could count on one hand how many actual paper letters I'd gotten in the mail in my entire life. It was probably Aunt Lillian. She wasn't very good with the technology.

"I think it's from Marion," Mrs. Ahlberg said, looking at me a little anxiously.

"Oh," I said, reaching out to take the thick envelope reluctantly.

Mrs. Ahlberg gave my shoulder a quick squeeze as she went

by. "We're here if you need to talk about anything," she said, heading toward the kitchen. "Always."

"I know. Thanks. I'll take it upstairs." I set my laptop aside and went slowly up the stairs to my room, holding the thick envelope away from my body as though it were fragile or contained explosives.

I sat down on the bed, turning the letter over a few times before getting enough courage to open it. I pulled out the carefully folded paper and looked down at the unfamiliar handwriting. It could have been anyone's. Marion had hardly ever left notes. She always had her tablet with her and I couldn't remember the last time she'd written me anything on actual paper.

Dearest Astrid, it began, *Merry Christmas a little early, Darling. I hope that you are doing well. First of all, I want you to know that we've both missed you so much and we both wish that things could have ended differently this summer.*

Yeah, me too, I thought bitterly.

Caprice suddenly jumped up on the bed and came right over to me, sniffing intently at the envelope, her little tail wagging back and forth.

"Leave it, Caprice, you can't possibly miss them. Can you?"

She wagged again and settled down next to me, resting her nose on my knee.

I can't tell you how beautiful the scenery is here, the landscape is so wild and rugged and well, vibrant. I think of you all the time and how much you'd love it here, even though I know you wouldn't like being away from Red and the farm too long. There are actually horses this far north, which was a surprise. Your father pulled over a few days ago so we could give a herd of them carrots over the fence. Can you imagine? He's a whole different person out here, Astrid, we both are.

I wanted to let you know that we sold the motor home and have bought a tiny cabin at the edge of a lake. In the mornings, we get up early and have our coffee on the front porch, watching the sun rise. There's something about this stark landscape that makes you feel so alive and vibrant. Our cabin isn't big, and it's rustic, but it feels more like home than our condo ever did. It's the perfect place to be with family.

"Uh oh, I hope she's not planning on trying to force us to move there with them," I said to Caprice. "She has the biggest fight on her hands if she's expecting me to pack up everything and leave here."

I smoothed out the paper from where my anxious fingers had crumpled the edges and kept reading.

We think of you often, Astrid, of how wonderful and strong you are, and of the mistakes we made. There will never be a stronger regret than the way we left things that awful night. I know we both hurt you deeply. I hope that with time we will be able to heal and that you will able to rejoice with us in our good news. Astrid, we've been given such an amazing chance to do things over again, to do it better this time and we hope that you'll choose to be a part of that.

I frowned down at the letter, waiting for her words to make sense.

Astrid, it is with great joy that we tell you we're expecting a baby. You're going to have a little sister.

"No," I gasped, putting a hand over my mouth, feeling sick. "That is impossible, you two are too OLD and you were terrible, terrible parents the first time around. You hate mess and noise and dirt. And Dad's a controlling freak. How is this poor baby going to survive?"

I know you must have very mixed feelings about this. We were so surprised when we found out the good news. I didn't think I could have children but by some miracle I conceived. We didn't want to tell you until we were very sure, but now I am four months along so we thought it was safe to share the news with you. We love you and want to make sure you get a chance to know your little sister.

We will make plans for a visit once she is born or you are welcome to come here, either to visit or permanently, whenever you wish.

We love you so much, Astrid.

Cordially,

Marion

Oh. My. Gosh. I sat there with the letter in my lap, hardly able to believe what I'd just read.

"This is impossible. I must have read it wrong." But a second and third reading confirmed what I already knew. It wasn't some horrible dream. I was going to have a sister to worry about now.

I was *already* worried about her and she hadn't even been born, an innocent little baby just waiting to be thrust into a world where she'd be told right from day one that she wasn't good enough.

No, that's not fair, I thought guiltily, *maybe they've changed. I guess it's possible. And Marion was always kind to me in her own way. Maybe it will be different since this baby will be her own kid; maybe she'll protect her more than she did me.*

Caprice whined and pushed her nose under my hand, looking anxiously up into my face.

"It's okay, girl," I said, sighing heavily.

"Astrid?" There was a soft knock on the door and Mrs.

Ahlberg poked her head inside. She frowned when she saw the letter that had dropped to the floor at my feet. "Oh honey, what's the matter? Was it bad news?"

"Yes," I said bitterly, "no, I don't know. They think it's good news, I guess."

I scooped the papers up off the floor and handed them to her wordlessly.

She started to read and then sat down on the edge of my bed, her eyebrows raised so high they nearly disappeared.

"Well," she said finally. "That was completely unexpected. How are you feeling?"

"Awful. It's pretty gross, really. They're *old*, for one thing, and they don't even like kids. How is Marion supposed to change diapers and clean up vomit and stuff? She can hardly handle dust let alone all the things that come out of a baby."

Mrs. Ahlberg choked back a laugh and put a hand on my shoulder.

"First of all, your parents are not that old," she said, smiling. "Marion's younger than I am."

"Hmm," I said noncommittally. I couldn't imagine Hilary's mom just randomly having another baby, either.

"But, you're right; they are certainly going to have a lot of challenges ahead of them. I hope they're up for it and that the child is raised in a loving home."

"Ha, I doubt it." My eyes suddenly began to water and the room went blurry around me.

"Oh, Astrid, I know it's upsetting, but really, it has nothing to do with you. You don't ever have to go back there, remember? Not unless you choose to. You just have to concentrate on school and sports and on being a happy teenager."

"I know," I said, sniffing and wiping impatiently at my eyes. "But, that's the thing. She hasn't even been born and I feel responsible for protecting her. I know it doesn't make sense but what if I have to do the same thing for her one day that I had to do for Caprice?"

"Sweetheart, no. That's not your responsibility and hopefully, your parents have learned something and do a better job than they did raising you. I'm sorry, I know it's wrong of me to say that but it's true. But, if you are ever in the position of having to protect her then you know now that you are not alone. You call Ronald and me and let us handle it. We want to be able to handle things for you, Astrid, so that you don't have to worry. I guess it's probably the same way you feel about this new little sister of yours; we want to protect you and let you just have a happy life. Won't you let us do that for you?"

I stared at her blankly and then something in my heart just sort of melted and that last barrier I'd held up to keep the Ahlbergs from getting too close dissolved into nothing.

"Okay," I said quietly.

I hadn't realized before then that a part of me hadn't trusted them to keep me, not forever like they'd said, I'd been waiting for the other shoe to drop, for them to get bored of me and kick me out. For Hilary's ever-changing moods to become too much. I'd sort of been holding my breath and waiting for this good life to end as abruptly as it had begun.

Her gaze softened even more, and this time when she hugged me, I leaned into it and felt my tension drain away.

"Hey, what's going on in here and why wasn't I invited?"

Hilary asked, standing in the doorway. "Nobody said there'd be hugs."

"Come on in, sweetie," her mom said, waving her over, "there's more than enough to go around."

"I don't know, lately it seems like Astrid gets it all."

I sighed and shook my head. "Sorry, Hilary, I'm too tired to fight with you right now."

"Oh come on, isn't that what sisters are supposed to do?" Hilary asked, coming to sit on the bed beside us and leaning her shoulder up against mine. "We're not best friends anymore, Astrid, once you're a member of this family then you're officially my sister, and that means you'll have to accept that I'm a little crazy sometimes and that once in a while I like a good fight."

I looked up to see her smiling at me mischievously.

"Okay, fine," I said, laughing, "then there's one more fight I need your help with."

Chapter Forty-eight

"Thank you for meeting with me," I said to Hilary's dad, carefully pouring his cup of tea and sitting down across from him.

"Of course," he said, trying not to smile. I could tell that he thought Hilary and me calling an emergency meeting with him was hilarious, but I was determined that he take me seriously.

I pulled my clipboard toward me and studied my notes then turned to Hilary.

"Astrid and I would like to discuss the purchase of some livestock," she said, folding her hands on the table.

"Oh yes, what did you have in mind?" He put his tea cup down and sat up straight, studying us both with curiosity.

"I'd like to acquire one lamb on behalf of my Aunt Lillian, to be part of her breeding stock and I'd like to buy Portia for myself. As a companion for Red, not for eating," I added quickly.

"I see." He looked back and forth between us and sighed. "Astrid, the whole point of raising sheep is so we can feature our homegrown meat at our restaurant, and at the bed and breakfast. If we sell off stock then that will cut into our supply."

"We've thought of that," Hilary said firmly. "Dad, you will

have at least twelve more lambs born this year, more if anyone has triplets. We did some research and, as gross as it is to say, this breed produces about 50 lbs. of meat after processing, so that's 600 lbs. of meat this year. You can't deny that that's more than enough meat for one small bed and breakfast."

"Well, I suppose," he said slowly.

"Furthermore, as you know, Astrid's aunt has begun running sheep on her ranch. She is prepared to trade you one of her lambs for Portia's lamb. That way you can get some unrelated breeding stock for next year."

"Oh," he said, sitting up and looking interested, "what sort of sheep does she have?"

"Registered Khatadins, they're actually worth more money than your sheep, Dad, so technically it's a good deal for you."

"Yes, yes it is," he said thoughtfully, "not a bad deal at all for me, but what about Lillian? How does it benefit her?"

"Well, two ways; first, she gets new breeding stock too, and secondly, you're going to throw Portia into the deal and give her to Astrid."

"Well, I don't know about…"

"That's the deal, Dad. Portia's not worth anything to you now except as sausages. Astrid will keep her as a companion to Red."

"But what are supposed to do in the Spring? What's to keep her from getting bred by accident again? I doubt Hamlet will stay in his paddock if he knows she's down here."

"We've thought of that. Astrid is going to pay to get her spayed."

"Spayed? Like a dog? Can you even do that?"

"Yes, you can," I threw in quickly, "I called a vet in town and

GENEVIEVE MCKAY

I just have to book her an appointment and take her in."

"Isn't that expensive, though?"

"It's doable," I said carefully. "I have a little bit from selling Ellie and my parents sent me money for Christmas. It's the least they can do for going ahead and springing their awful surprise baby on me."

"Okay, okay," he said, laughing. "You've convinced me then. It sounds like a good deal for me anyway. Shall we have some cake to celebrate?"

"Yes, please," Hilary said, smiling at him. "but only if we can take it down to the barn and celebrate with Portia. She's the one who gets to live, after all."

But really, I thought later on, once I was tucked into bed with Caprice snuggled up beside me, *it's me who gets to live, too.*

These last few months had been difficult but it had been sort of like healing from a wound. That terrible night when I'd run away had damaged me, maybe more badly than I'd recognized at the time, but in my own way, and in my own time, I'd healed. Maybe I was a little scarred and battle-worn, and maybe I wasn't the exact same person I'd been before. But I was stronger now, too.

And in just a week, it would be Christmas with my new family and a whole holiday spent with my extended barn family, and with Rob and Darius. And a whole season of archery and riding stretched out in front of me, full of promise.

Maybe I wouldn't get better at archery overnight, but I would *eventually,* and maybe my distant dream of going to the Olympics wouldn't stay just a dream very long.

I was going to fantastic places in the New Year. Whether I was ready for it or not.

Resources

Are you interested in learning more about Classical Dressage? Visit Sylvia Loch's Classical Riding Club (http://www.classicalriding.co.uk) for links, videos, articles and books to help you improve your position, connection and relationship with your horse. It's free to join and anyone is welcome no matter what their riding level; it's all about learning. There are even online tests and lessons you can do from the comfort of home.

Some of my favourite non-fiction horse books are; The Classical Rider by Sylvia Loch, Centered Riding by Sally Swift, That Winning Feeling by Jane Savoie, The Complete Training of Horse and Rider by Alois Podhajsky and Dressage for the New Age by Dominique Barbier. There are so many more. Do you have a favourite training book to recommend?

Are you interested in learning more about Horseback Archery? The International Horseback Archery Alliance has links to organizations in various countries as well as postal matches where you can compete from home and send in your scores. https://www.horsebackarchery.info/links

If you enjoyed Defining Gravity, Flight, Freefall or any of my other books, I'd love if you'd take a moment to write a review on any of the platforms where they are sold.

Astrid's Series

Defining Gravity
Flight
Freefall
Riding Above Air

Short Stories and Collections

The Horses of Winter

Greystone Manor mystery series (under G.M. Mckay)

The Curse of the Golden Touch (coming June 2019)
The Sting of the Serpent's Blade (coming Fall 2019)

The Strange Adventures of Carolina Brown

The Opposite of Living
An Aching in the Bone
Wayfarer's End

Visit my website at www.genevievemckay.com
Follow on Twitter @Geners_Mckay
Follow my pics on Instagram: @mckaygenevieve
Or join my Facebook author page:
www.facebook.com/authorgenevievemckay

Acknowledgments

Huge thanks to my fabulous editor Jinxie Gervasio who always laughs and cries in the right places and is full of good advice.

Massive appreciation, in no particular order, to Heather Stewart of Sweet Water Stables, Marti Oltmann, Helen Cartwright, Helen Yeo, Mariko Brown, Jennifer Warburton, Jules Kirby, Helen Kwong, Honey Johnston and the rest of the Advanced Reading team. Your help was invaluable!

Fabulous cover design credit goes to *Cover Design by James, GoOnWrite.com*

Interior design credit goes to the wonderful folks at *Polgarus Studio.*

And last, but not least, thanks to all the fantastic teachers, both two-legged and four-legged, who have helped me on my journey to be a better writer and a better horse-person. The path has not always been smooth but it sure has been quite a ride!

Genevieve Mckay is a seven-time novelist and horse enthusiast living with her family on the wet and wonderful West Coast.

Made in United States
North Haven, CT
07 November 2021

10914634R00189